Math tools

GRADES 3–12

Math Tools

GRADES 3–12

64 WAYS TO DIFFERENTIATE INSTRUCTION AND INCREASE STUDENT ENGAGEMENT

HARVEY F. SILVER
JOHN R. BRUNSTING
TERRY WALSH

For information:

Corwin Press
A SAGE Company
2455 Teller Road
Thousand Oaks, California 91320
www.corwinpress.com

SAGE Ltd.
1 Oliver's Yard
55 City Road
London EC1Y 1SP
United Kingdom

SAGE India Pvt. Ltd.
B 1/I 1 Mohan Cooperative Industrial Area
Mathura Road, New Delhi 110 044
India

SAGE Asia-Pacific Pte. Ltd.
33 Pekin Street #02-01
Far East Square
Singapore 048763

Printed in the United States of America.

Library of Congress Cataloging-in-Publication Data

Silver, Harvey F.
Math tools, grades 3–12: 64 ways to differentiate instruction and
increase student engagement/Harvey F. Silver, John R. Brunsting, and Terry Walsh.
p. cm.
Includes bibliographical references and index.
ISBN 978-1-4129-5781-6 (cloth)
ISBN 978-1-4129-5782-3 (pbk.).
1. Mathematics—Study and teaching (Elementary)—United States. 2. Mathematics—Study and teaching (Secondary)—United States. 3. Effective teaching—United States. 4. Learning strategies—United States. I. Brunsting, John R. II. Walsh, Terry. III. Title.

QA135.6.S55 2008
372.7—dc22 2007026281

This book is printed on acid-free paper.

07 08 09 10 11 10 9 8 7 6 5 4 3 2 1

Acquisitions Editor: Cathy Hernandez
Editorial Assistants: Megan Bedell and Cathleen Jane Mortensen
Production Editor: Nancee McClure
Copy Editor: Sara Bierling
Typesetter: C&M Digitals (P) Ltd.
Proofreader: Joyce Li
Indexer: Sheila Bodell
Cover Designer: Rose Storey
Graphic Designer: Lisa Miller

Contents

Acknowledgments

This book represents the collective and creative teaching ideas of an incredible number of classroom mathematics teachers. With great pleasure we acknowledge the many, many colleagues who directly or indirectly shaped the purpose and substance of *Math Tools, Grades 3–12: 64 Ways to Differentiate Instruction and Increase Student Engagement*.

This group of inspirational and thoughtful educators shared both their angst over a myriad of classroom learning challenges and their hopeful thoughts about instructional remedies. A significant number of those teachers are Chicago-area educators who, like classroom teachers everywhere, seek ways to help every child learn and dare to believe that children can enjoy mathematics. Our professional conversations, combined with our ongoing search through the teaching and learning research, have produced this collection of strategic and effective tools.

The writing of this book has been a long-term labor of love, and we would be remiss not to specifically acknowledge a few individuals whose names you will not see among the authors. First, there is Susan Morris, who in the early days of writing was a constant source of encouragement, support, and inspiration. Second, there is Matthew Perini, whose wordsmithing skills fleshed out these pages with prose that made our thoughts and ideas come to life. Next, there is Justin Gilbert, who managed countless pieces of text and graphics while helping design and illustrate many of the figures you will see throughout the book. We would also like to thank the entire staff of Thoughtful Education Press, including Peta Feiner and Dan Strong, for their assistance to the writing team throughout the development of this book. A special thanks is due to NCTM and McREL, two organizations whose work helped shape the math tools matrices that introduce Chapters 2 through 5.

Finally, there is Rachel Livsey, who while at Corwin Press nurtured *Math Tools* from concept to manuscript, and Cathy Hernandez, who took over the project and guided it through to publication. We further thank those at Corwin Press who believe that these pages will provide instructional ideas that will benefit teachers and foster a deeper understanding of mathematics in those whom we all serve—our students.

About the Authors

Harvey F. Silver, president of Silver Strong & Associates and Thoughtful Education Press, was named one of the 100 most influential teachers in the country. He has conducted numerous workshops for school districts and state education departments throughout the United States. He was the principal consultant for the Georgia Critical Thinking Skills Program and the Kentucky Thoughtful Education Teacher Leadership Program. Harvey is the author of several educational bestsellers, including *So Each May Learn: Integrating Learning Styles and Multiple Intelligences* (2000) and *The Strategic Teacher* (2007), both published by the Association for Supervision and Curriculum Development (ASCD). With Richard Strong, Harvey developed *The Thoughtful Classroom*—a renowned professional development program based on the commitment to "make students as important as standards."

John R. Brunsting is a mathematics teacher, staff development specialist, and author. John serves schools as a *Thoughtful Classroom* trainer and coach as well as a mathematics consultant on practical, style-based tools and strategies. He is the coordinator for Illinois Advanced Placement Institutes and cofounder of Mathematics and Technology Institutes, training organizations committed to the instructional excellence of teachers. Previously an Advanced Placement Calculus Exam Committee member, John coauthored *Preparing for the AP Calculus Examination* (2006). He has presented at national and international conferences for the National Council of Teachers of Mathematics (NCTM), ASCD, the Japan Association for Supervision and Curriculum Development (Japan ASCD), Teachers Teaching with Technology (T^3), and the International Conference on Computers in Education.

Terry Walsh has been a mathematics trainer and consultant for more than a decade. He is a mathematics teacher and one of the founding editors of the *Eighty Something!* graphing calculator newsletter. He has developed and implemented mathematics applications of *Thoughtful Classroom* concepts in his own classes and has coached other mathematics teachers in the use of these tools and strategies for increasing student understanding. Terry has presented at international, national, and regional professional mathematics conferences sponsored by such organizations as NCTM, the Illinois Council of Teachers of Mathematics, the Metropolitan Math Club of Chicago, and T^3.

1

A User's Guide to Learning Styles and Math Tools

The journey of developing this book began almost five years ago. After over sixty combined years of service in schools, two of us—John R. Brunsting and Terry Walsh—were coming to the end of our careers as mathematics instructors and administrators. For most of those sixty years, we had the pleasure of working together in Hinsdale Central High School in Hinsdale, Illinois, where we met Harvey Silver and were introduced to the *Thoughtful Classroom* professional development model he designed with Richard Strong. What we quickly came to learn is that the *Thoughtful Classroom* really works. Whenever we implemented *Thoughtful Classroom* strategies in our classrooms or worked with other teachers to help them implement *Thoughtful Classroom* strategies in their own classrooms, the effect on student learning was palpable—students became more engaged, discussions got richer, student thinking went deeper, and test scores went up.

There was, however, one particular *Thoughtful Classroom* text that always seemed to make the biggest difference in classrooms in the shortest amount of time. That text was *Tools for Promoting Active, In-Depth Learning* (Silver, Strong, & Perini, 2001; Silver, Strong, & Commander, 1998). The idea behind *Tools for Promoting Active, In-Depth Learning* is simple. It is a collection of classroom-tested tools, or simple teaching "moves," that teachers can use to foster active, in-depth learning. These tools are based on the principles of effective learning and brain-based instruction and require little or no planning. As such, the tools can serve as "on-the-fly" techniques whenever a learning episode begins to lag, or they can be planned into a lesson or unit ahead of time in order to meet specific objectives.

As we—John and Terry—ended our careers in classrooms and began new ones as staff developers, we began exploring a new question with Harvey: What would a tools-based approach to mathematics instruction look like? Or, more specifically, rather than adapting generic tools to the demands of mathematics instruction, why not develop a new book, one that would respond directly to the concerns of mathematics teachers? The idea of a math-specific tools book excited all three of us, so we set out to align what we were doing in mathematics staff development with this new "math tools" venture. We worked with teachers of mathematics from around the country to select tools that were most relevant to mathematics instruction. We modified other tools to make them more math-centered, and we developed some new ones along the way.

As we added tools to our list, we organized them into four distinct styles of instruction: a *Mastery* style that emphasizes skill acquisition and retention of critical mathematical terms; an *Understanding* style that builds students' capacities to find patterns, reason and prove, and explain mathematical concepts; a *Self-Expressive* style that capitalizes on students' powers of imagination and creativity; and an *Interpersonal* style that invites students to find personal meaning in mathematics by working together as part of a community of problem-solvers. However, the more we discussed our aim to develop a book that would provide teachers of mathematics with a repertoire of instructional tools that they could use to differentiate instruction according to different styles, the more we heard a common refrain. It sounded like this: We know that different students have different ways of learning and that we need to engage them all, but isn't mathematics a worst-case scenario for differentiation?

It isn't difficult to see why mathematics might seem like a worst-case scenario for differentiated instruction. The quantitative nature and sequential organization of mathematical content can make considerations of student differences seem marginal. Add to this the realities of teaching in an age marked by standards, high-stakes tests, and teacher accountability laws—an age when you can pick up almost any mathematics journal and find a piece that sounds the alarm for all-out reform, a piece that sounds like this:

> Efforts to improve the quality of mathematics education in the United States have been under way for the past half-century. According to the 2007 National Assessment of Educational Progress (NAEP), however, more than half of our fourth graders and almost 70% of our eighth graders still fail to achieve proficiency in mathematics. Our students also continue to fare poorly on international assessments of mathematics achievement. On the 2003 Program for International Student Assessment (PISA) exam, which tests students' mathematical literacy and problem-solving abilities, students from 23 out of the 39 participating countries significantly outperformed students from the United States. Even our top students lagged behind their counterparts from other nations. Despite decades of reform, then, it is clear that we still have a serious mathematics problem in the United States. Because we live in a world where individuals who possess well-developed mathematical skills are more likely to go to college, more likely to be employed, and more likely to earn higher salaries than those who do not, it is even clearer that we must find a solution.

Clearly, the refrain of mathematics teachers about the difficulties in differentiating instruction had some real wisdom behind it. What they were asking was: Can I *afford* to differentiate? With the stakes so high, how much attention can I really pay to the differences among my students? After all, the standards I'm being asked to meet aren't differentiated; they're uniform, the same for every single student regardless of style or ability level.

What we've discovered during our journey as teachers of mathematics, administrators, professional developers, and authors is that *differentiation is not in the way of meeting high standards, it is the key to meeting them.* Our students' perceptions of mathematics as a discipline, their academic success in our classrooms, and their development as math-literate citizens all depend on our ability to engage all our students, not just our "math whizzes" and high achievers. And no, mathematics is not a worst-case scenario for differentiation. Mathematics can be differentiated as easily as language arts or social studies or any other subject for that matter. All you need to understand are two little words: *learning styles.*

WHAT ARE LEARNING STYLES AND WHY DO THEY MATTER?

Few ideas in education have stood the test of time as well as learning styles. The history of style stretches all the way back to the work of Carl Jung (1923), one of the founding fathers of modern psychology. What Jung discovered is that the ways in which people process and evaluate information tend to develop into particular personality types. Years later, Kathleen Briggs and Isabel Myers (1962/1998) took Jung's work and expanded on it to create a comprehensive model of cognitive diversity. The fruit of Briggs and Myers' efforts is the world-renowned Myers-Briggs Type Indicator, which, according to recent estimates, some two million people take each year to better understand their strengths and liabilities as learners, workers, and individuals. In the years since the development of the Myers-Briggs Type Indicator, new generations of educational researchers including Bernice McCarthy (1982), Carolyn Mamchur (1996), Edward Pajak (2003), Gayle Gregory (2005), and Harvey F. Silver, Richard Strong, and Matthew Perini (2007) have adapted and refined these ideas and helped educators across the globe put learning styles to work in classrooms and schools.

In a development of special interest to teachers of mathematics, Harvey F. Silver, Ed Thomas, and Matthew Perini (2003) applied the research on learning styles specifically to the study of mathematics. Out of their work came the identification of four distinct mathematical learning styles, outlined in Figure 1.1.

It goes without saying that no student falls completely into one style category. Learning styles should never be used to reduce students to a set of identifiable behaviors neatly summarized in a three-inch by three-inch box. However, most of us tend to develop clear preferences for certain styles, while seeking to avoid other styles.

To get a better sense of what the four mathematical learning styles look like in the classroom and to help you discover which styles you prefer, let's look in on the classrooms of four different teachers of mathematics. While students in each of these four mathematics classrooms are all studying area and perimeter, each teacher is

Figure 1.1 The Four Types of Mathematics Students

The Four Types of Mathematics Students	
Mastery Math Students . . .	**Interpersonal Math Students . . .**
Want to . . . learn practical information and set procedures. *Like math problems that* . . . are like problems they have solved before and that use algorithms to produce a single solution. *Approach problem solving* . . . in a step-by-step manner. *Experience difficulty when* . . . math becomes too abstract or when faced with non-routine problems. *Want a math teacher who* . . . models new skills, allows time for practice, and builds in feedback and coaching sessions.	*Want to* . . . learn math through dialogue, collaboration, and cooperative learning. *Like math problems that* . . . focus on real-world applications and on how math helps people. *Approach problem solving* . . . as an open discussion among a community of problem solvers. *Experience difficulty when* . . . instruction focuses on independent seatwork or when what they are learning seems to lack real-world application. *Want a math teacher who* . . . pays attention to their successes and struggles in math.
Understanding Math Students . . .	**Self-Expressive Math Students . . .**
Want to . . . understand why the math they learn works. *Like math problems that* . . . ask them to explain, prove, or take a position. *Approach problem solving* . . . by looking for patterns and identifying hidden questions. *Experience difficulty when* . . . there is a focus on the social environment of the classroom (e.g., on collaboration and cooperative problem solving). *Want a math teacher who* . . . challenges them to think and who lets them explain their thinking.	*Want to* . . . use their imagination to explore mathematical ideas. *Like math problems that* . . . are non-routine, project-like in nature, and that allow them to think "outside the box." *Approach problem solving* . . . by visualizing the problem, generating possible solutions, and exploring among the alternatives. *Experience difficulty when* . . . math instruction is focused on drill and practice and rote problem solving. *Want a math teacher who* . . . invites imagination and creative problem solving into the math classroom.

SOURCE: Silver, Thomas, Perini (2003).

approaching the content in a different way. William Merkel, Sandy Horowitz, Bruce Wong, and Julia Lacomba all teach sixth-grade mathematics, and each teacher has developed a different activity for students to complete. Which of these classrooms would you want to be in the most? Which of these classrooms would you want to be in the least? Once you are familiar with the four classroom activities, rank them in order of preference from most preferred to least preferred.

Mastery Activity

In William Merkel's classroom, students have just reviewed the formula for finding the area and perimeter of a rectangle. William wants to assess his students' progress to see if they have mastered the procedure. He provides each student with the drawing of an irregular shape and explains, "We have gone over how to find the area and perimeter of a rectangle. Today we are going to look at an irregular shape. I want you to apply the formulas you already know about area and perimeter to compute the area and perimeter of this irregular shape."

Figure 1.2 Mathematics Classroom—Mastery Activity

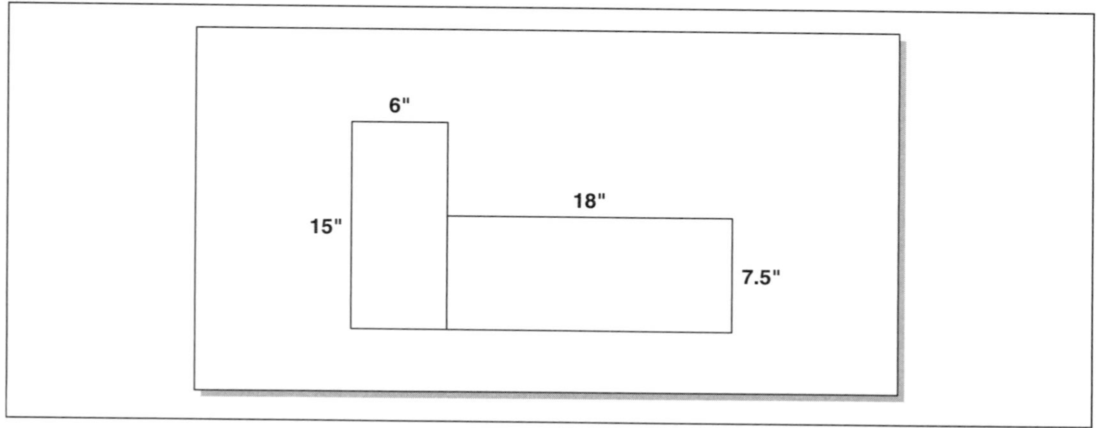

Understanding Activity

Sandy Horowitz wants to see if her students understand what measurements are needed to correctly calculate area and perimeter. Her students are familiar with the procedures for finding area and perimeter, and today she is also challenging students with an irregular shape. Sandy starts by providing her students with a diagram without any measurements. She continues, "I want you to figure out what would be the fewest measurements needed to accurately calculate both the area and perimeter of this irregular shape. Then, I want you to explain the process you used to figure out your answer."

Figure 1.3 Mathematics Classroom—Understanding Activity

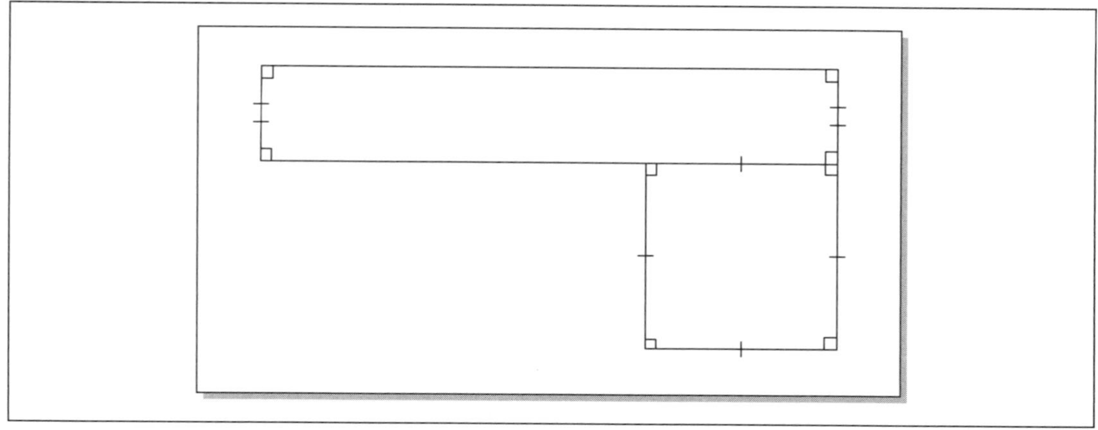

Self-Expressive Activity

After studying area and perimeter with his class, Bruce Wong wants to inspire his students to think more divergently about mathematics. Today, Bruce's class will be working on an open-ended assignment. Bruce tells his students that they will be working with four shapes—one rectangle, one square, one trapezoid, and one equilateral triangle. He elaborates on the assignment, "I want each of you to create your own area and perimeter problem by connecting these four shapes. The shapes can be of any measurement you choose. You can arrange the shapes in any way you want, but you have to be able to solve your problem using only four measurements." For his students that finish the assignment early, Bruce challenges them to create another problem connecting the same four shapes in a different way. However, this time students must be able to solve the problems they create using only three, two, or even one measurement.

Interpersonal Activity

Julia Lacomba always tries to have her students find personal relevance in mathematics, and the topic of area and perimeter is no different. Today, Julia is asking her students to draw up a floor plan of their homes, illustrating the dimensions of each room. "I want each of you to picture your home. It doesn't matter how big or small it is, or whether you live in an apartment or a house. Think about each room in your home. What are the dimensions of each room? How do the rooms connect to each other? Draw a floor plan for your home that includes the dimensions of each room." After students have finished their floor plans with estimated measurements, Julia challenges students to answer these two questions: "Suppose that you wanted to carpet each room of your home (except the bathroom and kitchen). How much carpet would you need? What if you wanted to install crown molding or put up a new wallpaper border in each of these rooms? How much total molding or border would you need?"

Each of the four teachers we have just met wants his or her students to learn and understand what area and perimeter are, and how to calculate area and perimeter in different ways. However, each of these teachers has developed a very different activity to use. So, which classroom activity would you enjoy most? Which would you like least or try to avoid? If you have a preference for one activity over the others, then this is the first signal of your mathematical learning style. Your style influences the types of activities you enjoy and how you approach learning and teaching.

If you enjoyed William Merkel's activity, then your dominant style preference is most likely *Mastery.* Students who prefer the Mastery style learn best step-by-step and enjoy activities with clear procedures and one correct answer.

If you selected Sandy Horowitz's activity, then your dominant style preference is most likely *Understanding.* Students who prefer the Understanding style enjoy analytical tasks where they have to figure things out and explain or prove their answers.

If you were drawn to Bruce Wong's activity, then your dominant style preference is most likely *Self-Expressive.* Students who prefer the Self-Expressive style thrive when they are given choices, have the opportunity to be creative, or are asked to explore alternative solutions to problems.

If you chose Julia Lacomba's activity, then your dominant style preference is most likely *Interpersonal.* Students who prefer the Interpersonal style learn best from others or when the content has a strong relevance to their lives. These students do well with activities that are personal, connected to their lives, or that result in helping others.

Now that you have a deeper understanding of how the four styles play out in mathematics instruction, ask yourself this: What happens if we combine the work of William, Sandy, Bruce, and Julia? What if over the course of the unit on area and perimeter, students completed all four of these activities? We get a differentiated mathematics classroom, one in which every learner gets what he or she wants and needs, while also growing underdeveloped capacities by working in weaker styles. In short, we get an instructional program that asks students to:

- Apply formulas, compute accurately, and reinforce skills through practice (Mastery).
- Discover patterns, make generalizations, and develop mathematically sound explanations (Understanding).
- Think creatively, develop new problems, and try out a variety of problem-solving approaches (Self-Expressive).
- Make personal connections and solve real-world math problems (Interpersonal).

Thus, style-based mathematics instruction is more than a way to invite a greater number of students into the teaching and learning process. Style-based instruction is, plain and simple, good math—balanced, rigorous, and diverse. Fifth-grade teacher Barb Heinzman puts it this way:

> What I saw right away was that not only did different students approach mathematics using different learning styles, but real mathematical power required using all four styles. Think about it: If you can't compute accurately, explain your ideas, discover solutions, and apply math in the real world—you don't know math. Miss even one of these and you miss the boat. The problem with most math programs is they emphasize just one of these and leave out the rest. By building every unit so it includes all four styles of learning, I support all my students, and I stretch them into areas where they wouldn't naturally go. (Strong, Silver, & Perini, 2001, p. 79)

Barb's experiences as a teacher of mathematics are borne out by current research showing that style-based teaching leads to improved learning and higher levels of achievement. For example, Robert J. Sternberg (2006) and his colleagues conducted a remarkable series of studies involving diverse student populations including students from Alaskan Eskimo villages, rural Kenya, and a wide range of student populations from across the United States. In these studies, students were taught mathematics (along with other subjects) in five different ways:

- A memory-based approach emphasizing identification and recall of facts and concepts;
- An analytical approach emphasizing critical thinking, evaluation, and comparative analysis;
- A creative approach emphasizing imagination and invention;
- A practical approach emphasizing the application of concepts to real-world contexts and situations; and
- A diverse approach that incorporated all the approaches.

Out of these studies, Sternberg and his colleagues drew two conclusions. First, whenever students were taught in a way that matched their own style preferences, those students outperformed students who were mismatched. Second, and even more important, students who were taught using a diversity of approaches outperformed all other students on both performance assessments and on multiple-choice memory tests. Sternberg (2006) goes on to say, "In other words, even if our goal is just to maximize students' retention of information, teaching for diverse styles of learning still produces superior results. This approach apparently enables students to capitalize on their strengths and to correct or to compensate for their weaknesses, encoding material in a variety of interesting ways" (pp. 33–34).

So now that we know what learning styles are, what they look like when applied in the mathematics classroom, and that teaching with learning styles in mind leads to improved teaching and higher levels of learning, how do we incorporate them into our own classrooms? By using a variety of tools. Chapters 2 through 5 of this book each contain a set of tools that support one of the four mathematical learning styles. Mastery tools (Chapter 2) increase retention of critical terms and deepen students' computation and practice skills. Understanding tools (Chapter 3) challenge students to take an analytical approach to mathematics. Self-Expressive tools (Chapter 4) allow students to use their creativity and imagination to explore mathematical ideas. Interpersonal tools (Chapter 5) draw out the personal and social aspects of mathematics.

HOW DO I SELECT THE RIGHT TOOL FOR THE RIGHT LEARNING SITUATION?

A quick glance at the table of contents shows that the four mathematical learning styles serve as the framework for this book. Chapters 2 through 5 contain tools that support Mastery, Understanding, Self-Expressive, and Interpersonal styles, respectively. Chapter 6 provides four different strategies for combining tools from all four styles to design more powerful tests, lessons, assessment systems, and units of study. Our intent in designing the text around styles is to make the important goal of differentiating mathematics instruction eminently manageable for teachers. By selecting tools from different chapters of the book, teachers naturally accommodate and challenge learners of all four styles.

However, helping teachers of mathematics diversify their teaching practices has not been our sole purpose in writing this book. More generally, *Math Tools* has been written to provide all mathematics teachers with a repertoire of high-impact instructional techniques that they can begin using tomorrow, techniques that:

- Help students meet rigorous academic standards.
- Are backed by a reliable research base.
- Can be used to meet a host of instructional objectives, from preparing students for new learning all the way to developing performance-based assessments that ask students to show what they have learned.

That's why we begin Chapters 2 through 5 with a Math Tools Matrix. Each Math Tools Matrix lays out the tools within the chapter and provides the reader with an at-a-glance overview of each tool. Take a look at the Math Tools Matrix for Chapter 2 (pages 18–19). Notice how the tools are listed and described down the left side of the matrix. If you follow the top row across the two pages, from left to right, you'll also notice that the columns are broken up into three distinct sections labeled

"NCTM Process Standards," "Educational Research Base," and "Instructional Objectives" (also known as "The Seven P's"). By tracking a tool across the matrix, you can gather the vital statistics for that tool to help you determine how well it fits your purposes. To see how this process works, let's use the first tool in the book, Knowledge Cards, to take a quick tour of a Math Tools Matrix.

Vital Statistic 1: Title and Flash Summary

The name of a particular tool is often not enough to give new readers a sense of how a tool works or to jog the memories of readers who are using *Math Tools* more like a reference text. So, after the page number that tells you where to find the tool, the first thing you'll see is the tool's name and a "flash summary" that describes it in one sentence or less. Figure 1.4 below shows this title and flash summary cell for the Knowledge Cards tool.

Figure 1.4 Math Tools Matrix—Knowledge Cards Title and Summary

Knowledge Cards—Students create "flash cards" to visualize and remember complex terms and concepts.

Vital Statistic 2: NCTM Process Standards

In developing ten comprehensive standards for mathematics instruction, the NCTM has provided all mathematics instructors with a map of the terrain—an overarching set of goals to drive decisions about planning, teaching, assessment, and curriculum design. The first five of these standards address specific areas of mathematical content. You will not find these NCTM Content Standards on the Math Tools Matrix. Why? Because tools are not content-specific; they can be used to deliver instruction in any content—from addition facts to the use of geometric principles in Renaissance art.

But while tools are not content-specific, they are thinking-specific. That is to say, each tool engages students in one or more mathematical thinking processes. That's where the back half of the NCTM Standards, known as the Process Standards, come into the picture (National Council of Teachers of Mathematics, 2000). These five standards help teachers keep teaching and learning focused on the development of the following key mathematical thinking processes.

1. *Problem Solving,* or building students' capacity to analyze problems, develop and implement problem-solving strategies, and evaluate the effectiveness of their solutions.

2. *Reasoning and Proof,* or developing students' ability to support claims mathematically, explain how the mathematics they learn works, and justify the choices they make as problem solvers.

3. *Communication,* or helping students clarify and deepen their thinking through listening, reading, writing, and exchanging ideas with fellow learners and problem solvers.

4. *Connections,* or expanding students' opportunities to explore the deep relationships between mathematical concepts as well as how mathematics is used in the world beyond school.

5. *Representation,* or helping students explore and gain proficiency in the different ways in which mathematical ideas can be expressed and translated into alternate forms.

If you follow the Knowledge Cards row across the page (or look at Figure 1.5), you will see that the Communication and Representation fields contain darkened circles, while the other three Process Standards have empty fields. This tells you that using Knowledge Cards will help you and your students meet the Communication and Representation standards.

Figure 1.5 Math Tools Matrix—NCTM Process Standards for *Knowledge Cards*

MASTERY				
NCTM PROCESS STANDARDS				
Problem Solving	Reasoning and Proof	Communication	Connections	Representation
		●		●

Vital Statistic 3: Educational Research Base

When it comes to instruction, we know better than ever before which techniques and strategies work. Numerous "meta-analytic" studies—studies that combine the results from many other research studies to create a larger and more reliable field of data—have helped the educational community to identify a set of best practices that consistently yield results in the classroom. Of these meta-analytic studies, there is one in particular that stands out: Robert Marzano, Debra Pickering, and Jane Pollock's *Classroom Instruction That Works: Research-Based Strategies for Increasing Student Achievement* (2001). By comparing the effects of different instructional strategies on student performance, the researchers at Mid-continent Research for Education and Learning (McREL) identified and ranked the nine classroom practices that lead to the greatest gains in student achievement (Marzano, Pickering, & Pollock, 2001).

1. *Identifying similarities and differences:* Comparisons, analogies, metaphors, and classification strategies.

2. *Summarizing and note taking:* Teaching students how to collect, record, and condense information.
3. *Reinforcing effort and providing recognition:* Developing a positive classroom environment in which student work and achievement are a significant part of the classroom conversation.
4. *Homework and practice:* Strategies that allow students to rehearse and retain their learning both in the classroom and on their own.
5. *Nonlinguistic representation:* Using visualization, icons, symbols, and graphic organizers to represent learning.
6. *Cooperative learning:* Creating structures that allow students to work, learn, and develop products and performances as part of productive teams.
7. *Setting objectives and providing feedback:* Helping students identify goals, monitor progress, and develop plans for improvement.
8. *Generating and testing hypotheses:* Developing students' abilities to infer, interpret, and explain through inquiry and investigation.
9. *Cues, questions, and advance organizers:* Helping students activate prior knowledge, connect to new learning, and see the "structure" of what they're about to learn.

Every tool in this book has been chosen or designed with this essential research in mind. In making this strong connection to Marzano, Pickering, and Pollock's research, we have attempted to give teachers of mathematics an easy way to plan and implement research-based lessons. Whenever you select a tool for use in your classroom, you can be sure that it has a reliable research base behind it. Plus, this connection to *Classroom Instruction That Works* gives you a simple way to document how your lesson plans incorporate current and widely respected research.

If you follow our left-to-right tour across the Math Tools Matrix on pages 18–19, you'll see that to Marzano, Pickering, and Pollock's nine categories, we have added two more: *Vocabulary* and *Writing*. Here's why:

10. *Vocabulary:* A large number of studies show that direct vocabulary instruction focused on the most critical academic terms (as opposed to long lists of unprioritized words) yields significant improvement in student comprehension and achievement. In fact, Marzano (2004) shows that effective vocabulary instruction can increase student comprehension by as much as 33 percentile points. Put another way, a student whose understanding of content puts him at the 50th percentile without any vocabulary instruction can move all the way to the 83rd percentile if his teacher provides direct instruction in essential academic terms.
11. *Writing:* "Writing," Douglas Reeves (2002) tells us, "improves performance in all academic areas" (p. 5). And it's not hard to see why. When students are given meaningful opportunities to process ideas in writing, to stop the flow of content and summarize, or elaborate on, or explore connections to other disciplines or their own lives, or develop their own imaginative responses to new content (mathematical or otherwise), the depth of their understanding increases dramatically.

Figure 1.6 below shows this second set of columns labeled "Educational Research Base" on the Math Tools Matrix. The Knowledge Cards tool, with its emphasis on sketching and summarizing critical math terms incorporates three different research-based practices: summarizing and note taking, nonlinguistic representation, and direct vocabulary instruction.

Figure 1.6 Math Tools Matrix—Educational Research Base for *Knowledge Cards*

EDUCATIONAL RESEARCH BASE										
Identifying similarities and differences	Summarizing and note taking	Reinforcing effort and providing recognition	Homework and practice	Nonlinguistic representations	Cooperative learning	Setting objectives and providing feedback	Generating and testing hypotheses	Questions, cues, and advance organizers	Vocabulary	Writing
	●			●					●	

Vital Statistic 4: Instructional Objectives

Any time we select a tool to use in our classroom or incorporate into our lesson or unit designs, we are seeking a way to meet specific instructional objectives or questions. For example:

- How will I **p**repare students for new learning?
- How will I **p**resent new content in a way that is engaging?
- How will students **p**ractice new skills effectively?
- How will students **p**rocess new content deeply?
- How will I engage students in meaningful **p**roblem solving?
- How will students demonstrate or **p**erform what they know and understand?
- How will students **p**ersonalize their learning so that it is meaningful to them?

This list of questions is called the Seven P's (for more on how to use the Seven P's to design comprehensive lessons and units, see pages 253–256). The Seven P's are based on our synthesis of the work of a number of educational researchers concerned with lesson and unit design, including Madeline Hunter (1984), Grant Wiggins and Jay McTighe (2005), and Robert Marzano (2003). By adapting this work to fit the specific demands of the mathematics classroom, the Seven P's serve as a simple framework for matching tools to your own classroom objectives.

So now let's complete our tour of the Math Tools Matrix. If we follow the Knowledge Cards row all the way down to the last set of columns labeled "Instructional Objectives," which contain The Seven P's, we see two different P's represented: *Processing* and *Personalizing* (see Figure 1.7 below).

Figure 1.7 Math Tools Matrix—Instructional Objectives for *Knowledge Cards*

INSTRUCTIONAL OBJECTIVES						
Preparing	Presenting	Practicing	Processing	Problem Solving	Performance	Personalizing
			●			●

This means that as an instructional tool, Knowledge Cards can be used to meet either purpose or both depending on how you use it. For example, you can use Knowledge Cards relatively early in the learning process, thereby offering students a way to process new terms deeply through images and words. On the other hand, you might ask students to work in groups to create a set of Knowledge Cards at the end of a unit. In this context, Knowledge Cards are less about processing new content and more about developing a personally meaningful way to review and remember the important content in the unit. In both cases, however, elements of both processing and personalizing are present. The difference lies in which P gets the greater emphasis.

FIVE WAYS TO USE MATH TOOLS

So far, we have put the lion's share of our attention on the conceptual underpinnings for this book: What are tools? What are learning styles? What's the relationship between tools and styles? What's the relationship between tools and other critical factors in instructional decision making, from NCTM Process Standards to current instructional research to elements of quality lesson and unit design? We end this introduction by refocusing our attention on practical issues. So, before taking the plunge into the 64 tools that make up the remainder of this book, here are five different ways you can put these tools into effective practice.

1. ***Try one out.*** Every tool in this book is here because it makes a difference in the mathematics classroom. After all, a tool, by our standards, is only a tool if it addresses NCTM Process Standards, has a research base behind it, and plays a vital role in making lessons come to life. In other words, tools *work.* So, pick a tool, any tool, and watch what happens. Then try a few more. Before you know it, you and

your students will have your own personal favorites, and a new teaching and learning dynamic will be in full swing in your classroom.

2. ***Use tools to help you meet a particular standard or objective.*** Looking for ways to increase students' mathematical reasoning skills? Just use the Math Tools Matrices to find tools that address the NCTM Process Standard for Reasoning and Proof. Or maybe you're looking to build students' comprehension by helping them master critical concepts and terms or by infusing writing into the curriculum. Use the matrices to locate vocabulary tools or writing tools, respectively. The point is, the tools in this book can help you and your students meet those standards and objectives that matter most in your particular classroom, even as they shift throughout the year.

3. ***Individualize instruction.*** Remember that the tools in this book are organized according to the learning styles they naturally engage. So perhaps you're working with a highly creative Self-Expressive student who just can't seem to memorize and follow the steps in a critical problem-solving procedure. Try a tool like Math Recipes, which will allow students to make a creative comparison between cooking and problem solving and design a "recipe card" that outlines the steps in the procedure. If you want to help Interpersonal learners who wilt during independent seatwork to increase their proficiency as problem solvers, tap into their social nature with tools that either connect problem solving to the world beyond school (e.g., Real-World Connections or Who's Right?) or that challenge them to work as part of a productive problem-solving team (e.g., Cooperative Structures for Promoting Positive Interdependence). Style-based individualization works because every style has identifiable patterns of strength and weakness. Mastery learners may have no problem memorizing terms or following procedures, but often experience real difficulty with open-ended problems ("You mean there is no right answer?!") or high levels of abstraction. Understanding learners may be great at thinking their way through challenging problems, but their hearts often drop into their stomachs when they're asked to work as part of a team. As Robert Sternberg (2006) has shown, allowing students of mathematics to think and work in their strong styles gives them a much better chance at mastering key content and skills. Even better, when students' preferences are accommodated, they become more likely to try to stretch as learners, meaning you can use tools to teach to their strengths and to challenge them to try working in new styles that they might otherwise avoid.

4. ***Differentiate instruction for the entire class.*** While personalized instruction is a powerful teaching and learning model, the truth is that teachers do not often have the luxury of working like doctors, who see their patients one at a time. Teachers work with entire classes, groups of students brought together largely by virtue of their age and by scheduling logistics. The question that this model consistently raises is, *How can I work optimally with* all *of my students?*

Math tools, organized by style, make the work of differentiating instruction and assessment for every learner a manageable proposition. All you need to do is rotate the tools you use in your classroom across all four styles. That way, you can rest assured that your:

- Mastery learners are getting the routine and direction they thrive on while they develop their ability to think conceptually and creatively.
- Understanding learners have the opportunity to think logically and independently while growing their capacities as thoughtful team members.

- Self-Expressive learners get the chance to use their imaginations while learning how to manage and master mathematical procedures.
- Interpersonal learners can learn as part of a problem-solving community, where mathematics connects strongly to the real world, while they build their critical reasoning skills.

As you implement new tools, keep track of which styles you seem to favor and which tools seem to make the biggest impact among your students. And don't forget about Task Rotation (page 222), a strategy that uses tools from all four styles to create truly differentiated assessments.

5. ***Design more powerful lessons, assessments, and units.*** While tools work well on their own, they can also be used as "instructional building blocks." In Chapter 6, you'll find a set of strategies for selecting and combining tools to create larger designs, from lesson plans, to differentiated tests and assessments, to standards-based units of study. These strategies will help you develop a tools-based approach to thinking your way through the bigger picture of lesson planning and unit design.

2

Mastery Math Tools

MASTERY MATH STUDENTS

Want to . . . learn practical information and procedures.

Like math problems that . . . are like problems they have solved before and that use set procedures to produce a single solution.

Approach problem solving . . . in a step-by-step manner.

May experience difficulty when . . . math becomes too abstract or when faced with open-ended problems.

Learn best when . . . instruction is focused on modeling new skills, practicing, and feedback and coaching sessions.

—Silver, Thomas, & Perini (2003)

Mastery Math Tools Matrix

PAGE	MATH TOOL	NCTM PROCESS STANDARDS: Problem Solving	Reasoning and Proof	Communication	Connections	Representation
20	**Knowledge Cards**—Students create "flash cards" to visualize and remember complex terms and concepts.			●		●
23	**Memory Box**—Students collect ideas and images from their memories related to a specific topic.			●		●
25	**Most Valuable Point (MVP)**—Students choose a detail/idea/rule that is most valuable to a concept and explain the decision succinctly.			●		●
27	**Mathematical Summaries**—Students review a concept and explain its meaning in a concise summary.			●		
29	**Fist Lists and Spiders**—Students summarize and synthesize concepts by collecting 5–8 ideas or details about a topic.			●	●	●
32	**Procedural Notes**—Students record the steps in a procedure, perform the steps, and explore the reasoning behind each step.	●	●			
34	**Mathematical Conventions**—Students decide which practice out of two options is more practical/accepted and explain why.		●			
38	**What's Wrong?**—Students examine incorrect answers, make corrections, and explain what went wrong.	●	●			
39	**Mastery Review**—Students solve equations and check their work against the teacher's solutions.	●				
40	**Convergence Mastery**—Students take quizzes with peer review until all students demonstrate complete mastery of the content.			●		
45	**Practice Makes Perfect**—The teacher reviews a skill with students, providing less help each time, until students can perform it by themselves.	●	●			
47	**Mental Math War**—A "War"-like card game to help students practice solving equations with their peers.				●	
49	**Vocabulary Knowledge Rating (VKR)**—Over a unit, students rate their knowledge of terms and reflect on their understanding.			●		
52	**Glossaries**—Students create a short list of terms, define them, and use visualizations and examples to make terms memorable.			●	●	
54	**Word Walls**—A wall-mounted vocabulary reference chart that places critical math vocabulary at the center of learning.			●	●	
57	**Vocabulary Organizers**—Structures that facilitate memorization and make relationships between critical terms explicit.				●	●

MASTERY MATH TOOLS

EDUCATIONAL RESEARCH BASE											INSTRUCTIONAL OBJECTIVES							
Identifying similarities and differences	Summarizing and note taking	Reinforcing effort and providing recognition	Homework and practice	Nonlinguistic representations	Cooperative learning	Setting objectives and providing feedback	Generating and testing hypotheses	Questions, cues, and advance organizers	Vocabulary	Writing	Preparing	Presenting	Practicing	Processing	Problem Solving	Performing	Personalizing	MATH TOOL
	●			●					●					●			●	Knowledge Cards
	●			●					●	●		●		●			●	Memory Box
	●			●					●	●				●			●	MVP
	●		●						●			●		●			●	Mathematical Summaries
	●			●				●	●					●			●	Fist Lists and Spiders
			●					●				●	●		●			Procedural Notes
●								●			●		●	●				Mathematical Conventions
			●				●						●		●			What's Wrong?
			●			●							●		●			Mastery Review
		●	●		●	●							●			●		Convergence Mastery
			●		●	●					●	●	●		●	●	●	Practice Makes Perfect
			●		●								●					Mental Math War
								●	●					●			●	VKR
	●			●					●			●		●			●	Glossaries
									●	●	●			●				Word Walls
				●				●	●		●			●				Vocabulary Organizers

SOURCE: Marzano, R. J., Pickering, D. J., & Pollock, J. E. (2001). *Classroom instruction that works: Research-based strategies for increasing student achievement.* Alexandria, VA: Association for Supervision and Curriculum Development.

KNOWLEDGE CARDS

Purpose

Knowledge Cards are great tools for helping students rehearse procedures, remember laws and theorems, and identify important mathematical terms and topics. When creating Knowledge Cards for mathematics vocabulary, students compose definitions or descriptions in their own words; they also create icons, graphs, or pictures that will help them remember the content of the card. Knowledge Cards lead students toward mastery of mathematical concepts by allowing them to create their own visual and written descriptions, and then using their Knowledge Cards to review and study essential vocabulary.

Overview

Most students remember using flash cards at some point early on in their academic careers, or are at least familiar with the notion of flash cards. Flash cards are commonly used with younger students, but as students grow older and mathematics content becomes more abstract and complex, flash cards begin to fall out of favor. This is unfortunate for two reasons. First, much of the mathematics that students encounter at the middle- and high-school level incorporates plotting, graphing, and drawing, or necessitates some other form of visual representation. Second, when working with content that is more conceptual, having students visualize abstract concepts helps deepen their understanding. Using Knowledge Cards in any mathematics classroom helps students to:

- Make mathematical concepts their own; students write definitions and descriptions in their own words and draw their own icons or pictures.
- Use their imagination to understand mathematics; by creating their own Knowledge Cards, students have the opportunity to explore concepts and to define vocabulary in ways that are especially meaningful to them.
- Remember, practice, and master mathematics vocabulary and concepts; Knowledge Cards are effective and fun for students to use independently, in pairs, or within small groups.

Once students have created their Knowledge Cards, the cards become ideal tools for helping students rehearse new learning so that they can commit important concepts to their permanent memories. As research on effective practice shows, early practice sessions should be short but frequently occurring. As students become increasingly comfortable with the material, practice periods should be spaced out over longer intervals (Marzano, Norford, Paynter, Pickering, & Gaddy, 2001). Here are five quick ideas for using Knowledge Cards to make these practice sessions effective and fun.

- *Independent practice:* Students quiz themselves using their Knowledge Cards. As students approach mastery of the content, the cards with the most explicit concepts should be removed.
- *Class opener:* The teacher circulates around the room and quizzes students by showing the class a Knowledge Card. The teacher then calls upon a student to provide the correct term or definition.
- *Class closer:* For the last few minutes of the class period, students work in pairs to quiz and coach their partners by using their Knowledge Cards.

- *Class competition:* Students are divided into two equal teams. One team is shown a Knowledge Card by the teacher and has a limited amount of time to provide the correct answer. If there is an incorrect answer given, then the opposing team has a chance to answer. Depending on the class and the content, the teacher may elect to award points for correct answers and keep score.
- *Home reinforcement:* for homework or in preparation for an in-class test, a parent or older sibling quizzes students. They then exchange roles and continue exploring the content.

Steps

1. Identify a concept, topic, or idea.
2. Generate a list of essential vocabulary words for your chosen topic.
3. Show students what sample Knowledge Cards look like.
4. Provide students with index cards or other materials on which they can create their Knowledge Cards.
5. Remind students that their Knowledge Cards must have a term with a graph, icon, or drawing that describes it. On the back of students' Knowledge Cards there must be a definition or explanation written in their own words.
6. Discourage students from copying textbook definitions word-for-word or from using words and phrases that they don't completely understand.
7. Encourage students to be clear, descriptive, and creative when composing both sides of their Knowledge Cards.

Examples

Figure 2.1 Student's Knowledge Cards for *Translation* and *Reflection*

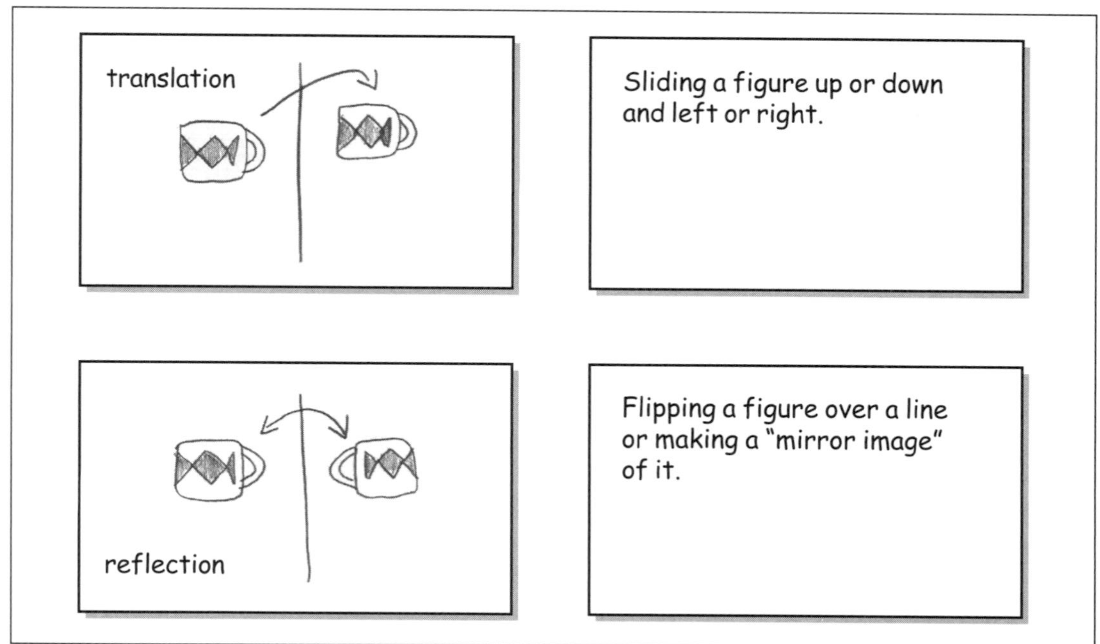

Figure 2.2 Student's Knowledge Cards for *Tangent* and *Secant*

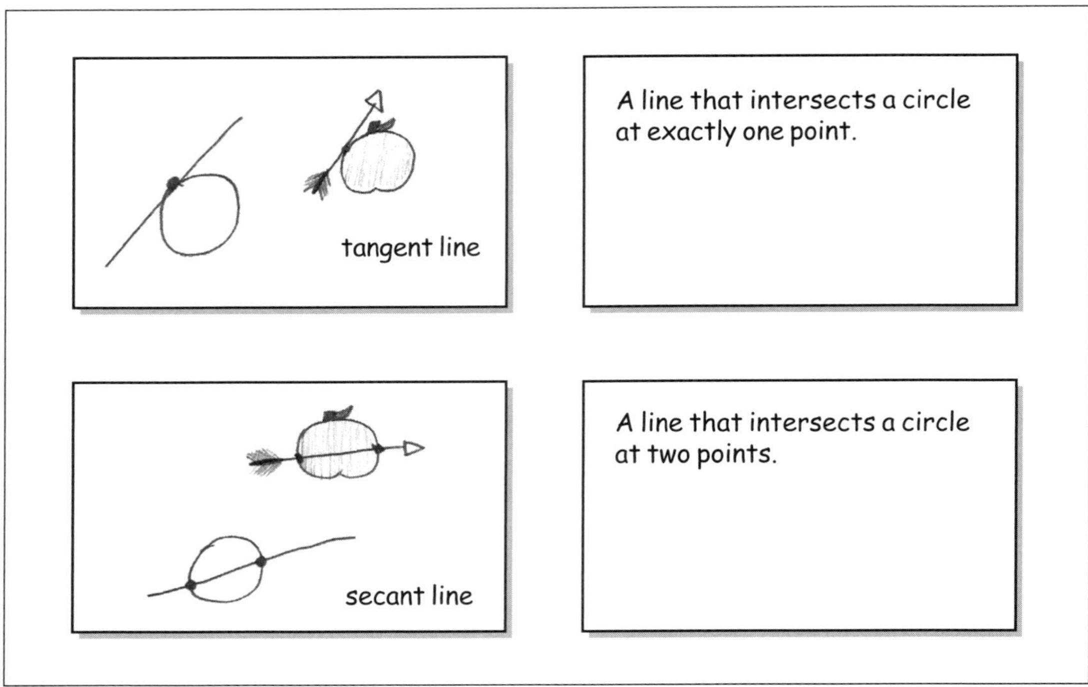

tangent line
A line that intersects a circle at exactly one point.
secant line
A line that intersects a circle at two points.

Figure 2.3 Student's Knowledge Card for *Scale Drawing*

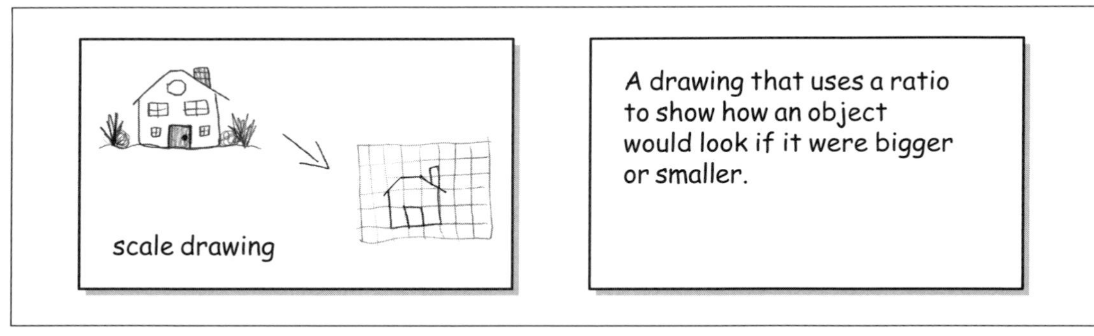

scale drawing
A drawing that uses a ratio to show how an object would look if it were bigger or smaller.

Figure 2.4 Student's Knowledge Card for *Absolute Value*

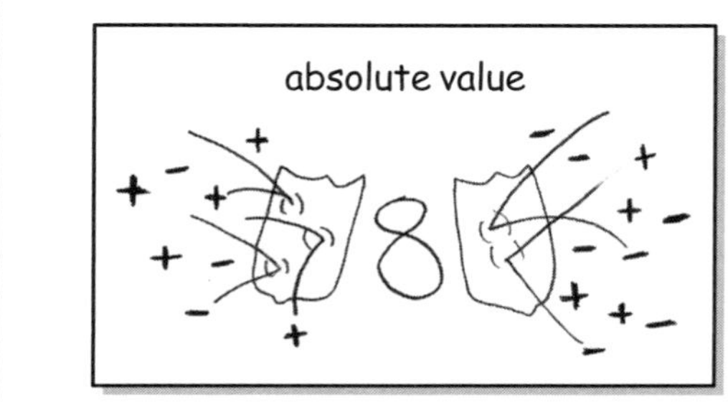

The units a number is from zero on the number line without being positive or negative.

MEMORY BOX

Purpose

Memory Box encourages students to tap into their prior knowledge and let the contents of their memories flow freely onto paper, where they are collected to become a set of meaningful visual and written notes. As students create Memory Boxes, they are reflecting upon what has been taught by accessing new and prior knowledge.

Overview

The Memory Box technique is used to prompt students to think about a topic that has been previously presented. Whether students are asked to recall information from earlier in the day or earlier in the marking period, the process is the same. With their textbooks and notebooks put aside and armed only with an empty box drawn on a blank sheet of paper, students retrieve as much information as they can from their memories. Students explore what they know and remember about a topic, filling their Memory Boxes with words, numbers, symbols, and doodles.

Students' unique Memory Boxes can be:

- Kept as a set of personal and creative notes.
- Compared and contrasted in pairs.
- Used as the basis for a competitive review game (see Math Boggle on pages 212–213).
- Used to focus their attention on the big or important ideas related to the topic (see MVP on pages 25–27).

Steps

1. Present or review a topic with students.
2. Allow students time (usually 3–5 minutes) to take new notes or to review previously taken notes.
3. Have students put away their textbooks and notebooks.
4. Distribute copies of (or have students draw) a blank Memory Box.
5. Prompt students to explore their memories and retrieve any relevant information about the topic.
6. Encourage students to be creative as they fill their Memory Boxes with words and pictures.

Examples

Figure 2.5 Student's Memory Box for *Fractions*

My Memory Box:

Fractions help you break things up equally = 1/4

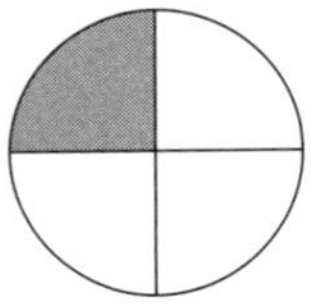

Part of a whole

$\frac{\text{numerator}}{\text{denominator}}$ $\frac{\text{parts under consideration}}{\text{total number of parts in whole}}$

If you add and subtract a fraction the denominator needs to be the same.
1/2 + 2/8 = 4/8 + 2/8 = 6/8

always change a fraction into its simplest form so . . . 6/8 = 3/4

a fraction is another way of writing a division problem

Types of fractions:

Proper: 1/2, 2/5 Mixed improper: $1\frac{1}{2}$, $2\frac{2}{4}$, 5/4, 6/5

Common denominator

Equivalent fractions 1/2 = 2/4 = 3/6

Fractions can be decimals

Figure 2.6 Student's Memory Box for *Circles and Ellipses*

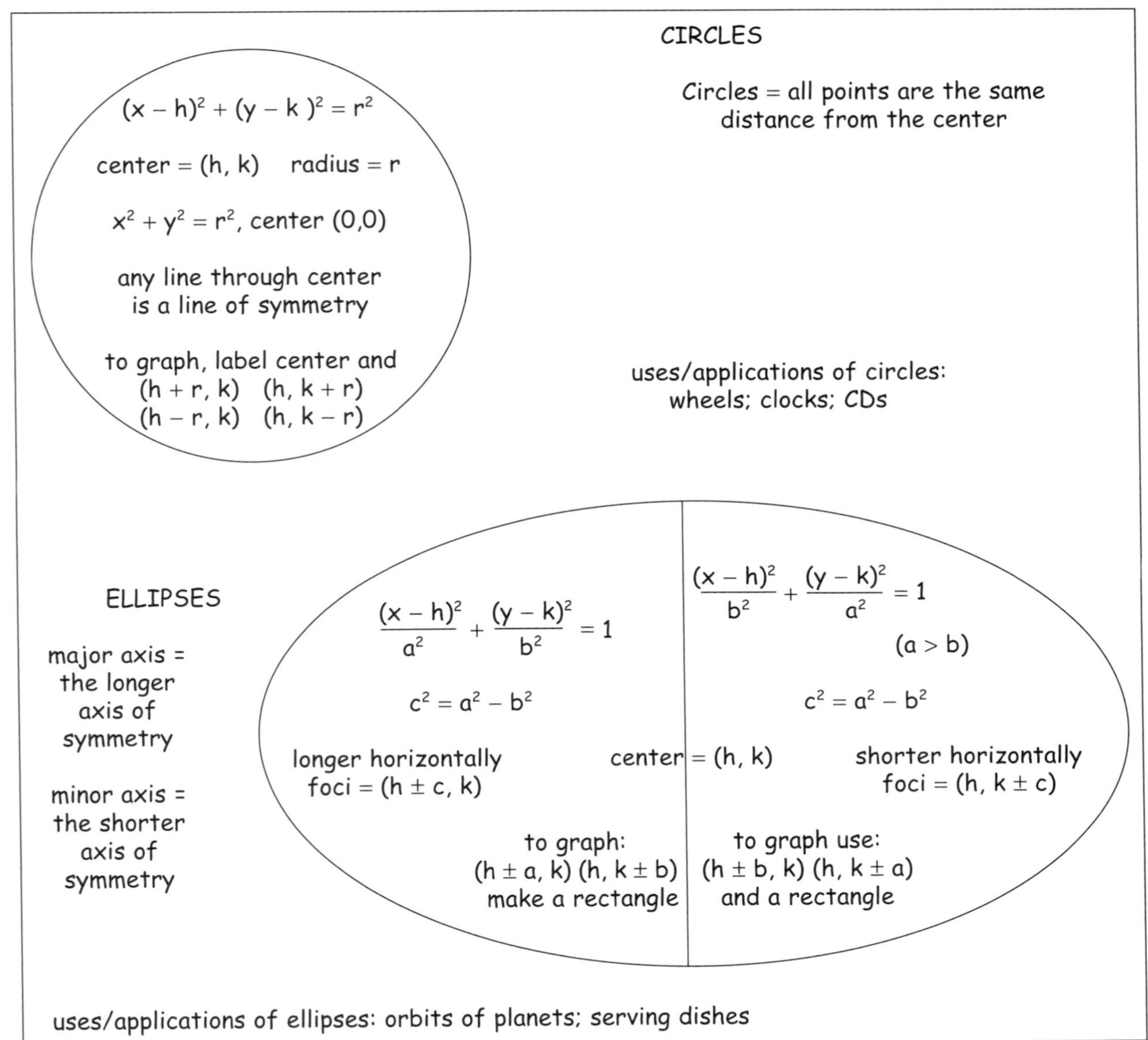

MOST VALUABLE POINT (MVP)

Purpose

Too often we fail to ask students to reflect on their learning; we do not encourage students to elaborate on what they think are the most important concepts they are studying. Having students identify and explain the Most Valuable Point (MVP) from their own notes, lists, or classroom products is a way to engage students in deeper and more critical thought about mathematical concepts.

Overview

When using the MVP technique, the teacher starts by presenting (or reviewing) a topic and giving students time to go over their notes. As students look over their notes, they think about the important and essential elements of the topic and zero in on what they believe is the MVP. The teacher then has students elaborate on their chosen MVP and explain their selection by writing for five minutes. Students then share their MVP selections within small groups or with the entire class.

MVP is easily implemented into any lesson where students generate notes, lists, drawings, or other written or visual products. While MVP is a concise and effective way for students to analyze and consider their own notes and work, MVP also works very well when used in conjunction with the Memory Box and Math Boggle tools (see pages 23–25 and 212–213). By putting all three tools together (Memory Box—MVP—Math Boggle), you can create a powerful memory and review process in which students collect their prior knowledge (Memory Box); identify and elaborate on the most essential information and share their elaborations with their peers (MVP); and then exercise what they have learned and memorized in a competitive review game (Math Boggle).

Steps

1. Have students complete an activity where notes, pictures, and/or lists are generated as part of the process.
2. Allow students time to review their notes.
3. Ask students to think deeply about their work before highlighting what they feel is the MVP.
4. Have students explain their selections for MVP by writing for 5 minutes.
5. Encourage students to share their choices for MVP with their peers, either in small groups or together as a class.

Examples

On the following page is an MVP, accompanied by a set of notes that a high-school student composed after a lecture on the connections between geometry and art.

Figure 2.7 Student's MVP for *Geometry and Art*

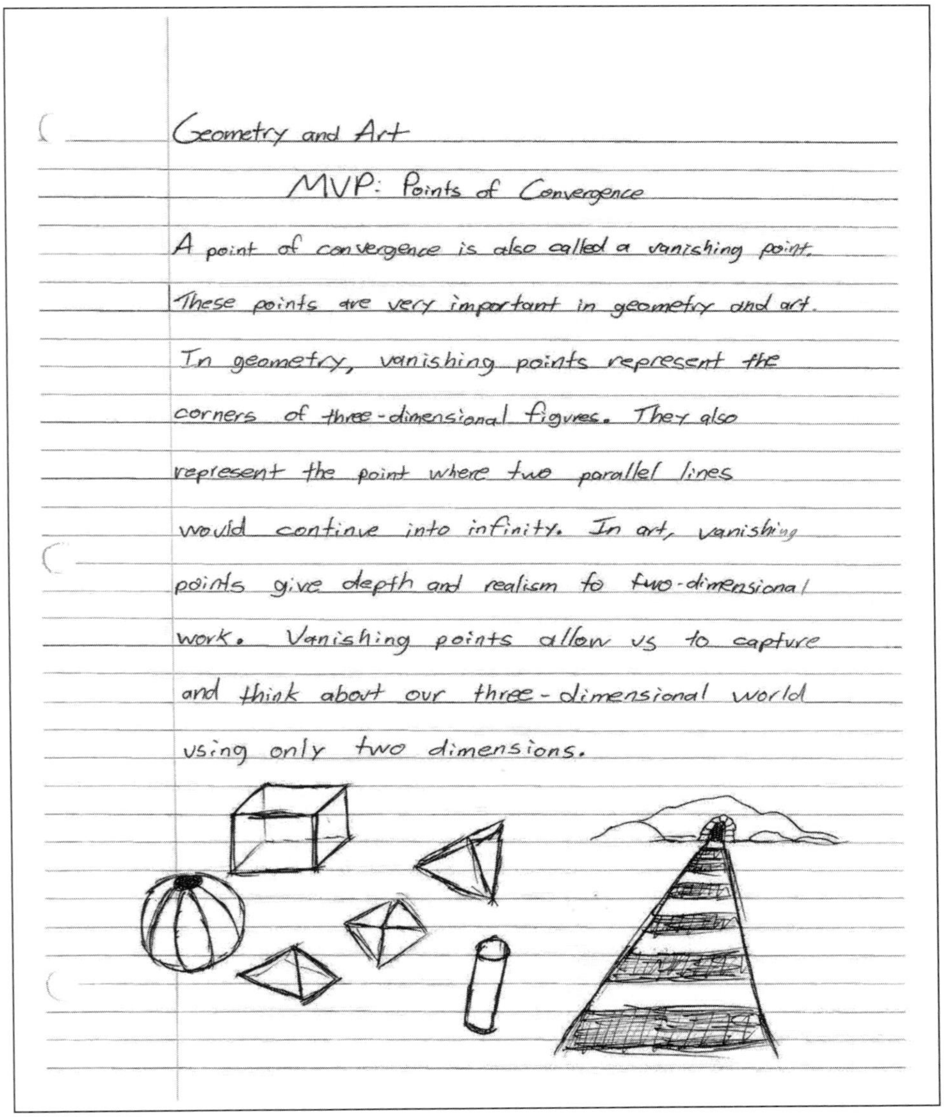

Geometry and Art

MVP: Points of Convergence

A point of convergence is also called a vanishing point. These points are very important in geometry and art. In geometry, vanishing points represent the corners of three-dimensional figures. They also represent the point where two parallel lines would continue into infinity. In art, vanishing points give depth and realism to two-dimensional work. Vanishing points allow us to capture and think about our three-dimensional world using only two dimensions.

MATHEMATICAL SUMMARIES

Purpose

Summarizing, as Rick Wormeli (2005) tells us, is one of the most powerful teaching and learning strategies available to teachers. Yet, in the classroom the power of summarizing is often overlooked. Nowhere is this truer than in mathematics classrooms, where teaching students how to focus their attention on the biggest and most important ideas is often sacrificed in the name of content coverage. But how will students be able to comprehend or remember what we teach them if they don't know how to prioritize information or how to separate the crucial from the marginal? How will students build new learning on top of old learning if they can't call up and restate that learning in the first place?

Mathematical Summaries provides students with a simple, but powerful way to transform a wealth of information into that clear and concise package called a summary.

Overview

Mathematical Summaries begins with a source of information—anything from a reading to a visual prompt to the students' notebooks. Whatever source of information is chosen, the goals of Mathematical Summaries remain the same: encouraging students to take a closer look at the mathematics they are studying, giving them the opportunity to explain content in their own words, and helping them take ownership of the concepts they are learning.

Mathematical Summaries can take several forms. You can ask students to:

- Read or listen to a passage and summarize in their own words the mathematics concepts being discussed.
- Review their notes (including homework, quizzes, and classroom examples) and pick out the critical concepts and key terms.
- Look over a table, chart, or graph (even maps, artwork, or architecture) and explain the mathematics at work.

Steps

1. Direct students to their textbooks or notebooks, or select a relevant passage to discuss.
2. Read the selection with students or have students read the selection independently.
3. Have students review and summarize the selected material then retell what they have read, listened to, or observed using their own words.

Examples

Lemonade Stand

Think about the word problem we solved yesterday about Malcolm's lemonade stand. Write a paragraph that explains Malcolm's problem with the lemons and how we solved it. Include how we figured out which information was important and how we used mathematics to solve Malcolm's problem.

Pythagorean Theorem

Before we continue to learn more about the applications of the Pythagorean Theorem, take some time to think about what you already know. Each of you has a piece of cardstock cut into a right triangle. On one side of the triangle, write down everything you know or think you know about the Pythagorean Theorem. On the reverse side of the triangle, write down at least one question that you have about the Pythagorean Theorem or about Pythagoras himself.

Calculus Integration

Work with a partner and review your notes on the washer method and cylindrical shells method of calculus integration. One student in each pair will review the washer method and the other student will review the cylindrical shells method. Use your notebooks, homework, and written examples to help you review. After you have reviewed your method, present a clear summary for your partner that addresses all of the major points. The person listening to the summary will check for accuracy. Each person in the pair will have a turn at summarizing a method and listening to a summary.

FIST LISTS AND SPIDERS

Purpose

Fist Lists and Spiders help students build and master critical vocabulary by mapping out the connections between mathematical ideas. When creating a Fist List or Spider, students identify and then visually connect important ideas, words, attributes, characteristics, or procedures that are strongly related to the mathematical concept at hand.

Overview

A word is a label that represents an abstract idea; however, words need other words to help them "express themselves." Fist Lists and Spiders are simple mapping techniques that help students generate ideas about a mathematical concept. The visual organizer on which students collect their ideas is either an outline of a hand or an eight-legged spider. Students write the mathematical concept in the center then generate either five or eight ideas, one for each digit on the hand or leg of the spider. Having students create simple maps increases their capacity to commit key information to memory, helps them see critical relationships, and allows them to use both linguistic and visual information to build deep conceptual understanding. Since students cannot simply rephrase a textbook definition or give a single preconceived answer, Fist Lists and Spiders force students to build personally meaningful definitions of the concepts they learn. Fist Lists and Spiders work well with students of all ages: a concept map on coins and their values is every bit as meaningful to a second-grader as a map on logarithms is to a high-school student. Younger students will also enjoy creating their maps by tracing their hands or giving "personalities" (fangs, fuzz, etc.) to their spiders.

Steps

1. Identify a mathematical concept or critical term for students to consider.
2. Provide students with a Hand or Spider Organizer, or allow students to create their own.
3. Have students write the mathematical concept or term being discussed in the center (either the palm of the hand or the body of the spider).

4. Allow students time to think about the focus of their maps and to generate ideas. Have students write down their five or eight best ideas, one in each digit of their Fist List or on each leg of their Spider.
5. Have students share and discuss their maps with a partner or within a small group.
6. Encourage students to share their Fist Lists or Spiders with the entire class and explain the connections that they made between their key ideas and the central mathematical concept or term.

Examples

Figure 2.8 Student's Fist List for *Order of Operations*

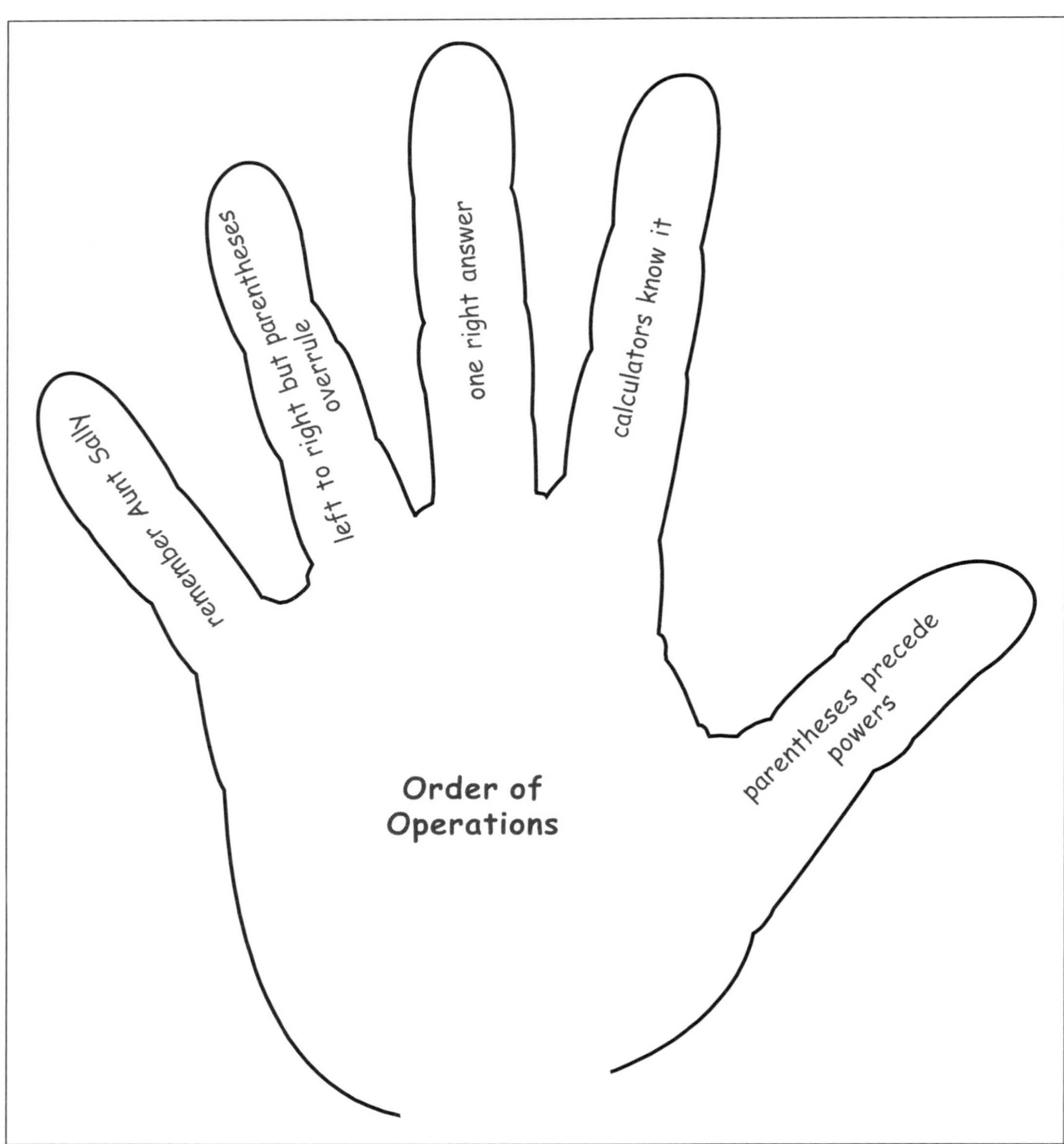

Figure 2.9 Student's Spider Organizer for *Graphs*

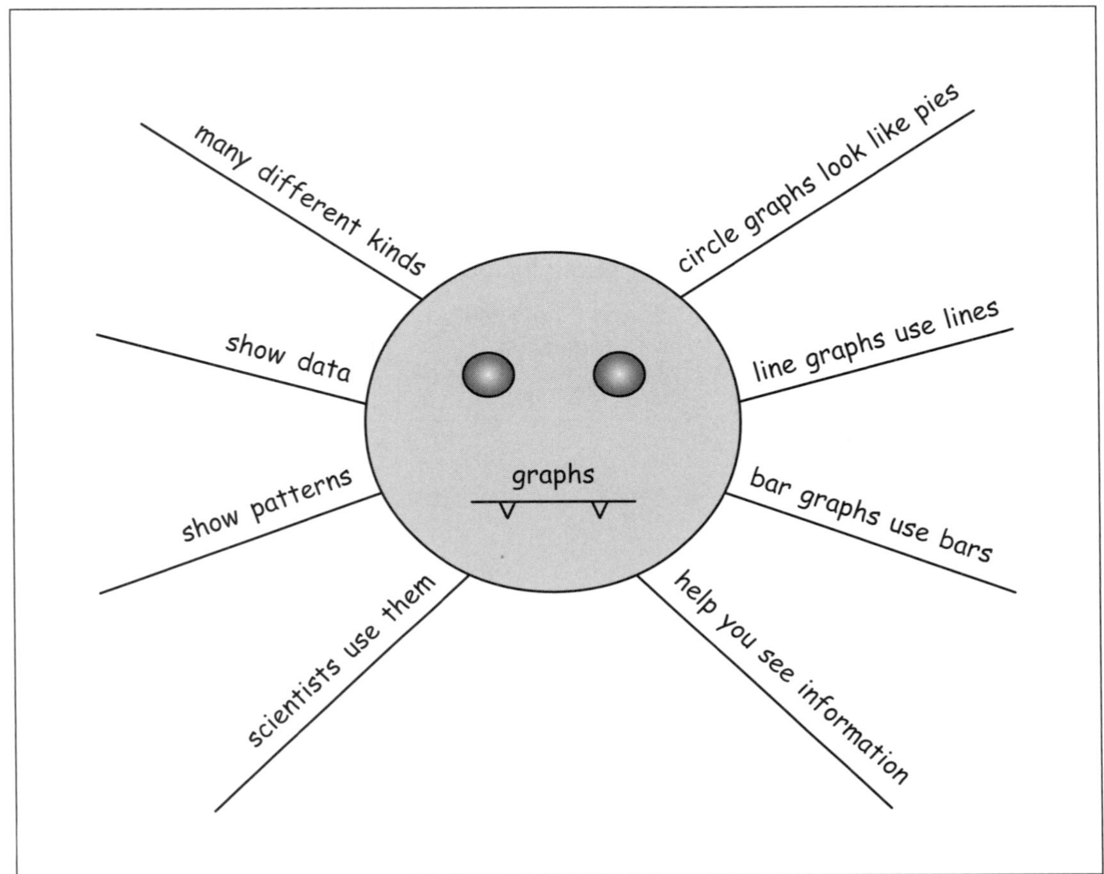

Fist Lists and Spiders can also be restructured to challenge students to think inductively. For example, reversing the Fist List technique by providing students with five related ideas, one at a time, requires students to employ reasoning and critical-thinking skills to correctly identify the mathematical concept in question. These types of Fist Lists are relatively simple for teachers to create and ask students to only listen and process the information as it is presented. The first of the five related ideas (which function now as clues) is the most general. As clues are revealed, they become more specific and usually end with an equation, formula, or some other type of mathematical sequence that represents the essence of the hidden concept. Figure 2.10 shows how this process works with two different concepts: the Pythagorean Theorem in geometry and the Law of Cosines in trigonometry.

Figure 2.10 Alternative Fist List Clues and Concepts

Reversed Fist List Clues Leading to Concepts		
(Geometry)		**(Trigonometry)**
theorem	1st Related Idea/Clue	theorem
triangle	2nd Related Idea/Clue	triangle
relationship among sides	3rd Related Idea/Clue	relates sides and angles
right angle	4th Related Idea/Clue	side-angle-side
$a^2 + b^2 = c^2$	5th and Final Related Idea/Clue	$a^2 + b^2 - 2ab * \cos C = c^2$
Pythogorean Theorem	Concept	Law of Cosines

PROCEDURAL NOTES

Purpose

Procedures are the engine of mathematics. Yet as critical as procedures are, too many students have a hard time explaining why key procedures are important or how they work. The Procedural Notes activity leads students through a close examination of the steps in a mathematical procedure, such as finding the square root. But the tool does more than expose students to algorithmic procedures; students are asked to determine the reasoning behind the procedures and not simply mimic their steps.

Overview

Procedural Notes are less formal than geometric proofs. But, like geometric proofs, Procedural Notes focus students' attention on the individual steps, sequence of steps, and mathematical logic that make up a procedure. It is important for students to learn more than *where* and *when* it is appropriate to apply a procedure; students who achieve at high levels understand *how* and *why* a procedure works.

Procedural Notes can be used in a variety of ways in any mathematics classroom. Procedural Notes may ask students to:

- Produce work that demonstrates that mathematical procedures have been followed and checked.
- Identify the individual procedural steps on their way to solving a problem or equation.
- Explain the mathematical reasoning behind each step in a procedure when given the calculations and solution to a problem.

Steps

1. Introduce (or review) the mathematical procedure that students will investigate.
2. Model how the steps in the procedure work using a sample problem.
3. Explain the reason behind each step in the sequence.
4. Have students copy the steps and the reasons as they work through the problem.
5. Assign problems for students to solve using Procedural Notes.

Examples

Figure 2.11 Student's Procedural Notes for *Order of Operations*

$60 \div 18\ (3 \cdot 2) + 2\ (9 - 1)$		
Steps	**Calculations**	**Reasons**
1. Rewrite the problem	$60 \div 18\ (3 \bullet 2) + 2\ (9 - 1)$	Increase awareness of problem elements.
2. Work inside grouping symbols	$60 \div 18 \bullet 6 + 2 \bullet 8$	Order of operations; calculations inside parentheses or brackets first.
3. Multiply and/or divide left to right!	$\frac{10}{3} \bullet 6 + 2 \bullet 8$ $20 + 2 \bullet 8$ $20 + 16$	Multiplication and division before addition and subtraction. Always left to right, whichever operation appears first.
4. Add and/or subtract left to right!	36	Addition and subtraction from left to right, do whichever operation appears first.

Figure 2.12 Student's Procedural Notes for *Quadratic Equations*

$7x^2 + 3x = 4$		
Steps	**Calculations**	**Reasons**
1. Express equation in form: $ax^2 + bx + c = 0$	$7x^2 + 3x = 4$ $7x^2 + 3x - 4 = 0$	Standard equation form for quadratic.
2. Identify values of a, b, and c	$a = 7$ $b = 3$ $c = -4$	Identifies variables for use in quadratic formula.
3. If $a \neq 0$, write "quadratic." If $a = 0$, write "not quadratic" and stop.	quadratic	Confirms that equation is quadratic and that the quadratic formula is applicable.
4. Write quadratic formula and replace variables a, b, and c.	$x = \frac{-b \pm \sqrt{b^2 - 4ac}}{2a}$ $x = \frac{-3 \pm \sqrt{3^2 - 4 \cdot 7 \cdot (-4)}}{2 \cdot 7}$	Clarifies relationship of a, b, and c to the quadratic formula.
5. Simplify.	$x = \frac{-3 \pm \sqrt{121}}{14}$ $x = \frac{-3 \pm 11}{14}$	Expresses solution in useable form.
6. Express solution in set notation.	$\left\{\frac{4}{7}, -1\right\}$	Mathematical convention; solutions are in a solution set.

MATHEMATICAL CONVENTIONS

Purpose

The world of mathematics is filled with procedures, notations, and common practices that, while seemingly insignificant to many students, help to clarify abstract concepts and make calculations manageable. We call these common protocols conventions. A mathematical *convention* is a:

- General agreement or acceptance of certain practices or attitudes.
  - By convention, on a graph the axes are labeled.
  - Polynomials are written with terms in decreasing order.
  - There are conventions for writing restrictions when theorems, problems, or properties include variables in the denominators of fractions.
- Procedure, or technique widely accepted by a group; a custom.
  - Restrictions associated with answers are explicitly stated if not clearly understood, e.g., $a^{-1} = \frac{1}{a}$, $a \neq 0$.
  - In some classrooms, the teacher requires three points to be graphed on a line instead of two points.

Students need to make decisions about when conventions are being used appropriately and explain why they made their choices. In this way, Mathematical Conventions technique helps students to see mathematics terms and notations, not just as jargon or glyphs, but as helpful and useful expressions of mathematical concepts.

Overview

The Mathematical Conventions technique enables students to increase their fluency in the language of mathematics. To use the Mathematical Conventions technique, the teacher identifies the conventions associated with a lesson or unit. These conventions can be words, rules, symbols, notations, or protocol for formatting or simplifying expressions.

Built into the Mathematical Conventions technique is an assessment process in which students examine two options (one that uses the convention correctly and one that does not). Students select the accepted, or more correct, convention and then justify their choices by writing a brief explanation.

Steps

1. Identify all of the relevant conventions that will be used for a lesson or unit and explain the rationale for each convention.
2. Allow students time to briefly review the conventions.
3. Provide students with a worksheet that has accepted conventions paired up with common alternatives.
4. Have students choose which item in each pair is the preferred, or more correct, use of the convention. Students then explain in writing the thinking behind their choices.

Examples

In all of the examples of Mathematical Conventions that follow, students are asked to pick between two options and to explain their choices in the spaces provided.

Figure 2.13 Mathematical Conventions for *Simplifying Fractions*

	Option I	Option II	Explanation
A	$\frac{3}{1}$	3	
B	$\frac{4}{8}$	$\frac{1}{2}$	

(Continued)

Figure 2.13 (Continued)

	Option I	Option II	Explanation
C	$\frac{5}{7}$	$\frac{-5}{-7}$	
D	6x	$\frac{6x}{1}$	
E	$-\frac{2}{9}$	$\frac{2}{-9}$	
F	$\frac{7}{6}$	$1\frac{1}{6}$	
G	$\frac{2}{0}$	undefined	

Figure 2.14 Mathematical Conventions for Finding the *Area of Geometric Figures*

	Option I	Option II	Explanation
A	Triangle $A = \frac{b \bullet h}{2}$	Triangle $A = \frac{1}{2}h(b_1 + b_2)$	
B	Circle $A = \pi r^2$	Circle $A = r \bullet r \bullet 3.14159$	
C	Trapezoid $A = \frac{1}{2}bh$	Trapezoid $A = h \bullet \frac{b_1 + b_2}{2}$	
D	Square $A = b \bullet h$	Square $A = s^2$	

Figure 2.15 Mathematical Conventions for *Solving Equations and Inequalities*

	Option I	Option II	Explanation
A	$-\frac{-2}{-3}=\frac{2}{-3}$	$-\frac{-2}{-3}=\frac{-2}{3}$	
B	$\frac{1}{x-1}-\frac{x}{x-1}=\frac{1-x}{x-1}$ $=-\frac{x-1}{x-1}$ $=-1$	$\frac{1}{x-1}-\frac{x}{x-1}=\frac{1-x}{x-1}$ $=-1,\quad x\neq 1$	
C	$-2x+8>4$ $\frac{-2x+8}{2}>\frac{4}{2}$ $-x+4>2$ $-x>-2$ $(-1)(-x)<(-1)(-2)$ $x<2$	$-2x+8>4$ $-2x+8-8>4-8$ $-2x>-4$ $\frac{-2x}{-2}>\frac{-4}{-2}$ $x<2$	

Figure 2.16 Mathematical Conventions for *the Physics of Speed and Velocity*

	Option I	Option II	Explanation
A	Speed $s=\frac{d}{t}$	Speed $d=s\bullet t$	
B	Interval of Time t_1-t_2	Interval of Time Δt	
C	Average Velocity $=\frac{\Delta d}{\Delta t}$	Average Velocity $=\frac{d}{\Delta t}$	

WHAT'S WRONG?

Purpose

Everyone makes mistakes. This is especially true of students who are learning new mathematical concepts. Whether students are analyzing a word problem or reviewing quizzes they have taken, the process of gathering information, looking at calculations, and rooting out errors is essential to future learning. What's Wrong? asks students to analyze problems, look for errors in computation, logic, or procedural application, and to debug these errors. As students become aware of common sources of confusion or patterns in their miscalculations, they increase their proficiency in computation and problem solving.

Overview

The What's Wrong? technique revolves around a word problem, series of calculations, or some other form of mathematical work containing errors. As students examine the work, they find the errors, correct them, and then explain the mistakes that were made and how they fixed them. Through this debugging process, students learn to appreciate the importance of checking the accuracy of their work, making sure their answers are reasonable, and not rushing through their calculations.

Steps

1. Present students with a work sample that leads to an incorrect answer or a work sample whose answer, though correct, was obtained by an incorrect method.
2. Allow students time to review the work and make the necessary corrections.
3. Have students explain what went wrong and how they fixed the problem.

Examples

What's wrong with geometric figures?

Correct the following statements about common geometric figures:

- *Rectangle:* a figure with four angles of equal measure.
- *Triangle:* a figure with three angles of equal measure and three sides of equal length.
- *Circle:* a figure with an area of πr^2, where the diameter (d) is one half the length of the radius (r).
- *Square:* a figure with opposite sides of equal length and opposite angles of equal measure.

What's wrong with the check?

You and three of your friends go out to dinner at a Spanish restaurant. All of you agree that you will split the bill into four equal shares. For dinner you order:

- 2 Garlic Shrimp appetizers @ $4.50 each
- 2 Chorizo appetizers @ $3.50 each
- 2 Paella entrées @ $9.00 each

- 2 Lemon chicken entrées @ $8.00 each
- 4 Iced teas @ $2.00 each

Your friend takes out his cell phone and uses the phone's calculator to figure out the cost of the meal. He enters the following sequence of keys:

$$2 \bullet 4.5 + 2 \bullet 3.5 + 2 \bullet 9 + 2 \bullet 8 + 4 \bullet 2 \div 4 = 1{,}468$$

You are shocked to find out that your friend's calculations resulted in $1,468 per person! What is wrong with the answer your friend found? What is the correct answer?

What's wrong with standardized testing?

Look at the sample multiple choice question below (you would find similar questions on the SAT). The correct answer to this question is B. The other four choices (A, C, D, E) are known as distracters and they represent answers that are the results of common mistakes in computation or logic. Look at the distracters and identify the error that leads to each incorrect answer.

For all numbers, a, b, and c, the operation $a \bullet b = a - ab$.

What is $a \bullet (b \bullet c)$?

A. $a - ab - ac - abc$
B. $a - ab + abc$
C. $a + ab - ac + abc$
D. $a^2 - ab^2 - abc$
E. $a^2 - ab^2 - a^2bc$

What's wrong with reducing fractions?

$$\frac{16}{64} = \frac{1\cancel{6}}{\cancel{6}4} = \frac{1}{4}$$

MASTERY REVIEW

Purpose

Mastery Review encourages students to manage their own learning by developing their abilities to make calculations and check their own work without direct teacher instruction.

Overview

Mastery Review is a technique where the teacher provides assistance to students without verbally giving the class step-by-step directions. Instead, students are provided with a problem to solve individually. Once students have started working on the problem on their own, the teacher begins to work through the problem correctly on the board (or with the help of a computer or overhead projector). As students begin to master the mathematical procedure, they will look to their teacher's work less for instruction and more to check their own answers.

Students should not wait for the teacher to begin working, nor should they be copying the teacher's work without attempting the problem on their own first.

Mastery Review continues in this way at a brisk pace with a series of problems. The teacher monitors student work during the Mastery Review activity to determine if the problems should remain similar or be made progressively harder. Once all students have completed and reviewed their work, the teacher asks students to reflect on the process and encourages them to raise questions about any elements of the process that they found difficult or confusing.

Steps

1. Identify a mathematical procedure to review with students.
2. Develop a series of problems for students to solve. Depending on classroom familiarity and proficiency with the procedure, the series of problems can be similar or increase in complexity.
3. Have students begin working through the first problem. As students work, complete the problem correctly for all students to see.
4. Invite students to check their work against your own and encourage them to fix any errors they have made.
5. Do not provide students with any instruction. Instead, allow students to compare their own work to the correct work on display. This enables students to see procedures in action and make the content their own.
6. Lead a discussion after the activity is completed where students reflect upon the process and have an open forum to ask questions.

Examples

Whether the topic is adding two-digit numbers in the third grade or learning basic integrals in high school calculus, Mastery Review is a versatile tool that can be used in any mathematics classroom. It is for this reason that explicit examples have not been included.

CONVERGENCE MASTERY

Purpose

Find a classroom where each student learns and masters content and skills at the same pace and you will find a classroom with an enrollment of one. Yet we know that real classrooms contain many students, each of whom must be given an equal chance to practice new skills and demonstrate mathematical competence. Convergence Mastery makes this level of differentiated learning possible for many different concepts and skills in mathematics classrooms by offering students a series of short quizzes with only two possible grades: 100% and Incomplete. Students who score 100% early in the process serve as coaches and study partners for students who have yet to achieve 100%. This way, all students converge toward mastery.

Overview

Convergence Mastery helps teachers to quickly see which students have mastered a particular skill. At the same time, the tool gives less-proficient students further opportunities to continue practicing the skill. Convergence Mastery can be used with virtually any skill from any area or level of mathematics. In preparing a Convergence Mastery activity, a teacher selects a focus skill and develops a series of short quizzes with problems or questions that call for the application of the focus skill. While the skill on the quizzes remains constant, the actual problems or questions will vary from quiz to quiz. Before taking the first quiz, students practice the skill and review in pairs or in small groups. Students then break away to take the first quiz individually. After all students have completed the quiz, students return to their pairs or small groups. The teacher provides the correct answers to the quiz, and students grade a classmate's quiz. There are only two possible grades:

- *Incomplete*—for students with 1 or more incorrect answers
- *100%*—for students who answer every question correctly

Students who achieve 100% on a quiz are not required to take any additional quizzes. Instead, they become responsible for helping their partners or group members review, make corrections, and prepare for the next quiz. Students who have yet to score 100% then take a subsequent quiz. The activity continues in this way until all students have scored 100%.

Steps

1. Identify a focus skill.
2. Develop a series of short quizzes. (Each quiz should include identical concepts and skills with different content and questions.)
3. Organize students into pairs or small groups.
4. Have students prepare for the first quiz by reviewing the skill and any relevant mathematical concepts.
5. Administer the quiz to all of the students. (Students complete their quizzes independently.)
6. Share the correct answers to the quiz.
7. Have students grade their partner's or another group member's quiz and then review and prepare for the next quiz.
8. Excuse any students who received a score of 100% from any further quizzes. Instead, have these students help their partners or group members correct errors and prepare for the next quiz.
9. Give a follow-up quiz to students who have not yet scored 100%.
10. Repeat the process (steps 5 through 9) until all students have mastered (or increased their proficiency of) the focus skill.

Examples

Figure 2.17 Convergence Mastery Questions for *Measuring Centimeters*

Quiz 1

Look at the ruler on the board. What millimeter mark are arrows A, B, C, and D pointing at?*

A: ____ **B:** ____ **C:** ____ **D:** ____

Use your ruler to measure these pencils to the nearest millimeter.

E. ____

F. ____

G. ____

Quiz 2

Look at the ruler on the board. What millimeter mark are arrows A, B, C, and D pointing at?*

A: ____ **B:** ____ **C:** ____ **D:** ____

Use your ruler to measure these pencils to the nearest millimeter.

E. ____

F. ____

G. ____

Quiz 3

Look at the ruler on the board. What millimeter mark are arrows A, B, C, and D pointing at?*

A: ____ **B:** ____ **C:** ____ **D:** ____

Use your ruler to measure these pencils to the nearest millimeter.

E. ____

F. ____

G. ____

Quiz 4

Look at the ruler on the board. What millimeter mark are arrows A, B, C, and D pointing at?*

A: ____ **B:** ____ **C:** ____ **D:** ____

Use your ruler to measure these pencils to the nearest millimeter.

E. ____

F. ____

G. ____

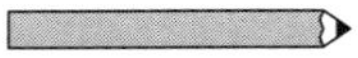

Quiz 5

Look at the ruler on the board. What millimeter mark are arrows A, B, C, and D pointing at?*

A: ____ **B:** ____ **C:** ____ **D:** ____

Use your ruler to measure these pencils to the nearest millimeter.

E. ____

F. ____

G. ____

**Ruler enlarged on the board*

Please note that the ruler is projected on to the board using a transparent metric ruler and an overhead projector; the teacher changes the position of arrows A, B, C, and D on the overhead for each quiz.

Figure 2.18 Convergence Mastery Questions for *Addition of Fractions*

Quiz 1

1. $\frac{2}{7} + \frac{5}{7} =$
2. $\frac{1}{3} + \frac{4}{3} =$
3. $\frac{2}{3} + \frac{1}{5} =$
4. $\frac{1}{3} + \frac{1}{7} =$
5. $\frac{1}{2} + \frac{7}{8} =$

Quiz 2

1. $\frac{1}{4} + \frac{3}{4} =$
2. $\frac{2}{5} + \frac{6}{5} =$
3. $\frac{2}{7} + \frac{1}{4} =$
4. $\frac{1}{2} + \frac{1}{5} =$
5. $\frac{1}{3} + \frac{7}{9} =$

Quiz 3

1. $\frac{2}{9} + \frac{7}{9} =$
2. $\frac{8}{7} + \frac{2}{7} =$
3. $\frac{3}{4} + \frac{1}{5} =$
4. $\frac{1}{4} + \frac{3}{5} =$
5. $\frac{4}{5} + \frac{3}{10} =$

Quiz 4

1. $\frac{3}{7} + \frac{4}{7} =$
2. $\frac{6}{5} + \frac{1}{5} =$
3. $\frac{4}{7} + \frac{1}{3} =$
4. $\frac{3}{4} + \frac{1}{5} =$
5. $\frac{3}{4} + \frac{5}{8} =$

Quiz 5

1. $\frac{4}{5} + \frac{6}{5} =$
2. $\frac{9}{7} + \frac{1}{7} =$
3. $\frac{2}{5} + \frac{1}{3} =$
4. $\frac{5}{6} + \frac{1}{7} =$
5. $\frac{2}{3} + \frac{5}{6} =$

SOURCE: Adapted from Thomas (2003a).

Figure 2.19 Convergence Mastery Questions for *Trigonometric Identities*

Trigonometric Identities

$\sin(-x) = -\sin x$
$\cos(-x) = \cos x$
$\tan(-x) = -\tan x$
$\sin(x + y) = \sin x \cos y + \cos x \sin y$
$\sin(x - y) = \sin x \cos y - \cos x \sin y$
$\cos(x + y) = \cos x \cos y - \sin x \sin y$
$\cos(x - y) = \cos x \cos y + \sin x \sin y$

$$\tan(x + y) = \frac{\tan x + \tan y}{1 - \tan x \tan y}$$

$$\tan(x - y) = \frac{\tan x - \tan y}{1 + \tan x \tan y}$$

Quiz 1

Write the trigonometric identities for each expression:

1. $\cos(x + y)$
2. $\cos(-x)$
3. $\tan(-x)$
4. $\sin(x - y)$
5. $\tan(x - y)$

Quiz 2

Write the trigonometric identities for each expression:

1. $\cos(x - y)$
2. $\sin(-x)$
3. $\sin(x - y)$
4. $\tan(-x)$
5. $\tan(x + y)$

Quiz 3

Write the trigonometric identities for each expression:

1. $\sin(-x)$
2. $\cos(x - y)$
3. $\tan(x + y)$
4. $\sin(x + y)$
5. $\cos(-x)$

Quiz 4

Write the trigonometric identities for each expression:

1. $\cos(-x)$
2. $\tan(-x)$
3. $\sin(x - y)$
4. $\cos(x + y)$
5. $\tan(x - y)$

Quiz 5

Write the trigonometric identities for each expression:

1. $\sin(x + y)$
2. $\sin(-x)$
3. $\cos(x - y)$
4. $\cos(-x)$
5. $\tan(x + y)$

SOURCE: Adapted from Thomas (2003b).

PRACTICE MAKES PERFECT

Purpose

Practice Makes Perfect is an ideal tool for teaching difficult or complex skills to students. The technique relies on a four-phase structure that maximizes skill acquisition. After teacher modeling, students practice applying the skill with less and less guidance from the teacher, until they can do it on their own. Because practice moves through four phases, the teacher has increased opportunity to provide the appropriate level of feedback and assistance to each student in the classroom.

Overview

Practice Makes Perfect moves through four distinct phases:

1. *Modeling.* During modeling, the teacher establishes the steps in the skill and demonstrates how to perform each step for students. The teacher should also think aloud during modeling, exposing the internal thinking that goes on during the performance of each step. Students observe and listen carefully, ask questions, and write down the steps in their notebooks. In establishing and modeling steps, keep students focused on the core of the skill by eliminating secondary or prerequisite procedures. For example, in teaching students how to graph a linear equation starting in the form $ax + by = c$, you would need to include solving for "$y =$ " and simplifying fractions if the coefficient of y is not 1. Also, you may need to review, or possibly re-teach, drawing the line from a given point with a given slope. You could use the following steps to model drawing the graph of the equation:

Step One: Write the problem:

$4x - 6y = 12$

Step Two: Change the problem into slope intercept form:

$$\begin{array}{rcl} 4x - 6y &=& 12 \\ \underline{-4x \qquad} && \underline{-4x \quad} \\ \dfrac{-6y}{-6} &=& \dfrac{-4x + 12}{-6} \\ y &=& \dfrac{2}{3}x - 2 \end{array}$$

Step Three: Identify the y-intercept, which equals –2 in this line, and plot the point (0, –2) on the y-axis.

Step Four: Identify and write the slope, which is $\frac{2}{3}$ in this problem.

Step Five: Starting at the y-intercept (0, –2), move vertically and horizontally using the slope to find and plot two more points. (As a Mathematical Convention, some teachers allow using only two points to plot a line.)

Step Six: Draw a line. Be sure to extend the line past the points.

2. *Directed practice.* Directed practice consists of the teacher and students working together to perform the skill or solve a set of problems that require the application of the skill. The teacher leads students through the steps in the skill using focusing questions. Focusing questions can be procedural, as in, "What is the first

step in graphing a linear equation in $y = mx + b$ form?" or conceptual, as in, "Why do we want to convert a linear equation into the form $y = mx + b$?"

3. *Guided practice.* The purpose of guided practice is to build student independence so that he or she can perform the skill without help. The teacher should assign a few highly focused problems or tasks. As students work, the teacher should circulate around the room to provide coaching and assistance as needed. Students should be reminded that this will be their last opportunity to receive guidance from the teacher, and they should be encouraged to ask questions and seek assistance. Guided practice is often organized into small student groups, affording students the chance to learn from each other.

4. *Independent practice.* For this final phase, students work on their own. They are now fully responsible for making decisions about how to complete the tasks or problems they are given. Often, independent practice comes in the form of homework. During independent practice, students should monitor what comes easily and which steps in the process are most difficult.

Steps

1. The teacher models the steps in the skill while thinking aloud (modeling).
2. The teacher leads students through a set of examples or problems by asking questions about each step in the skill (directed practice).
3. The teacher organizes students into small groups and assigns a few more examples or problems. As student groups work through the steps in the skill, the teacher observes, provides coaching, and encourages students to ask questions and seek help (guided practice).
4. The teacher assigns further examples or problems for students to work through on their own (often for homework). As students work on their own, they should keep track of when they are encountering difficulty (independent practice).

Examples

Use Practice Makes Perfect whenever you want students to master an important mathematical skill. Once you have completed your modeling session, you will need to provide students with examples or problems for each practice phase. For example, after modeling the steps involved in completing the square for quadratics with a leading coefficient of "1," an algebra teacher provided these examples for directed practice:

1. $x^2 + 6x - 3 = 9$
2. $x^2 - 12x - 8 = 0$
3. $x^2 + 5x + 8 = -11$

and these examples for guided practice:

1. $x^2 + 10x = 4$
2. $x^2 - 6x = 2$
3. $x^2 - 2x - 7 = 0$
4. $x^2 + 7x + 5 = 0$
5. $x^2 - 8x - 6 = -3$
6. $x^2 - 3x - 11 = -1$

The teacher then provided additional comparable problems for homework. She also asked students to write a summary of the process in their own words.

MENTAL MATH WAR

Purpose

Developed by Dr. Ed Thomas and built on the framework of the traditional War card game, Mental Math War provides a quick, engaging, and interactive way for students to practice working with variables, equations, and their solutions. Students playing Mental Math War process mathematical operations mentally as they work through equations containing variables. The technique also serves as a great way to introduce the concept of variables and equations—the very core of algebra—to young students.

Overview

Before starting Mental Math War, students are organized into groups of two with each pair given a deck of playing cards ("Jumbo" decks of playing cards printed with large numerals and characters are very helpful). Mental Math War can be played using a standard deck of playing cards composed of either fifty-two or fifty-four cards. Each card has a particular numeric value (see Figure 2.20).

Figure 2.20 Playing Card Values for Mental Math War

Mental Math War			
Name of Card	**Icon**	**Quantity**	**Value**
Ace	A	4	1
Deuce	2	4	2
Three	3	4	3
Four	4	4	4
Five	5	4	5
Six	6	4	6
Seven	7	4	7
Eight	8	4	8
Nine	9	4	9
Ten	10	4	10
Jack	J	4	10
Queen	Q	4	10
King	K	4	10
Joker	*J*	2	0

What brings the game together are the equations generated by the teacher. Regardless of the operations or numbers in an equation, all of the equations used in the game must contain the same variables: x, y, and z, where z represents the solution.

One student in each pair plays cards that represent the x variable and the other student plays cards that represent the y variable. Cards are played simultaneously, and the two players race to compute the equation mentally. So, if the x student plays a 7 and the y student plays a 3, and the equation is $2x + y = z$, the players would have to mentally compute $2 \bullet 7 + 3 =$. The first student to provide a correct answer collects both cards. If there is a tie, or neither player computes the answer correctly, the cards remain in the middle, to be collected with the new cards played in the ensuing round. When cards are played they should be placed in plain view of both students, but cards must be kept face down until they are played. After a certain amount of time has passed, the teacher changes the equation governing the game. While a new equation is being provided, students gather their cards, shuffle them, and redeal the deck. Some possible equations for Mental Math War include:

Figure 2.21 Mental Math War Equations

Today's Mental Math War Equations

$$x + y = z$$

$$x - y = z$$

$$2x + y = z$$

$$2x + 2y = z$$

$$x^2 + y = z$$

$$\frac{1}{2}x + 2y = z$$

$$2(x + 2) + y = z$$

$$xy = z$$

$$5xy = z$$

$$\frac{2xy}{2} = z$$

Steps

1. Review the concept of variables and their function in an equation.
2. Review the traditional War card game and explain the different rules and procedures for Mental Math War.

3. Group students into pairs.
4. Provide each pair of students with a deck of playing cards to be divided equally.
5. From each pair, assign one student to play cards for the x variable and one student to play cards for the y variable.
6. Remind students that cards must be kept face down until played, and that when played, the cards must be in full view of both students.
7. Start the game by writing or revealing an equation that includes the variables x, y, and z.
8. Pause the game and introduce a new equation (still using the variables x, y, and z) that will guide the next series of play.

VOCABULARY KNOWLEDGE RATING (VKR)

Purpose

One of the surest indications that students have a deep understanding of a mathematical topic is their ability to use essential vocabulary when they speak and write about that topic. Vocabulary Knowledge Rating (adapted from Blachowicz & Fisher, 2002; Harmon, Wood, & Hedrick, 2006) uses a simple double-assessment process to help students build their mastery over critical terms and concepts. Students assess their knowledge of essential vocabulary before the unit begins, which focuses their attention on the main ideas and key details. Then they assess their knowledge again—at the end of the unit—to see how their understanding has grown.

Overview

The Vocabulary Knowledge Rating (VKR) technique has students rate their knowledge of specific terms prior to learning new content. Students review the essential vocabulary then assess their understanding of each word using the following scale:

1 = I have never heard of this term.
2 = I have seen or heard of this term, but I am not sure what it means.
3 = I think I know what this term means.
4 = I know this term, and I can explain what it means.

For example, a fifth-grade teacher provided the VKR organizer shown in Figure 2.22 on the next page to her students prior to beginning a unit on fractions.

Over the course of a unit, students are asked to reflect upon their initial VKR. Once the unit has been completed, students again rate their knowledge of vocabulary and compare these ratings to their initial ratings. In this way, VKR serves as a powerful assessment tool. Students and teachers alike are able to see how students' understanding has increased, which words they know best, and which concepts are still giving them trouble.

Figure 2.22 Student's Vocabulary Knowledge Rating for *Fractions*

Fractions				
Terms	**Never heard of the term**	**I've seen or heard of the term**	**I think I know the term**	**I know and can explain the term**
fraction	1	2	**3**	4
numerator	1	**2**	3	4
denominator	1	**2**	3	4
proper fractions	1	**2**	3	4
improper fractions	1	**2**	3	4
equivalent fractions	**1**	2	3	4
mixed numbers	1	**2**	3	4
common denominators	1	2	**3**	4
least common denominators	1	2	**3**	4
inverting	1	**2**	3	4
Knowledge Rating: 22			**Date:** Sept 27, 2007	

Steps

1. Introduce students to the critical vocabulary they will encounter in the coming unit by reading the words out loud.
2. While reading the words to the class, pause and have students repeat each word.
3. Provide students with a VKR Organizer (see Figures 2.23 and 2.24 for examples).
4. Have students rate their knowledge of each word by selecting the appropriate number from the four-point scale. When finished, students add up all of the numbers and compute their initial rating.
5. Over the course of the unit, students reflect on their initial ratings and how their understanding of the vocabulary has changed.
6. After completing the unit, students again rate their knowledge of the vocabulary and compare this new rating to their initial rating.

Examples

VKR can be easily employed in any classroom, with any type of mathematical content, so long as there is vocabulary and concepts to be learned. For example, Figure 2.23 shows a VKR organizer for a unit on *quadratic functions.*

For younger students, the organizer can be simplified. For example, a third-grade mathematics teacher developed the organizer shown in Figure 2.24 for a unit on *graphs.*

Figure 2.23 Vocabulary Knowledge Rating for *Quadratic Functions*

Quadratic Functions				
Terms	**Never heard of the term**	**I've seen or heard of the term**	**I think I know the term**	**I know and can explain the term**
function	1	2	3	4
parabola	1	2	3	4
quadratic equations	1	2	3	4
zeros of functions	1	2	3	4
factoring	1	2	3	4
completing the square	1	2	3	4
quadratic formula	1	2	3	4
maximums	1	2	3	4
minimums	1	2	3	4
vertex of a parabola	1	2	3	4
axis of symmetry	1	2	3	4
discriminant	1	2	3	4
coeffecients	1	2	3	4
Knowledge Rating:			**Date:**	

Figure 2.24 Elementary Vocabulary Knowledge Rating Organizer for *Graphs*

Graphs			
Vocabulary Word	**I really don't know this word.**	**I've seen or heard this word used.**	**I know this word and can give an example!**
bar graph	1	2	3
line graph	1	2	3
picture graph	1	2	3
pie graph	1	2	3
data	1	2	3
vertical axis	1	2	3
horizontal axis	1	2	3
My Knowledge Rating:		**Today's Date:**	

GLOSSARIES

Purpose

Without a strong mathematical vocabulary, students will struggle with whatever content they are studying. Worse, students will be doomed to future difficulty as well. Why? Because when students have a hazy understanding of critical mathematical terms such as *product, denominator, area, equation, integer,* and *function,* their attempts to build new understanding will be thwarted by the initial lack of conceptual clarity. Glossaries provide students with the chance to focus their attention on the key terms that make up the discipline of mathematics. Students solidify and personalize their understanding of these key terms by recording definitions that work for them, creating meaningful visual representations for the terms, and periodically revisiting and revising their glossaries.

Overview

At the heart of a good student glossary are two critical attributes:

1. *Good glossaries focus on the most critical terms.* It is important that students not get bogged down with hundreds of words. A typical unit usually contains between 5 and 15 essential ideas. Focus student attention on those words. For example, for a unit on integers, the critical terms might be: *integers, whole numbers, positive, negative, sign, absolute value,* and *number line.*

2. *Good glossaries are personal.* Students must never simply copy definitions from their textbooks into their notebooks and call that a glossary. Remind students that they are creating personal records of their learning, as well as powerful study guides that will help them do well on quizzes, tests, projects, and exams. That's why students' glossaries should always contain definitions that make sense to the students themselves and are usually full of sketches, meaningful examples, metaphors, and the like.

Examples

Glossaries can be designed and maintained by students in any number of ways. At the most basic level, students should record the term, a definition that they understand personally, and an icon or visual representation that will help them remember the word and what it means. For example, Figure 2.25 shows a fourth-grade student's entry for the terms *perimeter* and *area.*

Figure 2.25 Glossary Entries on *Perimeter* and *Area*

Word	My definition	Visualization
Perimeter	The edge all around a flat shape.	Perimeter goes around the shape.
Area	The amount of surface inside a flat shape.	Area is inside the shape.

You can also ask students to use glossaries to generate initial definitions, check them against the actual definitions, and then note how their own definitions compare with their more technical counterparts. After their comparison, students create an icon or visualization. Figure 2.26 shows how this kind of entry works.

Figure 2.26 Glossary Entry for *Circle Graph*

Word	My definition	Glossary definition	Differences	Visualization
circle graph	A kind of graph that looks like a pie.	A graph used to compare parts of a whole. The pie-shaped "slices" in a circle graph are the parts. Together all the slices make up the whole, or 100%.	I was right about it looking like a pie, but I missed the stuff about parts of a whole.	

Glossaries also serve as great tools for students to refine or even revise their understanding of key terms as they learn more about them during a unit. Students can refine or revise understanding in a variety of ways. For example, students can:

- Draw a new picture or icon.
- Create a metaphor for the term.
- Rewrite their definitions in light of new information.
- List examples and non-examples of the term.
- Note a real-world application of the concept or procedure.

To accommodate this process of revisiting terms and then reviewing or revising them, have students keep the last columns in their glossaries blank. Then they can come back to the key terms later in the unit and make meaningful revisions. For example, while revisiting the key terms for a unit on graphs of functions, one student made the following revisions to his entry on parabolas (column four in Figure 2.27).

Figure 2.27 Revisited Entry for *Parabola*

Word	My definition	Visualization	Revisit and Refine
parabola	U-shaped figure generated by graphing certain functions. Follows form $f(x) = a(x+b)^2 + c$		The McDonald's golden arches logo looks like parabolas

WORD WALLS

Purpose

Research shows that the average student needs to interact with unfamiliar words four to six times in order to understand the meaning (Jenkins, Stein, & Wysocki, 1984). One of the biggest challenges teachers of mathematics face when it comes to vocabulary instruction is making sure students are regularly exposed to and using the new mathematical terms they are learning. Without this high level of exposure and use, students will not form the strong connections they need to hold onto new words.

Word Walls is an ideal strategy for creating a classroom culture that breeds that all-important, but often neglected, familiarity between students and the terms they encounter in their mathematics classes. The strategy also builds in the chance for students to incorporate vocabulary words into their writing and to refine their understanding of new words through discussion and use.

Overview

In developing a Word Wall, the students usually collect words they encounter during their reading and learning and share them with the class, while the teacher collects them in the Word Wall. However, some teachers prefer to select the words themselves in order to keep vocabulary focused on the most essential concepts and ideas.

There are basically two types of mathematics Word Walls: *Unit Word Walls,* containing the critical words in a unit of study, and *Thinking Word Walls,* focused on "thinking words" or words related to the thinking processes that students will engage in a discipline or unit.

The steps listed below correspond most closely with Unit Word Walls, but can be adapted easily for Thinking Word Walls as well. We have included two examples—one for each type of mathematics Word Wall—to show you how teachers in different content areas have adapted the tool to their needs and purposes.

Steps

1. Have students list any words that are new or unfamiliar to them over the course of a unit, or whenever they are engaged in new learning. (Even if the text goes on to define the word, it is important that students capture the new word.) Alternatively, you may choose to select the words yourself.
2. Encourage students to share the words on their lists during class. Record these words on a sectioned-off part of the board or on poster paper.
3. Ask students to define each recorded word and to generate one to three synonyms or brief definitions for each word.
4. Create the Word Wall by recording these brief definitions below each original word on the board or poster.
5. Have each student write a summary, response, or essay about a particular topic, using the words from the Word Wall. Students must use five to ten words correctly in their writing.

Examples

Third-Grade Unit Word Wall

Students in Anna Fiore's third-grade class are learning about weight, volume, and the relationship between the two concepts. So far, Anna and her students' Word Wall looks like Figure 2.28.

Figure 2.28 Third-Grade Unit Word Wall for *Measuring Weight and Volume*

Measuring Weight and Volume

rectangular prism
- a 3-D rectangle
- a prism with rectangular bases
-

bases
- the top and bottom of a rectangular prism

height of a prism
- distance between two opposite bases

volume
- amount of space inside a 3-D shape

cubic centimeter
- metric unit of volume
- a cube that is 1 centimeter on all sides

weight
- a measure of how heavy something is

capacity of a scale
- the most weight a scale can hold

precision
- getting more accurate measurements by using smaller units

faces
- the flat sides of a prism

Thinking Word Wall for Pre-Algebra

During the first week of Pre-Algebra, Amira Rosnan presents to students the thinking words they will be using not just for a particular unit, but for the entire year.

abstract
accelerate
addition
amplify
amount
apportion
attach
balance
change
chart
convert
decrease
deduct
deposit
difference
diminish
divide

double
effort
elaborate
equal
estimate
extend
factor
figure out
find
formulate
further
grade
gradual
graph
greatest
gross
group

guess
halve
increase
join
least
lose
loss
mix
more
multiple
odds
part of
product
propel
propagate
quadruple
quantity

ratio
reduce
remit
separate
shape
share
show
simplify
solve
step
sum
total
trace
transform
triple
value
withdraw

Rather than having students generate brief definitions for the words, Amira wants her students to see the different kinds of mathematical categories that these words fit under. So, she begins by having students examine the words, review new words, and start to put common words together under descriptive headings. For example:

Fractions	*Showing Math Visually*
halve	chart
part of	graph
ratio	shape

Over the course of the year, as students' exposure to new kinds of problems increases, Amira and her students revise and expand their Thinking Word Wall by adding words to their groups and creating new groups to accommodate students' new understanding.

VOCABULARY ORGANIZERS

Purpose

Vocabulary Organizers help students piece together the vocabulary words associated with a topic or unit to form a meaningful whole. The technique enhances comprehension by allowing students to construct a big picture of the content while minimizing students' need to remember the individual terms. Vocabulary Organizers succeed in lightening the load on students' memories by providing them with vocabulary terms and a structure for organizing the terms.

Overview

Vocabulary Organizers help students to understand the hierarchical relationships that bind together key concepts and critical vocabulary terms. Since students have access to the words, the focus is not on trying to remember important ideas. Instead, students are able to devote their attention to using the concepts correctly. For this reason, Vocabulary Organizers is a great tool for accommodating students with special needs and memory problems.

Steps

1. Review the key terms associated with a topic, unit, or reading.
2. Present the list of mathematical vocabulary words to students.
3. Create an organizer for students to fill in. (See Figures 2.30, 2.31, and 2.32 for examples of different Vocabulary Organizers.)
4. After students have placed the words in the organizer, review their work and help them assess their level of comprehension.

Examples

The use of Vocabulary Organizers can enhance students' comprehension of terms, procedures, and concepts in any mathematics classroom. In the different examples that follow, you will find three lists of vocabulary words and the sample Vocabulary Organizers that students completed for each.

Techniques for Graphing Statistics

bar graph
bell-shaped
cumulative frequency curve
frequency curve
histogram
interval scale
normal curve
positive slope
ratio scale
skewed curve
tail left
tail right

Figure 2.29 Techniques for *Graphing Statistics*

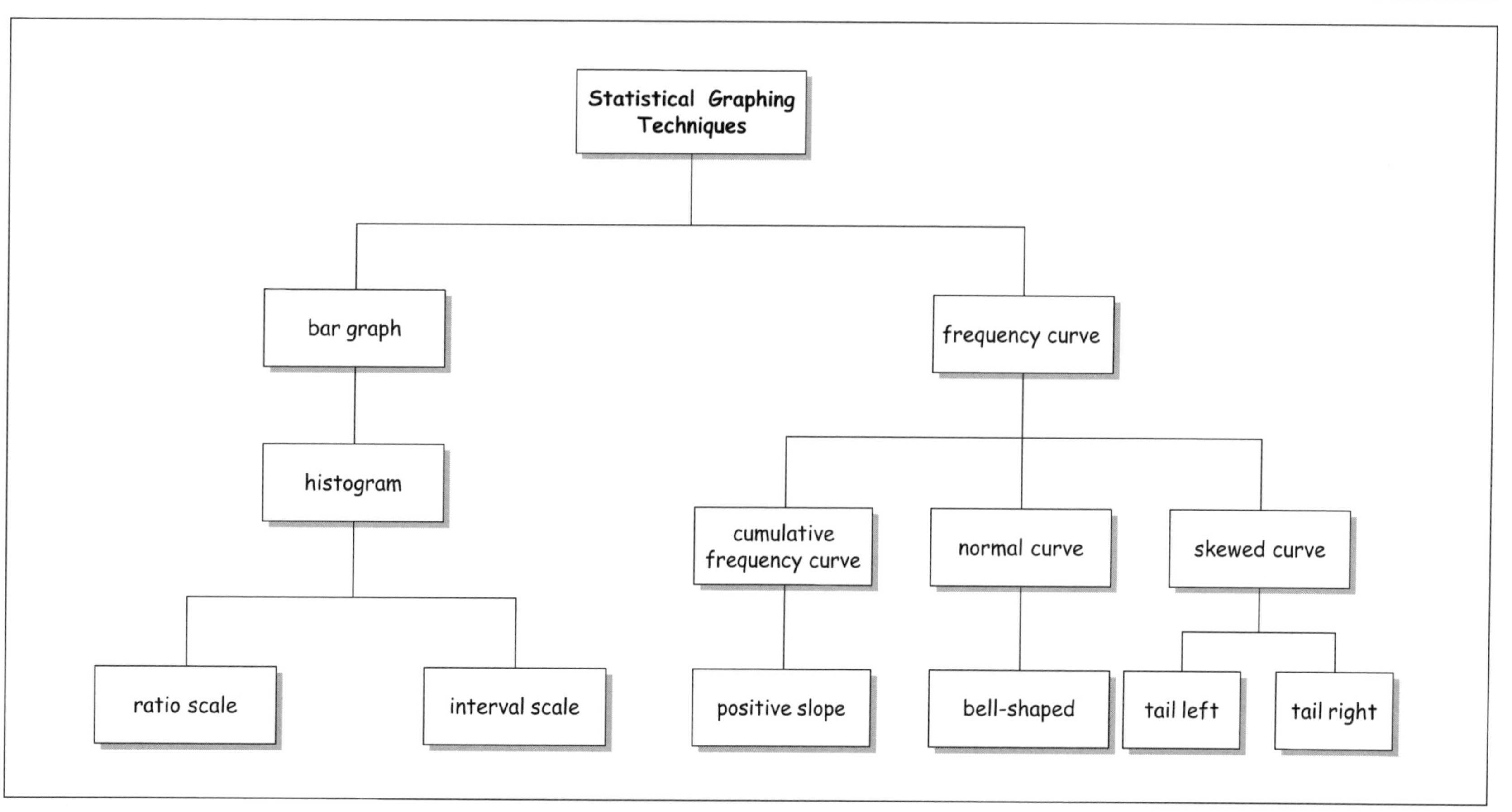

Sets of Integers

counting numbers
digits
even numbers
integers
natural numbers
negative integers
non-negative integers
odd numbers
positive integers
whole numbers
zero

Figure 2.30 Sets of Integers

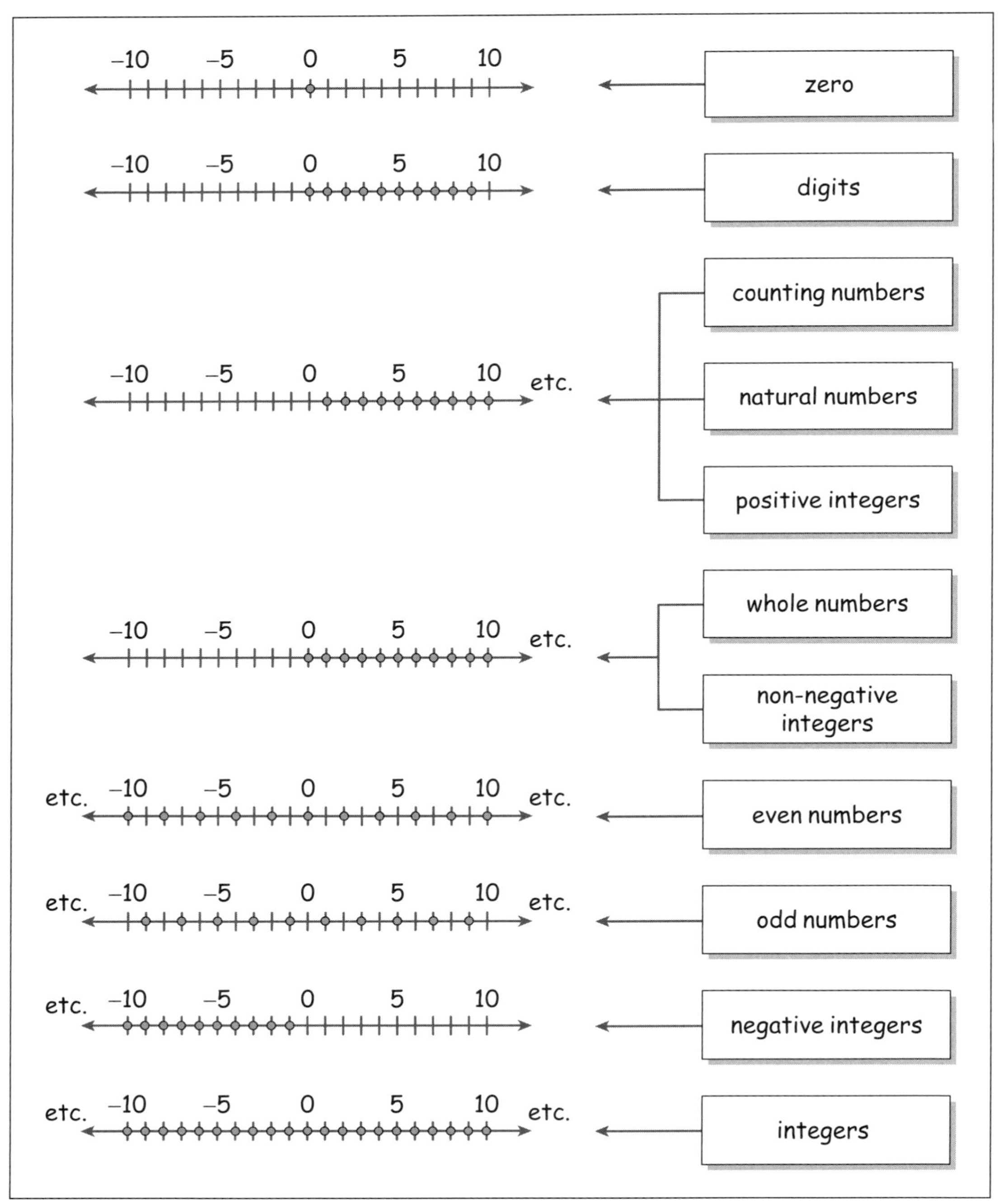

Special Quadrilaterals

isosceles trapezoid
kite
parallelogram
quadrilateral
rectangle
rhombus
square
trapezoid

Figure 2.31 Special Quadrilaterals

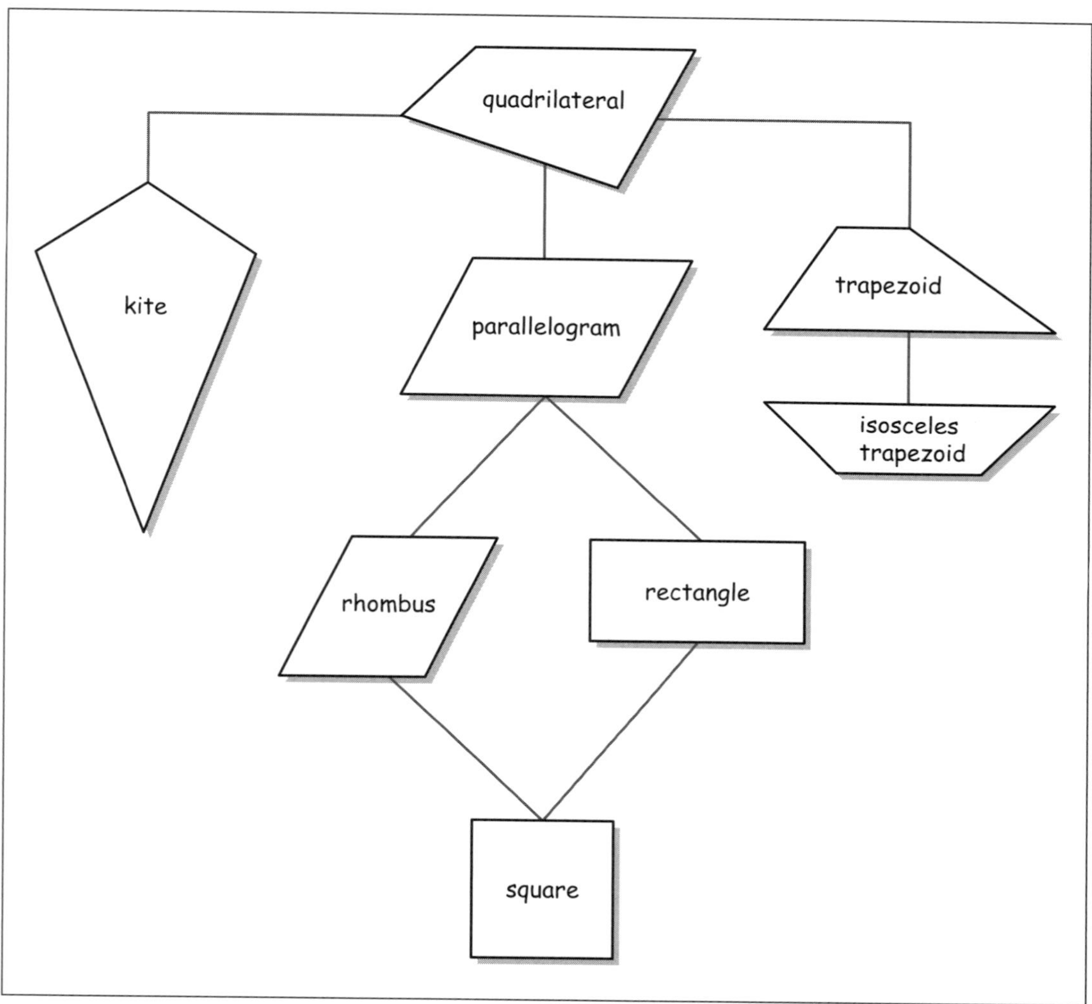

3

Understanding Math Tools

UNDERSTANDING MATH STUDENTS

Want to . . . understand why the math they learn works.

Like math problems that . . . ask them to explain, prove, or take a position.

Approach problem solving . . . by looking for patterns and identifying hidden questions.

May experience difficulty when . . . there is a focus on the social environment of the classroom (e.g., on collaboration and cooperative problem solving).

Learn best when . . . they are challenged to think and explain their thinking.

—Silver, Thomas, & Perini (2003)

Understanding Math Tools Matrix

PAGE	MATH TOOL	NCTM PROCESS STANDARDS: Problem Solving	Reasoning and Proof	Communication	Connections	Representation
66	**Always-Sometimes-Never (ASN)**—Students examine statements, decide if they are always, sometimes, or never true, and explain their reasoning.		●	●		
69	**Support or Refute**—Students review statements, decide whether or not they agree with them, and find evidence to support or refute.	●	●	●		
76	**Stake Your Claim**—Students use mathematical evidence to support or refute a mathematical claim.	●	●	●	●	
79	**Learning From Clues**—Students use clues to solve a problem or set of challenges.	●	●	●		
83	**Pattern Finding**—Students use patterns to solve problems and identify larger principles implied by those patterns.	●	●	●		
85	**Math Rulebook**—Students analyze examples and use inductive reasoning to identify and collect mathematical rules.		●	●		
88	**P's and Q's**—Students solve a problem by activating prior knowledge, making predictions, and developing plans.	●	●	●		
94	**Essential Question Notes (EQN)**—A notemaking tool for answering higher-order questions.	●	●	●	●	
98	**Compare and Contrast**—Students identify similarities and differences between two or more mathematical concepts.		●	●	●	
106	**Mathematical Analogies**—Students create and/or solve analogies to compare patterns, problems, and processes.		●	●	●	
108	**Three-Way Tie**—Students identify relationships between three terms or concepts, then develop a summary or interpretation.		●	●	●	●
112	**Which One Doesn't Belong?**—Students examine items, identify which one is most unlike the others, and explain why.		●	●	●	
114	**Yes, But Why?**—Students are challenged to explain, rather than simply state mathematical ideas.	●	●	●		
116	**Yes, But Why^3?**—Students solve a problem, then probe into the deeper meanings behind the answer.	●	●	●	●	
118	**Show Me**—Students demonstrate their understanding in four ways: identification, generating examples, illustrating ideas, and citing evidence.		●		●	●

UNDERSTANDING MATH TOOLS

EDUCATIONAL RESEARCH BASE											INSTRUCTIONAL OBJECTIVES							
Identifying similarities and differences	Summarizing and note taking	Reinforcing effort and providing recognition	Homework and practice	Nonlinguistic representations	Cooperative learning	Setting objectives and providing feedback	Generating and testing hypotheses	Questions, cues, and advance organizers	Vocabulary	Writing	Preparing	Presenting	Practicing	Processing	Problem Solving	Performing	Personalizing	**MATH TOOL**
							●				●			●				ASN
	●						●	●			●	●		●	●			Support or Refute
	●						●			●		●			●		●	Stake Your Claim
							●				●			●	●			Learning From Clues
●							●					●		●	●			Pattern Finding
●							●				●			●				Math Rulebook
●	●		●				●			●	●		●	●	●	●	●	P's and Q's
	●							●		●	●	●		●	●			EQN
●	●			●				●						●	●	●		Compare and Contrast
●							●		●					●			●	Mathematical Analogies
●	●							●	●	●	●			●				Three-Way Tie
●							●				●			●				Which One . . . ?
	●						●	●			●			●	●			Yes, But Why?
							●	●			●			●	●			Yes, But Why^3?
			●	●										●		●		Show Me

SOURCE: Marzano, R. J., Pickering, D. J., & Pollock, J. E. (2001). *Classroom instruction that works: Research-based strategies for increasing student achievement.* Alexandria, VA: Association for Supervision and Curriculum Development.

ALWAYS-SOMETIMES-NEVER (ASN)

Purpose

Always-Sometimes-Never (ASN) is a reasoning activity that focuses students' thinking around the important, and often subtle, facts and details associated with mathematical concepts. Students are asked to consider statements containing mathematical information and determine if what is stated is always, sometimes, or never true.

Overview

The ASN technique has students justify a statement as being *always true, sometimes true,* or *never true.* The teacher generates a series of statements for a particular mathematical concept, relates relevant background information or identifies parameters, and asks students to decide if each statement is always, sometimes, or never true. To ensure that students are thinking critically and not just making arbitrary choices, the teacher asks students to explain the reasoning behind their choices. Disagreements and discussions among students are encouraged. ASN can be used to help students:

- Tease out the critical attributes of mathematical concepts. For example, these two statements help students identify the critical similarities and differences between rectangles and squares:
  - A rectangle is a square. (Sometimes)
  - A square is a rectangle. (Always)
- Recognize the restrictions on a function's domain or range:
  - The equation of a vertical line can be expressed in slope-intercept form. (Never; vertical lines have undefined slope.)
  - The domain of a square root function is the set of all non-negative real numbers. (Sometimes; true for $f(x) = \sqrt{x}$ when $x \geq 0$, false for $g(x) = \sqrt{5-x}$ when $x \leq 5$.)
- Identify exceptions to mathematical rules. For example:
  - $\frac{a}{a} = 1$ (Sometimes; the statement is not true for a = 0.)
- Determine the applicability of a theorem or procedure to a given situation. For example:
  - If the sides of a triangle are a, b, and c then $a^2 + b^2 = c^2$. (Sometimes; true only when the triangle is a right triangle and c is the length of its hypotenuse.)

Steps

1. Provide students with a list of statements about a recently discussed or familiar mathematical concept or topic.
2. Allow students enough time to read and consider all of the statements carefully.
3. Have students think about each of the statements and decide whether each is *always true, sometimes true,* or *never true.*
4. Make sure that students explain the reasoning behind their choices.

Examples

ASN is a versatile tool that can be applied to mathematics across all grade levels (e.g., arithmetic, algebra, geometry, data analysis, advanced mathematics). For example, look at the ASN worksheet that a fourth-grade teacher developed for her unit on polygons (see Figure 3.1 on the following page).

While polygons and basic geometry provide the basis for one teacher's ASN activity, follow a few examples of activities that other teachers have developed and used in their classrooms.

Arithmetic: Addition and Subtraction

1. The sum of two 3-digit numbers is a 3-digit number. (Sometimes)
2. The sum of two even numbers is an odd number. (Never)
3. The difference of two odd numbers is an even number. (Always)
4. The sum of additive inverses is zero. (Always)
5. The difference of three odd numbers is an odd number. (Always)
6. The sum of three even numbers is zero. (Sometimes)
7. The sum of three odd numbers is zero. (Never)
8. The sum of two counting numbers is greater than the difference of the same numbers. (Always)

Statistics: Mean, Median, Mode

1. A list of numbers has a mean. (Always)
2. A list of numbers has a median. (Always)
3. A list of numbers has a mode. (Sometimes)
4. The mean of a set of numbers is one of the numbers of that set. (Sometimes)
5. The median of ten consecutive integers is one of those integers. (Never)
6. If the mode of a set of numbers is 14, then 14 is one of the numbers of that set. (Always)
7. The mean of a set of numbers is greater than the median of that set of numbers. (Sometimes)
8. The mode of a set of numbers, without repeated values, can be found by arranging the numbers in increasing order and then calculating the mean of the middle two numbers. (Never)

Trigonometry: Graph Analysis

1. The graph of a trigonometric function is periodic. (Always)
2. Doubling the amplitude of a trigonometric function doubles the period of the function. (Never)

Figure 3.1 Always-Sometimes-Never Worksheet on *Polygons*

Directions: Carefully read the following statements about polygons. In the box next to each statement, write an A if the statement is always true, S if it is sometimes true, and N if it is never true. Make sure you explain your reasoning for each statement.

☐ **1: A trapezoid is a rectangle.**

Reason: ____________________

☐ **2: A quadrilateral is a regular polygon.**

Reason: ____________________

☐ **3: Parallelograms are quadrilaterals.**

Reason: ____________________

☐ **4: A trapezoid has parallel legs.**

Reason: ____________________

☐ **5: The diagonals of a parallelogram bisect each other.**

Reason: ____________________

☐ **6: A rectangle is a square.**

Reason: ____________________

☐ **7: A square is a rectangle.**

Reason: ____________________

☐ **8: A rhombus is a rectangle.**

Reason: ____________________

☐ **9: A parallelogram has exactly three right angles.**

Reason: ____________________

☐ **10: A rhombus and a rectangle each have four sides of equal length and four angles of equal measure.**

Reason: ____________________

3. The graph of a cosecant function has an infinite number of asymptotes. (Always)
4. The period of y = sin $bx + h$ is equivalent to the period of y = sec $bx + k$. (Always; both $\frac{2\pi}{|b|}$)
5. A cosine function has both a maximum and a minimum value. (Always)
6. For numbers a and b, the graph of y = cos x on the interval $a < 0 < b$ is an increasing function. (Never)
7. Stretching the graph of a trigonometric function changes the period of the function. (Sometimes; true for horizontal stretches, false for vertical stretches.)
8. Applying a phase shift on a secant graph changes the location of vertical asymptotes. (Sometimes)
9. For any value of a, the graph of y = tan ax will have the y-axis as an asymptote. (Never)
10. Secant graphs have horizontal asymptotes. (Never)

SUPPORT OR REFUTE

Purpose

The Support or Refute tool is designed to slow down students' thinking—to invite them to think carefully and analytically about mathematical problems, situations, representations, and data. Support or Refute helps students develop a set of skills shared by all thoughtful problem solvers, including:

- Curtailing impulsivity.
- Accessing prior knowledge and using it to make sense of unknown situations.
- Separating the important information from the irrelevant information.
- Using evidence to develop logical deductions.
- Analyzing and discussing their own and other's mathematical interpretations.

Overview

A Support or Refute lesson begins with the students reviewing a set of four to eight statements about a problem, lesson, or other form of mathematical content. For example, before beginning a lesson on negative numbers, a fourth-grade teacher presented her students with these four statements:

1. There are no numbers that are less than zero on the number line.
2. You can subtract 5 from 3.
3. Negative numbers are only used when the temperature is extremely cold.
4. Negative 10 degrees is colder than 0 degrees.

After reviewing the statements carefully, students decide whether they agree or disagree with each statement. Then, during the lesson, reading, or problem-solving process, students collect evidence that supports or refutes each statement. Often, teachers will allow students to meet in small groups to share their observations and explore their interpretations. The lesson usually ends with a whole-class discussion on the content, the evidence-gathering process, and how students' initial ideas about the content have changed or been confirmed.

Steps

1. Generate four to eight statements about a lesson, word problem, or mathematical situation or representation.
2. Ask students to review the statements carefully and decide whether they agree or disagree with each one. (In the case of word problems or problems involving visual material, you need to provide the problem or visual along with the statements.)
3. As students learn more (through the lesson, through reading, through solving the problem, through a deeper investigation of the situation), ask them to collect evidence that supports or refutes each statement.
4. After students have collected evidence for all the statements, have them share and compare their findings in small groups.
5. Engage the class in a discussion of the content, as well as how their initial thoughts about each statement were challenged or confirmed.

Examples

Here's an example of the Support or Refute tool applied to angle relationships.

Figure 3.2 Angle Relationships

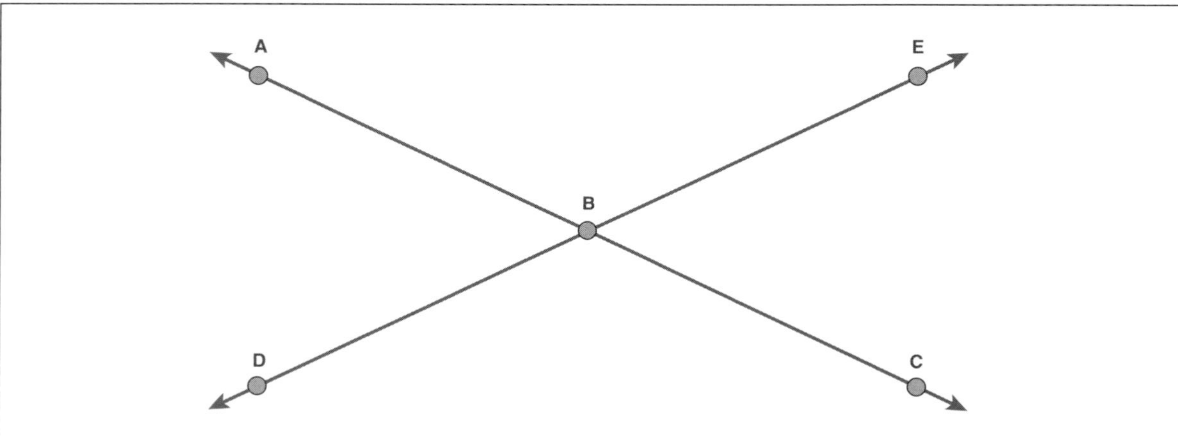

Examine the diagram above. Read the statements below. Put an "A" next to those you agree with and a "D" next to those you disagree with. Give your reasons for each of your positions in the boxes provided.

___ 1. When two lines intersect, they form angles.

Support	Refute

___ 2. $\overline{AC}$ and $\overline{DE}$ form four non-straight angles.

Support	Refute

___ 3. ∠ ABD and ∠ EBC seem to be obtuse angles.

Support	Refute

___ 4. ∠ ABE and ∠ DBC cannot both be acute angles.

Support	Refute

___ 5. ∠ ABD and ∠ DBC are supplementary to each other.

Support	Refute

(Continued)

Figure 3.2 (Continued)

___ 6. Although we don't know exactly what ∠ ABD and ∠ DBC measure, we do know that together the sum of their measures is 360.

Support	Refute

___ 7. Since ∠ ABD and ∠ EBC are vertical angles, as are ∠ ABE and ∠ DBC, both pairs of angles are congruent to each other.

Support	Refute

Support or Refute is also a great way to help students slow down the problem-solving process so they take the time to figure out what the problem is asking them to do, rather than leaping toward a solution. Figure 3.3, for example, is part of a Support or Refute lesson involving a word problem for which students need to set up a system of two equations with two variables.

Figure 3.3 Motorcycle Delivery

The Problem: A truck is on its way to three different motorcycle dealerships. The truck contains both mopeds and motorcycles. Maggie Sutton, who owns all three dealerships, receives an invoice which tells her that a total of 150 vehicles are on the truck but doesn't tell her how many of the vehicles are motorcycles and how many are mopeds. The invoice does show that the total mass of the vehicles is 34,800 lbs. It also shows that mopeds weigh 100 lbs. each while motorcycles weigh 320 lbs. How many mopeds and motorcycles are on the truck?

___ 1. The problem tells us the total number of vehicles on the truck.

Support	Refute

___ 2. The fact that there are three dealerships is critical to solving the problem.

Support	Refute

___ 3. The best way to solve this problem is to set up an equation with two variables.

Support	Refute

___ 4. Motorcycles have a greater mass than mopeds.

Support	Refute

___ 5. The solution requires two separate answers.

Support	Refute

Support or Refute can also be used to help students become more critical readers who can find evidence and use it to support their claims. For example, a high-school mathematics teacher presented his students with the organizer shown in Figure 3.4.

Figure 3.4 Pythagoras

___ 1. Pythagoras studied the 3-4-5 triangle because his followers thought it was magical.

Support	Refute

___ 2. Understanding a straightforward example can help you understand a more complicated problem.

Support	Refute

___ 3. Mathematics can surprise and disappoint even excellent mathematicians.

Support	Refute

___ 4. The Pythagorean Theorem came about only after Pythagoras began to explore a real-world situation.

Support	Refute

After deciding whether they agreed or disagreed with each statement, students were asked to collect evidence that supports or refutes each statement from the following reading:

A Secret Society

Imagine life in an economically and militarily powerful civilized society within which lies a small group of individuals who have created a secret society. Members of this secret society have their own method of identifying themselves in public so that they can recognize fellow members without betraying their membership to the general public. They firmly believe that they have the answers to all of the challenges facing all people in the world. What kind of people would belong to such a secret organization? What would their leaders be like? What would a psychiatrist say about such a group? How would you feel if you found out your brother or sister belonged to such a group? What would our modern society think of such a group?

Pythagoras was a philosopher and mathematician who lived in Greece around the sixth century BCE. He was the leader of a group called the Brotherhood of Pythagoreans. They were a secret society that studied mathematics. Like any secret society, they had special ways to identify one another. One way the Pythagoreans used to distinguish their members from the general public was a motto that the members alone knew. The Pythagorean motto was "All is number."

Ancient Greek and Egyptian land surveyors had discovered a method that allowed them to draw a line at right angles to another line on the ground when they needed to make perpendicular lines. The surveyors used a rope with the ends tied together, marked off into twelve equal parts by knots. They drove a stake into the ground on the line where they wanted the right angle to be. They drove another stake into the ground three rope sections away from the first stake, and then they looped the rope around the first two stakes. Next, they found the point that was four rope sections away from the first stake and five rope sections away from the second stake. They drove a stake there so that the rope looped around all three stakes. If the rope sections are all of equal length, the angle at the first stake will be a right angle. The Pythagoreans explored what they called the "magic 3-4-5 triangle." This triangle was called "magic" because any triangle with sides 3, 4, and 5 units always created a right triangle. The Pythagoreans found that in 3-4-5 triangles, the square of the hypotenuse (the longest side) equals the sum of the squares of the other two sides. They then generalized this rule for 3-4-5 triangles to apply to all right triangles.

The Pythagorean Theorem works with any right triangle; however, not all fit quite so neatly. Legend says when Pythagoras discovered that in some right triangles one or more sides needed to be non-repeating, non-ending decimals (and therefore irrational numbers), he and his followers sank into a depression that lasted many years. They felt almost betrayed by the numbers, which they believed should be supremely rational.

All three of the examples have shown how the same organizer is used by students to make an initial decision about the statements, collect details to support or refute each of their original decisions, and confirm or revise their original choices. When using Support or Refute with your class you can use the traditional Support or Refute Organizer (see Organizer 3-A) or you may want to develop your own organizer (see Figure 3.5).

Figure 3.5 Excerpt of Teacher's Alternative Support or Refute Organizer

Statement 1

Circle one	Supporting Details	Refuting Details	Final Thoughts. . .
Agree *Disagree*			*How did the details affect my intial choice?*

STAKE YOUR CLAIM

Purpose

Today's students are awash in unsubstantiated claims that involve mathematics: *You can lose three dress sizes just by taking this all-natural supplement once a day. Listening to these tapes while you sleep will increase your vocabulary by over 30% in just a month.* More than ever, we need to teach students how to use their mathematical knowledge to figure out when the claims they encounter are valid and when they are little more than hot air. Stake Your Claim teaches students how to subject claims to critical analysis by attacking them methodically and mathematically.

Overview

In a typical Stake Your Claim lesson, the teacher will model the problem-solving approach used to break down a claim and determine its validity:

- Identify the claim.
- Decide whether you agree or disagree with the claim.

Organizer 3-A Support or Refute Organizer

Name: ______________________________ **Date:** ____________________

Support or Refute Organizer

Name of text/article/information:

Statement 1:

Support	Refute

Statement 2:

Support	Refute

Statement 3:

Support	Refute

Statement 4:

Support	Refute

Statement 5:

Support	Refute

- Collect, organize, and display relevant data.
- Perform calculations.
- Draw a conclusion.
- Communicate your findings.

After the modeling session, students use the problem-solving approach independently by applying it to a new claim.

Steps

1. Present students with an unsubstantiated claim or with material that contains such a claim. (Advertisements often work well.)
2. Model the steps in the problem-solving approach.
3. Allow students to reflect on the approach and how they can use it on their own.
4. Present students with a new claim to analyze.
5. Give students the opportunity to communicate their findings in writing or to present them to the class.

Examples

Hamlet's Heart

Starting freshman quarterback Hamlet is a real heartthrob! Or at least Ophelia thinks so. Discussions about heartthrobs lead Ophelia's brother, Laertes, to make some calculations. Laertes declares that if Hamlet lives out his life as a healthy adult, his heart will beat about 3 billion more times. Is Laertes's claim valid? Show all of your work as well as any assumptions you made in analyzing the claim. (*Teacher's Note:* This problem is open to considerable variety in student answers depending on what they assume Hamlet's heart rate and lifespan will be. A simplified method based on 70 beats per minute and 70 more years in Hamlet's life is as follows: 70 beats/minute • 60 minutes • 24 hours • 365 days • 70 more years in Hamlet's life = 2,575,440,000 beats. These specific calculations show that Hamlet's heart would beat a little less than 3 billion more times in his lifetime.)

Listening to CDs?

As you're listening to the radio, you hear an ad that includes the following: "Thanks to the proven power of compound interest, you can make money fast by investing in our high-yield CDs. Our current interest rate is at an all-time high of 10% compounded annually. An investment of $1,000 can increase by more than 150% in only ten years!" Is the claim valid? How do you know?

(*Teacher's Note:* This problem is based on the assumption that students are not using a compound interest formula but are making the calculations year by year. So, a student's work might resemble the following calculations.)

Year	Amount	10% Interest
0	1,000	+ 100
1	1,100	110
2	1,210	121
3	1,331	≈133
4	1464	≈146
5	1,610	161
6	1,771	≈177
7	1,948	≈195
8	2,143	≈214
9	2,357	≈236
10	2,593	

Remember that this assumes the rate will remain at 10%. Since the rate is at an "all-time high," it is unlikely the rate will hold at 10%. Nevertheless, 10% can be used to get a sense of what ten years of compound interest will do to the initial investment. Since the calculations show an increase of 159% (2,593 – 1,000 = 1,593; 1,593 ÷ 1,000 = 1.593) in 10 years, the claim is true if the interest rate stays at 10%.

LEARNING FROM CLUES

Purpose

If students are to become powerful problem solvers, they must know how to examine what is known, determine what is to be found, then use both inductive and deductive thinking skills to reason their way to quality solutions. Learning From Clues is a reasoning strategy that builds these skills by tapping into our natural human affinity for solving mysteries. The strategy also increases students' abilities to retain content. When students investigate a problem or question under their own impelling curiosity, they are far more likely to force a deep connection with the information they gather along the way.

Overview

Learning From Clues activities can be designed around four distinct types of challenges:

- Logic games and problems
- Questions that puzzle or data that tease, which require students to use logical reasoning to explain and prove the answers
- Steps of a solution in mixed-up order, which require students to reorder the steps into a logical sequence
- Mathematical riddles

Steps

1. Select the type of challenge to be created.
2. Design an appropriate problem, providing sufficient clues for students to examine.
3. Have the students review the clues as individuals or as members of a small group.
4. Encourage students to use the clues to solve the challenge.
5. Make sure students can explain the logic they used to address and evaluate the effectiveness of their solution.

Examples

Type One: Logic Games and Problems

Consider the following: Teachers of mathematics always tell the truth. English teachers always lie. You walk into a room with three teachers, Teacher A, Teacher B, and Teacher C, and each says:

- Teacher A: "We're all English teachers."
- Teacher B: "Only one of us is a mathematics teacher."
- Teacher C: nothing at all

Who is a teacher of mathematics and who is an English teacher?

Type Two: Puzzles/Teasing Data

Here's a math mystery for you to solve. It starts with a set of simple tasks:

a. Pick a year in which something memorable happened to you (e.g., your team won the World Series, you visited a foreign country). Write the year out as a four-digit number (e.g., 2003).

b. Also write the year of your birth as a four-digit number (e.g., 1993).

c. Determine the number of years that have passed since your special year (e.g., 4, if it is 2007 and your special year was 2003).

d. Write down what your age will be at the end of the current year (e.g., 14, if it is 2007 and you were born in 1993).

e. Add up the numbers from a, b, c, and d from page 80:

$$\begin{array}{r} 2{,}003 \\ 1{,}993 \\ 4 \\ +14 \\ \hline 4{,}014 \end{array}$$

Now, compare your answer with a few classmates. Why are all your answers the same?

Type Three: Solutions in Mixed-Up Order

1. Seven equivalent expressions are written in the table below (Figure 3.6), but they are not in the right order. It is your job to use your mathematical expertise to sequence the expressions correctly. Examine the right column to identify which step comes in what order: #1 identifies the original expression, #7 is the simplified answer, and Steps #2 through #6 are the logical order of working from problem to answer.

Figure 3.6 Solutions in Mixed-Up Order

Step Order	Equivalent Expressions
	$51 + 16$
	$6 \bullet 3 + 5 \bullet 8 - 7 + 16$
	$6 \bullet 3 + 5(6 - 4)^3 - 7 + 4^2$
	67
	$18 + 40 - 7 + 16$
	$58 - 7 + 16$
	$6 \bullet 3 + 5(2)^3 - 7 + 4^2$

2. In the problem that follows, the steps and reasons of a geometric proof are shown, but they are out of order and scattered about the page. Work with a partner to determine the original given statement and the proven statement. Arrange all the steps and reasons in the proper order.

Figure 3.7 Scattered Geometric Proof

Given: ______________________

Prove: ______________________

Statements	Reasons
1.	1.
2.	2.
3.	3.
4.	4.
5.	5.
6.	6.

- $\angle$ BDA and $\angle$ BDC are right angles.
- $\angle$ BDA and $\angle$ BDC are congruent.
- The base angles of an isosceles triangle are congruent.
- Perpendicular lines form right angles.
- Right angles are congruent.
- Angle-Angle-Side.
- $\angle$ A and $\angle$ C are congruent.
- Given.
- Reflexive property of congruence.
- $\overline{BD}$ is congruent to $\overline{BD}$.
- Δ ABC is isosceles and $\overline{BD}$ is perpendicular to $\overline{AC}$.
- Δ BDA and Δ BDC are congruent.

SOURCE: Thomas, E. (2003b).

Type Four: Mathematical Riddles

1. I am a linear equation. My slope is the second smallest prime number and my x-intercept is the opposite of the greatest common factor of 24 and 56. Express my equation in slope-intercept form.
2. I am a trigonometric function. My reciprocal and I have the same number of letters in our full names, a number that is a multiple of 2. While my range is much greater than that of my reciprocal, my domain is not. What is my name?
3. I am a three-digit number. All of my digits are different, and they are all even. My digit in the ones place is greater than the digit in the tens place, but my digit in the ones place is also less than the digit in the hundreds place. If you add all of my digits together the answer will be 14. One of my digits is not a counting number. What number am I?
4. What are the coins in my pocket and how many do I have of each? I have exactly seven U.S. coins in my pocket. I have no coin worth more than 25 cents. If someone asked me if I could give him or her exact change for a quarter, I could truthfully say, "Yes." I have exactly one penny. The total value of my coins is more than a dollar.

PATTERN FINDING

Purpose

Successful students know that mathematics tends to operate in predictable and patterned ways. Pattern Finding asks students to pay close attention to the patterns as they analyze mathematical data, problems, or sequences. Once students have identified the patterns, they use them to extrapolate answers and make mathematically sound generalizations.

Overview

Much of the beauty of mathematics can be attributed to the inherent patterns in the behavior of numbers and geometric shapes. Pattern Finding puts students at the center of a set of mathematical data. The data can be almost anything—tables, shapes, number sequences, procedures—provided that there is a pattern in the data. Students analyze the data with three specific questions in mind:

- Can they identify the pattern?
- Can they use the pattern to find the missing information or solve the problem?
- Does the pattern imply a larger and more general principle? If so, can they express the principle or generalization?

Steps

1. Present the students with a set of mathematical data that follows an identifiable pattern.

2. Ask students to analyze the data and:
   a. Identify the pattern.
   b. Use the pattern to find the missing information or to solve the problem.
   c. Work to see if they can identify a larger principle implied by the pattern.
3. Conduct a follow-up discussion in which students discuss the pattern-finding process and their generalizations.

Examples

1. Consider the tables below. Identify and describe the pattern that converts decimals to equivalent percentages. Complete the missing table entries.

Figure 3.8 Percentage Tables

a.

decimal	percentage
.20	20%
.70	70%
.80	80%
	60%
.10	
	90%

b.

decimal	percentage
.15	15%
.79	79%
.07	7%
.93	
	38%
.01	

c.

decimal	percentage
.07	7%
.043	4.3%
.001	0.1%
	53.7%
1	
	2%

2. Identify and describe a pattern that you see within each set of numerical data. Use that pattern to determine the missing values, p and q.

Figure 3.9 Values

a.

x	y
–1	3
0	1
1	–1
2	–3
3	p
q	–7

b.

x	y
–2	5
–1	2
0	1
1	2
2	p
q	10

c.

x	y
–2	17
–1	3
0	1
1	–1
2	p
3	q

a. *Answers:*

$y = -2x + 1$

$p = -5$

$q = 4$

b. *Answers:*

$y = x^2 + 1$

$p = 5$

$q = 3$

c. *Answers:*

$y = -2x^3 + 1$

$p = -15$

$q = -53$

3. Given the infinite sequence: 1, 1, 2, 3, 5, 8, 13, *m*, *k*, *s* . . .
   a. Identify a pattern and use that pattern to find the values of *m*, *k*, and *s*.
   b. As can be seen above, the sixth term in the sequence, t_6, is 8. Write a formula for the general *n*th term of this sequence, t_n.
4. A three-sided polygon has zero diagonals, a four-sided polygon has two diagonals, a five-sided polygon has five diagonals, and a six-sided polygon has nine diagonals. A seven-sided polygon will have how many diagonals? How about an *n*-sided polygon?
5. Use patterns to answer the questions below:
   a. Following the same pattern, what numbers would be found in the next row of the pyramid?

Figure 3.10 Pyramid

1
1 1
1 2 1
1 3 3 1
1 4 6 4 1

   b. Binomial expansion can be accomplished by multiplying the appropriate binomial factors, i.e., $(x + 1)^5 = (x + 1)(x + 1)(x + 1)(x + 1)(x + 1)$. But binomial expansion also involves patterns similar to that in part a above. Use that pattern to help you expand both $(x + 1)^5$ and $(x + 1)^6$ below:

Figure 3.11 Binomial Expansion

$(x + 1)^2 = x^2 + 2x + 1$
$(x + 1)^3 = x^3 + 3x^2 + 3x + 1$
$(x + 1)^4 = x^4 + 4x^3 + 6x^2 + 4x + 1$
$(x + 1)^5 =$
$(x + 1)^6 =$

MATH RULEBOOK

Purpose

Math Rulebook asks students to examine specific mathematical content and to use it to derive general ideas and principles. The tool builds proficiency in key mathematical skills, including data analysis and describing patterns algebraically.

Overview

Math Rulebook is a highly inductive process. It requires students to look beyond—or behind—the given information. Students are provided with a set of examples that demonstrate an unstated rule. The tool requires them to step back and search for the underlying relationship that gives meaning to otherwise isolated bits of information. Students must then express the relationship they discover as a clear and concise mathematical rule. Often, teachers will ask students to collect the rules they discover, organize them by topic or concept, and develop a Math Rulebook for a unit or for the entire year.

Steps

1. Identify a mathematical rule.
2. Develop a set of examples that demonstrate the rule.
3. Ask students to analyze the examples and find the pattern or rule.
4. Have students write the rule out on paper and then test it with new examples.
5. Ask students to collect and organize rules to create a Math Rulebook.

Examples

Figure 3.12 Potpourri of Math Rulebook Activities

1. What's the rule that maps the numbers in column A to those in column B?

   Rule: ______________________________

   (*Rule:* $B = 3.5A$)

A	→	B
2	→	7
0	→	0
4	→	14
–2	→	–7

2. What's the rule that maps the numbers in column A to those in column B?

   Rule: ______________________________

   (*Rule:* $B = |A|$)

A	→	B
–3	→	3
0	→	0
2	→	2
–8	→	8

3. What's the rule that maps the numbers in column A to those in column B?

   Rule: ______________________________

   (*Rule:* $B = A^2$)

A	→	B
1	→	1
2	→	4
0	→	0
3	→	9

4. What's the rule that maps x → y in the set:
   {(x,y): (0,1), (1,0), (2,–7), (–1,2), (–2,9)}?

   Rule: ______________________________

   (*Rule:* $y = -x^3 + 1$)

5. What's the rule that maps x → y in the set:
   {(x,y): (1,10), (2,5), (3,$3.\overline{3}$), (10,1), (100,0.1)}?

   Rule: ______________________________

   (*Rule:* $x \to \frac{10}{x}$)

6. What's the rule that maps x to *g(x)*?

   Rule: ______________________________

   (*Rule:* $g(x) = -1/2\ x$)

x	→	g(x)
0	→	0
4	→	–2
6	→	–3
–1	→	1/2
–2	→	1

7. What's the quadratic rule that creates the graph of the function *f(x)* below?

   Rule: *f(x)* = ______________________________

   (*Rule:* $f(x) = 3 - x^2$)

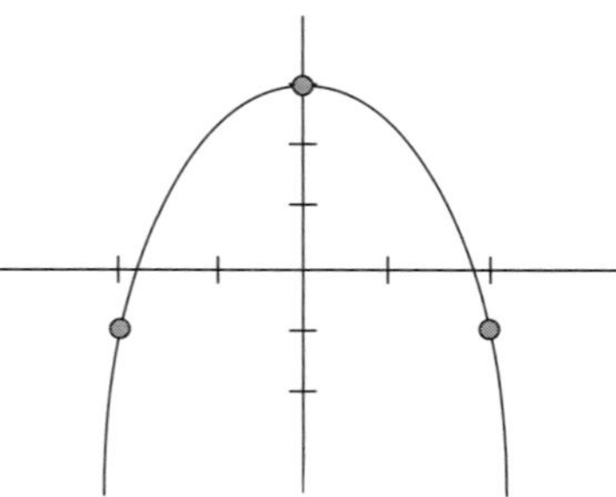

8. What's the rule that maps an ordered pair (*x*,*y*) to a single number *z* in the set:
   {(*x*,*y*) → *z*: (0,6) → 6, (3,4) → 5, (4,3) → 5, (2,4) → $2\sqrt{5}$, (5,12) → 13 }?

   Rule: ______________________________

   (*Rule:* $z = \sqrt{x^2 + y^2}$)

P'S AND Q'S

Purpose

Helping students become good problem solvers is the goal of every teacher of mathematics. P's and Q's is one tool for building students' powers as problem solvers. It gets students to stop, think, and make sure they understand mathematics problems and how to formulate a "plan of attack" before they try to generate solutions. By slowing students' thinking processes down and focusing their attention on the problems and questions that need to be resolved, P's and Q's teaches students how to:

- Preview the problem and read it carefully.
- Practice using their prior knowledge.
- Predict how the problem might be solved.
- Plan for problem solving.
- Put their plan into action by solving the problem.
- Prepare a similar problem for someone else.

Overview

The title of this tool comes with a bit of intrigue and an introductory "hook" built right in. A good way to begin a P's and Q's lesson is to ask students if they have ever heard the saying, "Mind your P's and Q's." After surveying student responses, you can explain to students that there are several competing stories of how this phrase came in to use. One common story claims that typesetters used the phrase back in the days when newspaper print was set using tiny letter blocks that were attached by hand to the printing press. Because lower-case *p* and lower-case *q* looked similar, the typesetter would always have to check the *p*'s and *q*'s carefully before running off copies. Regardless of the phrase's origin, the idea behind the phrase is always the same: be careful before you act to avoid making mistakes. The P's and Q's tool puts the wisdom of this phrase into practice in the mathematics classroom.

The tool uses the simple P's and Q's Poster (see Figure 3.13) that outlines the six P's of problem solving, along with the Q's, or questions, that a thoughtful problem solver asks along the way. The teacher shows students how to use the P's and Q's Poster by solving a sample problem step-by-step (or rather, p-and-q). Then, the teacher works with students collaboratively to solve a second problem, again using the P's and Q's Poster to guide the process. When ready, students can use the P's and Q's Poster as they work through mathematics problems on their own. Students should also be given the opportunity to reflect upon the benefits of the process and discuss the challenges they have encountered and any insights they have developed using P's and Q's.

After students have used P's and Q's several times, the teacher may ask them to select and then present or publish a piece of work that best illustrates their successful use of the P's and Q's tool.

Figure 3.13 P's and Q's of Problem Solving Poster

The P's and Q's of Problem Solving

Preview the problem and read it carefully

Q: What is the problem asking you to do?

Q: How can you write the problem in your own words?

Practice using your prior knowledge

Q: What other problems have you solved that are similar to this one?

Q: What did you do to solve those problems?

Predict how the problem might be solved

Q: What are some different ideas you have for solving the problem?

Q: What are some obstacles or difficulties you might face in solving this problem?

Plan for problem solving

Q: What strategy will you use to solve the problem?

Q: Why did you select this strategy?

Put your plan into action by solving the problem

Q: How did you arrive at your solution? Describe the steps in your answer.

Q: Are your calculations correct? Does your solution make sense?

Prepare a similar problem for someone else

Q: How would you design a similar problem for a friend to solve?

Steps

1. Explain the importance of understanding a problem before trying to solve it. Use discussion to connect this crucial idea to the phrase, "Mind your P's and Q's."
2. Distribute (or display a large version of) the P's and Q's Poster and explain how it is a helpful guide through the mathematical problem-solving process.

3. Select a sample problem. Model how you solve it by following the P's and Q's outlined on the poster.
4. Use a second sample problem to solve collaboratively with students, again using the P's and Q's Poster.
5. Encourage students to use the P's and Q's process on their own.
6. Provide opportunities for students to reflect on and discuss their applications of the P's and Q's process.
7. Allow students to select work that best exemplifies their use of P's and Q's and then to present or publish their work.

Examples

Preview the problem and read it carefully.

Q: What is the problem asking you to do?

Figure 3.14 Bill's Water Taxi Problem

While on vacation at Castaway Harbor, Bill decides to visit the Archipelago Aquarium at the far end of the harbor (look at the illustration below). The beach makes a "U" shape around the "square" harbor, which is roughly one square mile. Bill reaches a point on the beach where there is a water taxi stand. Bill can take a water taxi across the harbor to the aquarium in two different ways. First, he can pay $20 for a one-way pass to go anywhere on the harbor. Second, Bill can pay $5 plus mileage for crossing the water. Mileage is calculated as follows: first tenth of a mile is $3, and each additional tenth of a mile is $1. Assuming that the water taxi crosses the harbor in a straight path to the aquarium, which method of payment is cheaper for Bill?

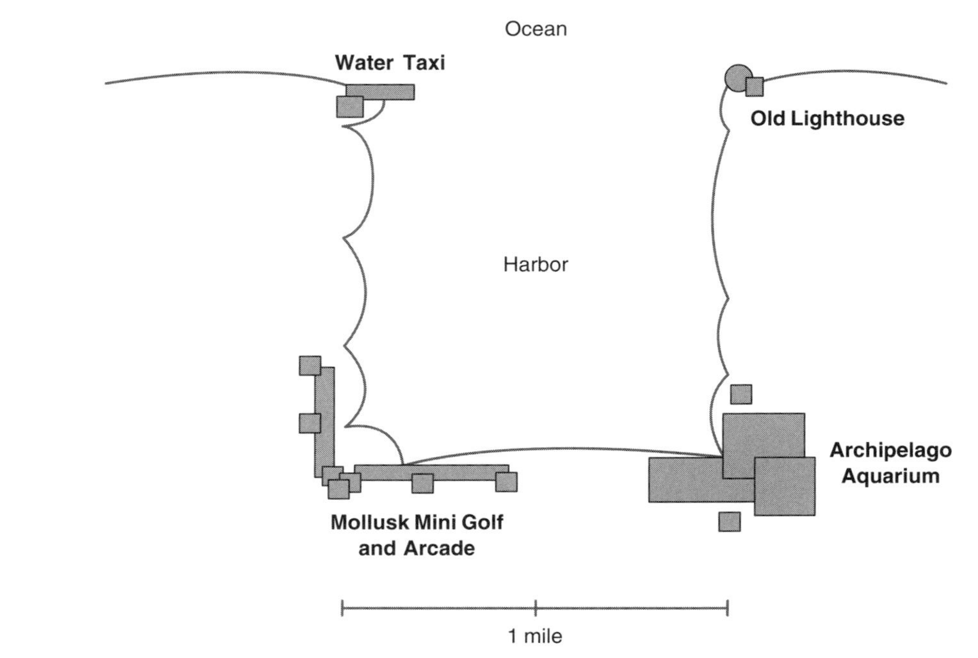

It's asking me to figure out how much Bill's trip will cost if he chooses to pay by the mile. It's also asking me to decide which option is cheaper for Bill.

Q: How can you write the problem in your own words?
Bill wants to get to the Archipelago Aquarium at the other end of Castaway Harbor. There are two choices: He can pay $20 for a one-way pass, or pay $5 for pickup, $3 for the first tenth of a mile, and $1 for each additional tenth of a mile. Which is the better value for Bill?

Practice using your prior knowledge.

Q: What other problems have you solved that are similar to this one?
[The student might connect this problem to several different past problems. First, any problems involving "pay-by-the-distance" such as taxi problems might come up. Second, problems involving solving for the hypotenuse of a right triangle are also relevant and may be considered by the student.]

Q: What did you do to solve those problems?
[Here, the student may refer to notes, textbooks, or call up memories in an attempt to reconstruct the P's and Q's processes from the poster.]

Predict how the problem might be solved.

Q: What are some different ideas you have for solving the problem?
[Students might brainstorm:

- Finding the length and height of the triangle made by bisecting the square across opposite corners.
- Setting up an equation for pay-by-the-mile versus simply doing several operations and having to add each one.]

Q: What are some obstacles or difficulties you might face in solving this problem?
There are several different things to be done and lots of calculations. Making the best choices and doing the mathematics correctly may be challenging.

Plan for problem solving.

Q: What strategy will you use to solve the problem?
Two strategies: First use the Pythagorean Theorem to find the distance to be traveled. Second use algebra to determine the cost of the pay-by-the-mile option.

Q: Why did you select this strategy?
In looking at different options, these two strategies seemed to be the most effective way to find the information needed to get the answer.

Put your plan into action by solving the problem.

Q: How did you arrive at your solution? Describe the steps in your answer.
First, I carefully looked over the illustration that was drawn for the word problem.
Next, I used what I know about squares to measure the harbor: The problem uses tenths of a mile, so if the harbor is 1 mile by 1 mile, then $10 \times 10 = 100$ gives me the area of the harbor in tenths of a mile.

Before I can figure out which option is cheaper, I need to know the distance from the Water Taxi dock to the Archipelago Aquarium. I can figure this out by using the Pythagorean Theorem:

Figure 3.15 Student's Sketch of Problem Using the Pythagorean Theorem

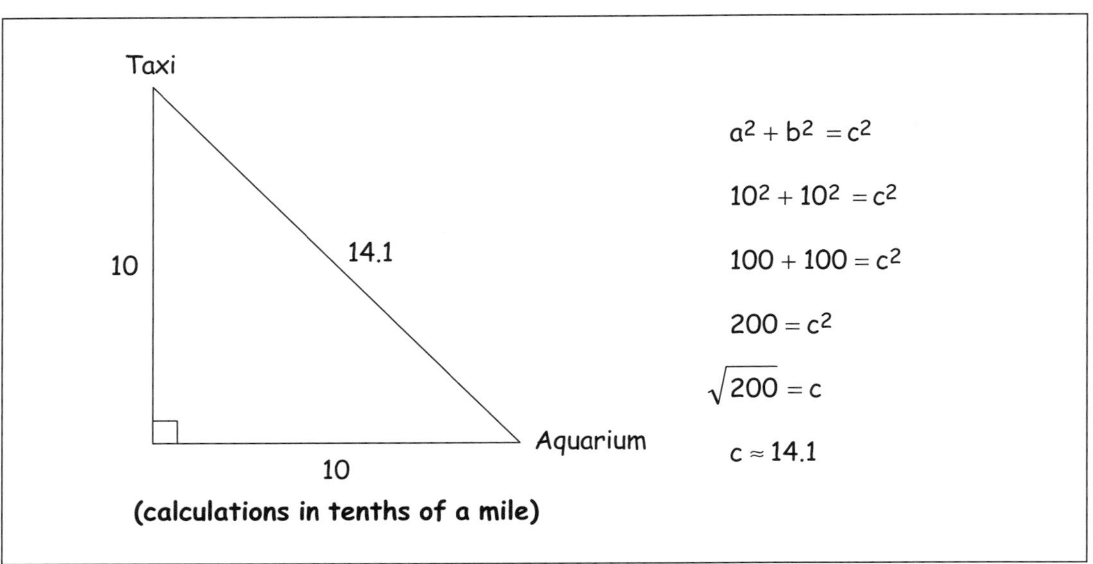

Now that I know that the distance from the Water Taxi dock to the Archipelago Aquarium is about 14.1 tenths of a mile, I can figure out which option is cheaper:

Figure 3.16 Student's Calculations

<u>Water Taxi pass</u>	<u>Water Taxi rate</u>
	\$5 for pick up
\$20 for one-way trip	\$3 for first tenth of a mile
	\$1 for each extra tenth of a mile
the distance from the water taxi stand to the aquarium doesn't matter since Bill is paying one price for the entire trip	the distance from the water taxi stand to aquarium is about 14 tenths of a mile
	pick up fee + first tenth of mile + extra tenths of a mile = cost of trip
	5 + 3(1) + 1(13) =
	5 + 3 + 13 = 21
cost of trip = \$20	cost of trip = \$21

Q: Are your calculations correct? Does your solution make sense?

My answer makes sense because the Water Taxi company makes almost the same amount of money either way.

Prepare a similar problem for someone else.

Q: How would you design a similar problem for a friend to solve?

When we play kickball outside, we play on the grass field used for Little League. Since it is 60 feet between each base, how far would you have to kick the ball to get it over second base and into the outfield?

Figure 3.17 Student's Problem for a Friend

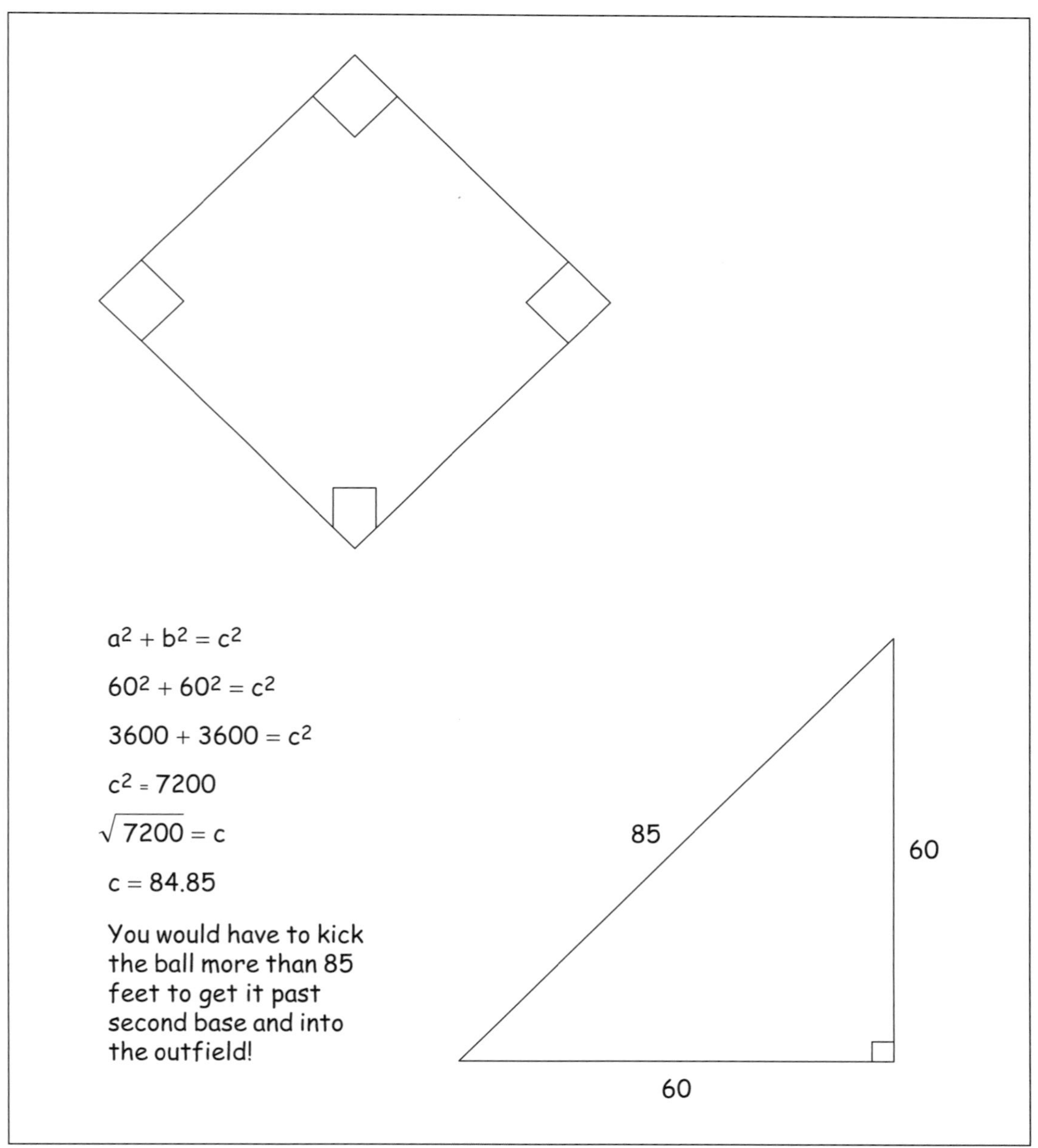

$a^2 + b^2 = c^2$
$60^2 + 60^2 = c^2$
$3600 + 3600 = c^2$
$c^2 = 7200$
$\sqrt{7200} = c$
$c = 84.85$
You would have to kick the ball more than 85 feet to get it past second base and into the outfield!
85
60
60

ESSENTIAL QUESTION NOTES (EQN)

Purpose

Essential Question Notes (EQN) provides students with a simple and friendly organizational structure for collecting information that helps them answer an essential question. EQN turns students into active learners and information managers rather than passive recipients of new content. This is important, especially in light of a wide body of research showing the importance of notemaking (or generating meaningful notes) to learning and recall. Students who make good notes during class remember more because they learn how to focus their attention on the critical content and how to develop a clear organizational structure for storing and retrieving information.

Overview

EQN is a notemaking device that requires students to organize their notes around an essential question. The organizer is made up of three columns: concepts, examples, and background information. The teacher begins the class by introducing the essential question. Over the course of the lesson, the teacher identifies concepts related to the question and provides examples of the concepts along with relevant background information. Students record the information in the appropriate columns. At the end of the class, the students use the completed organizer to answer the essential question.

Steps

1. Provide students with an overview of EQN.
2. Introduce the essential question for students to record at the top of the organizer.
3. Identify the essential concepts and instruct students to record the important information in the concept column.
4. Provide concrete examples for each concept.
5. Throughout the process, have students record important background information that is needed to understand the essential concepts and procedures.
6. At the end of the presentation, have students use their organizers to answer the essential question.

Examples

Figure 3.18 Student's Essential Question Notes for *Solving Equations*

Today's Essential Question:

How are equivalent equations used to solve an equation?

Concepts	Examples	Background Information
Solving equations - the objective is to use equivalent equations to isolate the variable on one side of the equation	$\boxed{X+5=9}$ subtract 5 from both sides: $X+5-5=9-5$ Answer: $\boxed{X=4}$ Check Original equation: $X+5=9$ Substitute: $4+5=9$ simplify: $\boxed{9=9}$ $\boxed{N-8=7}$ Add 8 to both sides: $N-8+8=7+8$ Answer: $N=15$ Check Original equation: $N-8=7$ Substitute: $15-8=7$ simplify: $7=7$	equivalent equation add, subtract, multiply or divide by the same term a term and its additive inverse add up to zero. the additive inverse of 5 is -5.

Figure 3.19 Student's Essential Question Notes for *Point-Slope Form*

Today's Essential Question:

How is Point-Slope Form used to write an equation of a line?

Concepts	Examples	Background Information
Point-Slope Form Objective: Identify required form information, variable substitution, simplification and check.	PS Form: $y - y_1 = m(x - x_1)$ Point (x_1, y_1)? Given (1, 5) so $x_1 = 1$ and $y_1 = 5$ Slope (m)? $3x + y = 5$ $y = -3 + 5$ $m = -3$ Substitute: $y - (5) = -3(x - 1)$ Simplify: $y = -3x + 8$ Check Answer: $y = -3x + 8$ Check slope: slope intercept form tells us $m = -3$ Substitute pt.: $x = 1$, $y = 5$ $(5) = -3(1) + 8$ $5 = 5$	equations of lines slope & slope-intercept form parallel lines & slopes of parallel lines meaning of a line containing a point simplification of expression substitution

Organizer 3-B Essential Question Notes Organizer

Name: ______________________ **Date:** ____________

Today's Essential Question:

Concepts	Examples	Background Information

COMPARE AND CONTRAST

Purpose

Research shows that teaching students how to identify similarities and differences is the single most effective way to increase understanding and raise achievement levels (Marzano, Pickering, & Pollock, 2001). Setting two concepts against one another and using each as a frame of reference for examining the other allows students to see deeply into the content they are studying and fuels new insights about mathematics. Plus, by learning how to make increasingly sophisticated comparisons, students become more adept at avoiding the most common pitfalls of mathematical learning. Comparisons help students:

- See the "invisible" (e.g., closure of sets under operations, mathematical structures).
- Clarify the "confusable" (e.g., expressions vs. equations, permutations vs. combinations).
- Notice the "neglectable" (e.g., divisibility by a variable that could have a zero value).

Overview

The human brain is hard wired to make comparisons. Compare and Contrast draws its power from this natural cognitive activity, but it also refines students' comparative skills by teaching them a four-phase process for making quality comparisons. First, students use a set of clear criteria to describe each item or concept separately. Then, students use a Comparison Organizer to draw out the similarities and differences between the two concepts. Next, students use their comparisons to form conclusions and explore the causes and effects behind key similarities and differences. Finally, students apply their learning by solving a new problem or completing a task.

Steps

1. Select two (or more) related concepts or mathematics problems.
2. Specify criteria for comparison.
3. Provide (or teach students how to create) graphic organizers for describing items and comparing them (see Organizers 3-C and 3-D for reproducible templates).
4. Guide students through the four phases of comparison:
    a. Description
        i. Establish purpose for the comparison.
        ii. Identify sources of information.
        iii. Clarify criteria for describing items.
        iv. Have students describe the two items using the Description Organizer (Organizer 3-C).

b. Comparison
   i. Provide students with a Comparison Organizer (Organizer 3-D).
   ii. Have students identify key similarities and differences on the organizer.
c. Conclusion
   i. Ask students to decide if the two items are more alike or more different.
   ii. Explore and discuss causes/effects of the differences.
   iii. Help students form generalizations.
d. Application
   i. Present students with a new problem or task.
   ii. Have students apply their learning to the new problem or task.

Examples

Compare and Contrast works equally well with concepts and procedures. Let's start with procedures. Compare and Contrast is a great way to help students discover the thinking and problem-solving demands behind different kinds of mathematical problems. For example, you might have students compare two different kinds of percentage problems:

Problem 1

Haylee sells kitchen equipment. As part of her salary, Haylee receives 12% commission on her sales. In February, Haylee sold $7,250 worth of kitchen equipment. How much commission should she receive?

Problem 2

For March, Haylee forgot to check her total sales figures. She received a commission of $825 for the month. How much did Haylee sell?

First, students describe the two problems using clear criteria, as shown in Figure 3.20.

Figure 3.20 Describing Two Percentage Problems

	Problem 1	Problem 2
How is the problem written? (What do you need to figure out?)	The problem is asking me to figure out what Haylee's commission will be.	The problem is asking me to figure out Haylee's total sales.
What formula or models can be used?	The proportion method $\frac{\text{P (part of the whole)}}{\text{B (base)}} = \frac{\text{R (rate, or percentage)}}{100}$	Same
How can you sketch the problem to better understand it?	 $7,250 Total sales (100%) Haylee's commission 12% This is what's missing—Haylee's commission in dollars	 Total sales (This is what's missing) Haylee's commission is $825
How did you solve the problem?	1. Reviewed the proportion method $\frac{P}{B} = \frac{R}{100}$ 2. Identified what I knew P is unknown R is 12% B is 7,250 3. Set up the proportion $\frac{P}{7,250} = \frac{12}{100}$ 4. Cross multiplied 100 P = 87,000 5. Divided both sides by 100 P = 870	1. Used the same method. $\frac{P}{B} = \frac{R}{100}$ 2. Identified what I knew P is 825 R is 12% B is unknown 3. Set up the proportion $\frac{825}{B} = \frac{12}{100}$ 4. Cross multiplied 12 B = 82,500 5. Divided both sides by 12 B = 6,875

Now, with their descriptions complete, students are in a position to conduct a powerful comparison, as shown in Figure 3.21.

Figure 3.21 Comparison Organizer

Differences

Problem 1	Problem 2
Total sales are given.	Total sales are missing.
Commission is missing.	Commission is given.
Problem asks what Haylee's commission will be in dollars.	Problem asks what total sales are in dollars.

Similarities

Both use the proportion method.

Both give the percentage of commission.

Both involve sales.

The diagrams look very similar.

After the conclusion phase, in which students decide if the two problems are more alike or more different and discuss how the differences affect the problem-solving procedure, you might ask them to apply their new understanding with a task like the following.

> To show what you've learned, create three new sales-commission problems. One problem should be like Problem 1 and the other should be like Problem 2. Then, since we noticed that Problem 1 asks you to solve for total commission and Problem 2 asks you to solve for total sales, create a new problem that asks you to figure out the rate (or percentage) of commission.

As we have already noted, Compare and Contrast works as well with mathematical concepts as it does with problem-solving processes. The tool is highly flexible and can be used at varying levels of depth. Students may simply be asked to generate as many similarities and differences as possible and quickly draw conclusions. Here are a few examples of this "down and dirty" approach to Compare and Contrast.

Whole Numbers and Counting Numbers

- Whole numbers are similar to counting numbers because ________________.
- Whole numbers are different from counting numbers because ____________.
- Between the two, the more interesting set of numbers is ________________ because ____.

Odd Numbers and Prime Numbers

- Odd numbers are similar to prime numbers because ___________________.
- Odd numbers are different from prime numbers because ________________.
- Between the two, the more interesting set of numbers is ________________ because ____.

Expressions and Equations

- Expressions are similar to equations because __________________________.
- Expressions are different from equations because _______________________.
- Between the two, the harder one to work with is ________________________ because ____.

Greatest Common Factor (GCF) and Least Common Multiple (LCM)

- A GCF is similar to an LCM because ________________________________.
- A GCF is different from an LCM because _____________________________.
- Between the two, the more useful is ________________________________ because ____.

Permutations and Combinations

- Permutations are similar to combinations because _______________________.
- Permutations are different from combinations because ___________________.
- Between the two, the more useful is ________________________________ because ____.

Of course, concepts also lend themselves to the full, four-phase Compare and Contrast process. By working with students to run two concepts through the four phases or the "full treatment," you are committing to the development of their reasoning and analytical skills. For example, you might ask students to:

- Describe *congruence* and *similarity* separately, according to these criteria: symbol notation, size of figures, and shape of figures.
- Identify key similarities and differences on a Comparison Organizer (see Figure 3.22).
- Decide if the two concepts are more similar or more different.
- Apply their learning to a task—a brief essay in which students discuss which concept is more useful in real life.

Figure 3.22 Description Organizer for Congruence and Similarity

Congruence	Similarity

Similarities

Organizer 3-C Blank Description Organizer

Name: ______________________ **Date:** ______________

	Problem 1	Problem 2
Problem		
How is the problem written? **(What do you need to figure out?)**		
How can you sketch the problem to better understand it?		
How did you solve the problem?		

Organizer 3-D Blank "Top Hat" Comparison Organizer

Name: ____________________ **Date:** ____________________

MATHEMATICAL ANALOGIES

Purpose

Analogies are great tools to get students to think deeply and in new and refreshing ways about mathematical content. What's more, analogies help students hone their logic and critical-thinking skills as they work to identify the relationship between two items, distill that relationship into a single sentence, and eliminate answers that do not express the same relationship as the original pair.

Overview

Mathematical Analogies put the power of analogical thinking to work in mathematics classrooms. When using analogies, it is important that you teach students what analogies are and that you provide a clear method for solving them. Here's a simple four-step method for teaching students how to work their way through analogies:

1. Examine the original pair. Ask yourself: what is the relationship between the two items? Some of the most common relationships include:

- intensity
- location
- opposites
- specific to general
- part to whole
- tool to use/user
- sequence
- cause and effect
- signs
- defining characteristics

So, for example, let's say the original pair is: trigonometry : triangles :: A student might say the relationship is "In trigonometry we study triangles."

2. Express the relationship as a simple sentence: "Trigonometry is the study of triangles."

3. Work through the list of potential answers by substituting the items in the potential answers into your sentence. Eliminate all answers in which the relationship between the items is not the same as the relationship in the original pair.

trigonometry : triangles ::

a. sports : football	(sports is not the study of football)
b. zoology : animals	(zoology is the study of animals)
c. sociology : surveys	(sociology is not the study of surveys)
d. English : Shakespeare	(English can be the study of Shakespeare)

4. If you cannot eliminate all but one answer, refine your sentence so that it is more specific:

"Trigonometry is a branch of mathematics designed to study triangles."

zoology : animals (Zoology is a branch of science designed to study animals.)

English : Shakespeare (I don't think English is a branch of anything. It is not designed to study Shakespeare only.)

The answer is:

b. trigonometry : triangles :: zoology : animals

Steps

1. Select or develop a set of analogies related to mathematical content.
2. Explain to students what analogies are and how they work.
3. Teach them the four steps for solving analogies.
4. Allow students to solve further analogies on their own.
5. As students become more comfortable with the process, encourage them to design their own Mathematical Analogies.

Examples

algorithm : answer ::

a. analogy : comparison
b. universe : star
c. angle : right triangle
d. line : line segment
e. highway : destination

The answer is e: An algorithm is a step-by-step process created to lead to an answer just as a highway leads to a destination.

point : pencil tip ::

a. plane : building
b. triangle : kite
c. picture : frame
d. line segment : piece of string
e. chapter : book

The answer is d: A pencil tip is a good physical representation of a point. A piece of string is a good physical representation of a line segment.

multiplication : addition ::

a. distributive : quantity
b. theorem : properties
c. division : subtraction
d. replenish : refill
e. real numbers : closed

The answer is c: Multiplication is repeated addition. Division is repeated subtraction.

angle : rays ::

a. circle : radius
b. polyhedron : planes
c. hexagon : equilateral triangles
d. triangle : line segments
e. rectangle : right angles

The answer is d: An angle can be defined to be the union of two rays sharing a common endpoint. A triangle is the union of three line segments sharing common endpoints.

meter : yard ::

a. shorter : longer
b. pound : 16 ounces
c. Fahrenheit : Celsius
e. stopwatch : race
f. fraction : percent

The answer is c: Meters and yards are different scale units that can be used to measure lengths. Fahrenheit and Celsius are two scales that can be used to measure temperature.

THREE-WAY TIE

Purpose

A deep understanding of mathematical content means more than knowing what the key concepts are; it also means understanding how these concepts are related, how they fit together to form a bigger picture. Three-Way Tie gives students the opportunity to focus their attention on these hidden relationships. Students identify the relationship between pairs of critical concepts or terms and then distill their understanding of the relationship into a single sentence.

Overview

Three-Way Tie uses a triangle organizer that connects three separate but interrelated terms. Students examine the terms, determine the relationships between each pair of words, and then explain the relationship in one sentence along each side of the triangle. (Figure 3.23 shows a completed Three-Way Tie Organizer.)

What makes Three-Way Tie such a potent technique is the way it forces students to cut to the heart of the content, to refine and communicate their thinking about three important concepts in only a few well-chosen words.

Figure 3.23 Completed Three-Way Tie Organizer

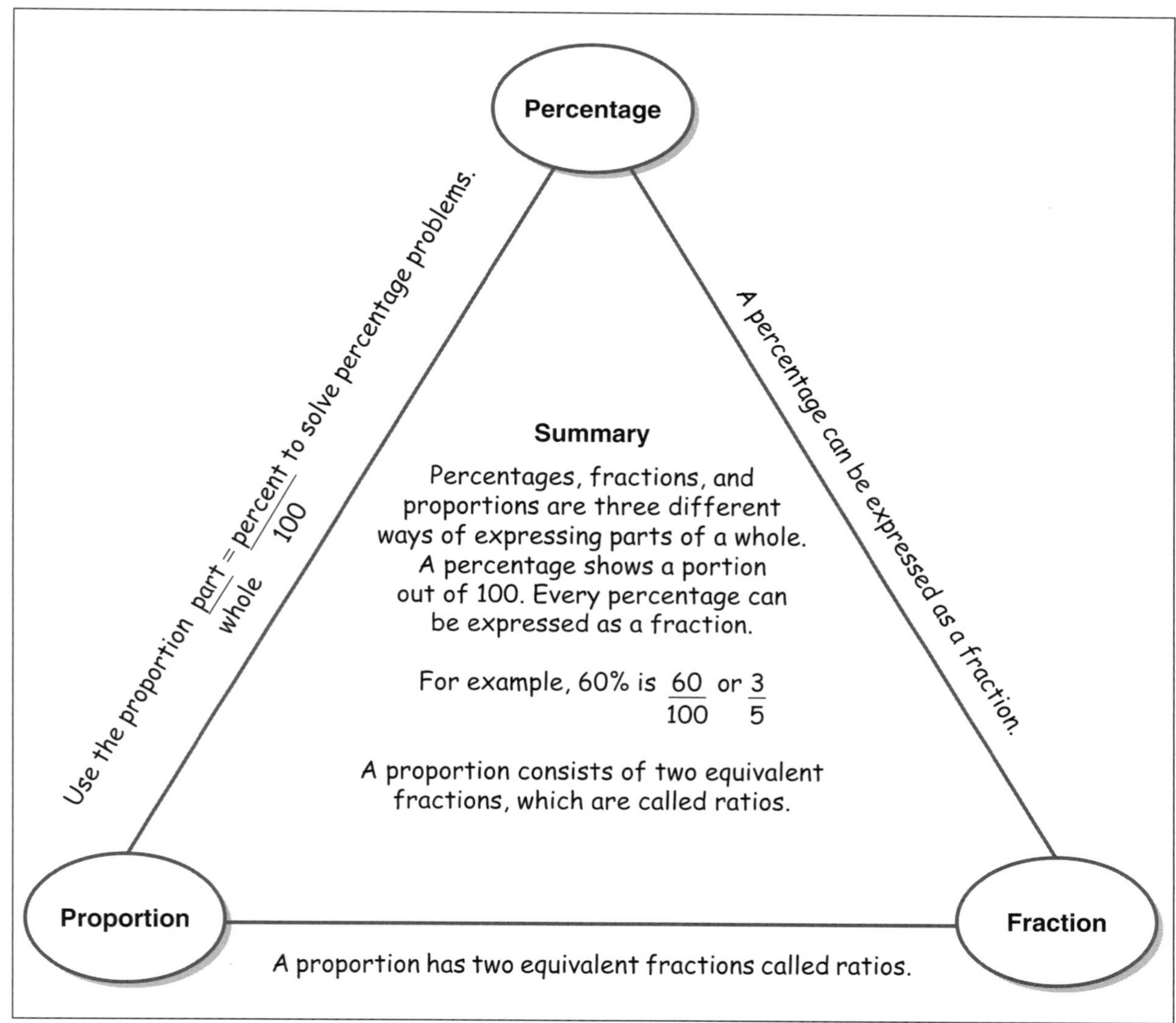

Steps

1. Identify an important mathematical concept.
2. Graphically "triangulate" the concept with two related terms or concepts. Alternatively, you can have the students generate the three terms themselves by selecting the three most important ideas in a reading or unit.
3. Along each side of the triangle, the student writes a sentence that clearly relates the two terms. (See Organizer 3-E for a blank Three-Way Tie Organizer.)
4. Have students use their three sentences to develop a brief summary of the concept.
5. Allow students time to share and explain what they wrote on their organizers.

Examples

Figure 3.24 Potpourri of Three-Way Tie Examples

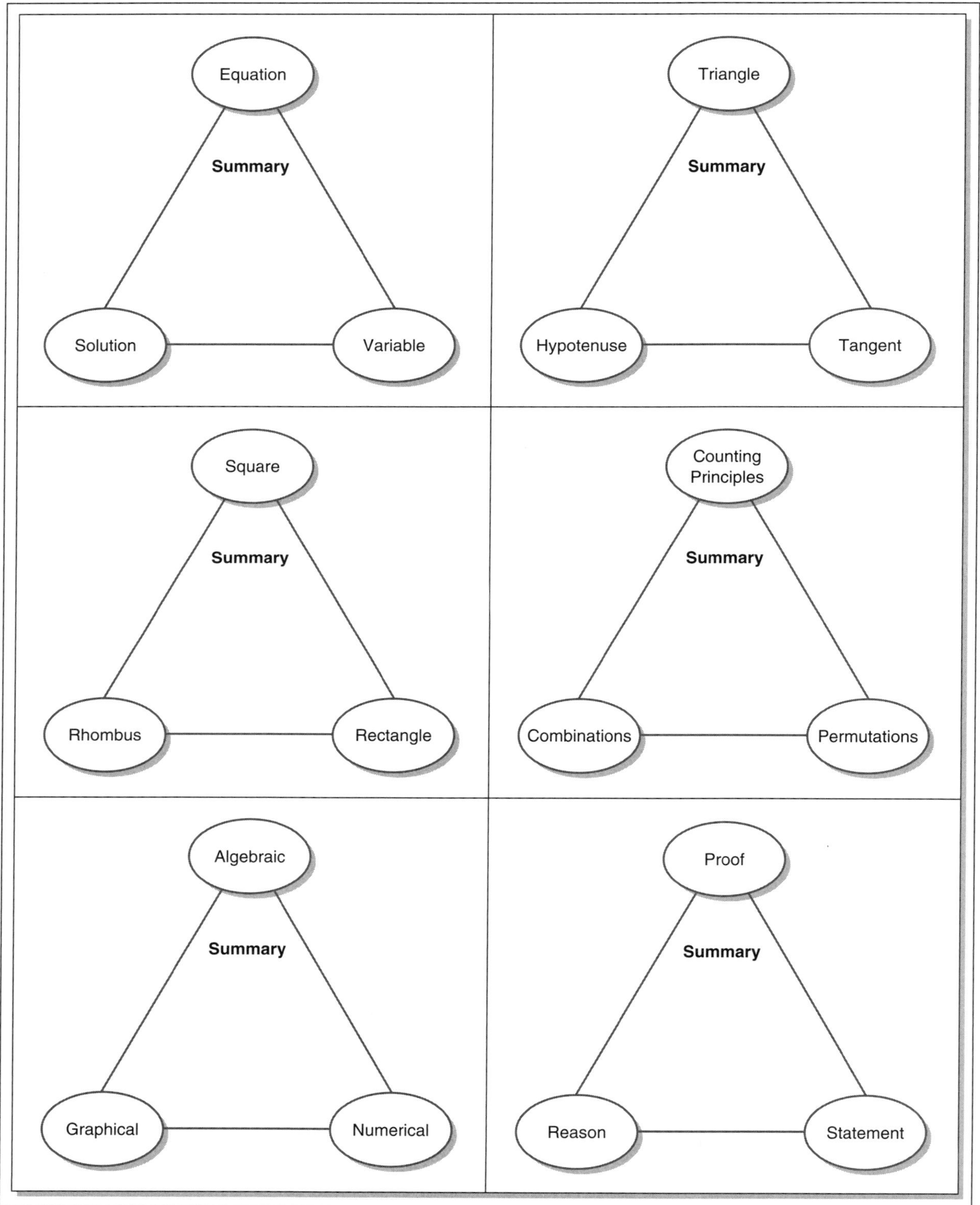

Organizer 3-E Blank Three-Way Tie Organizer

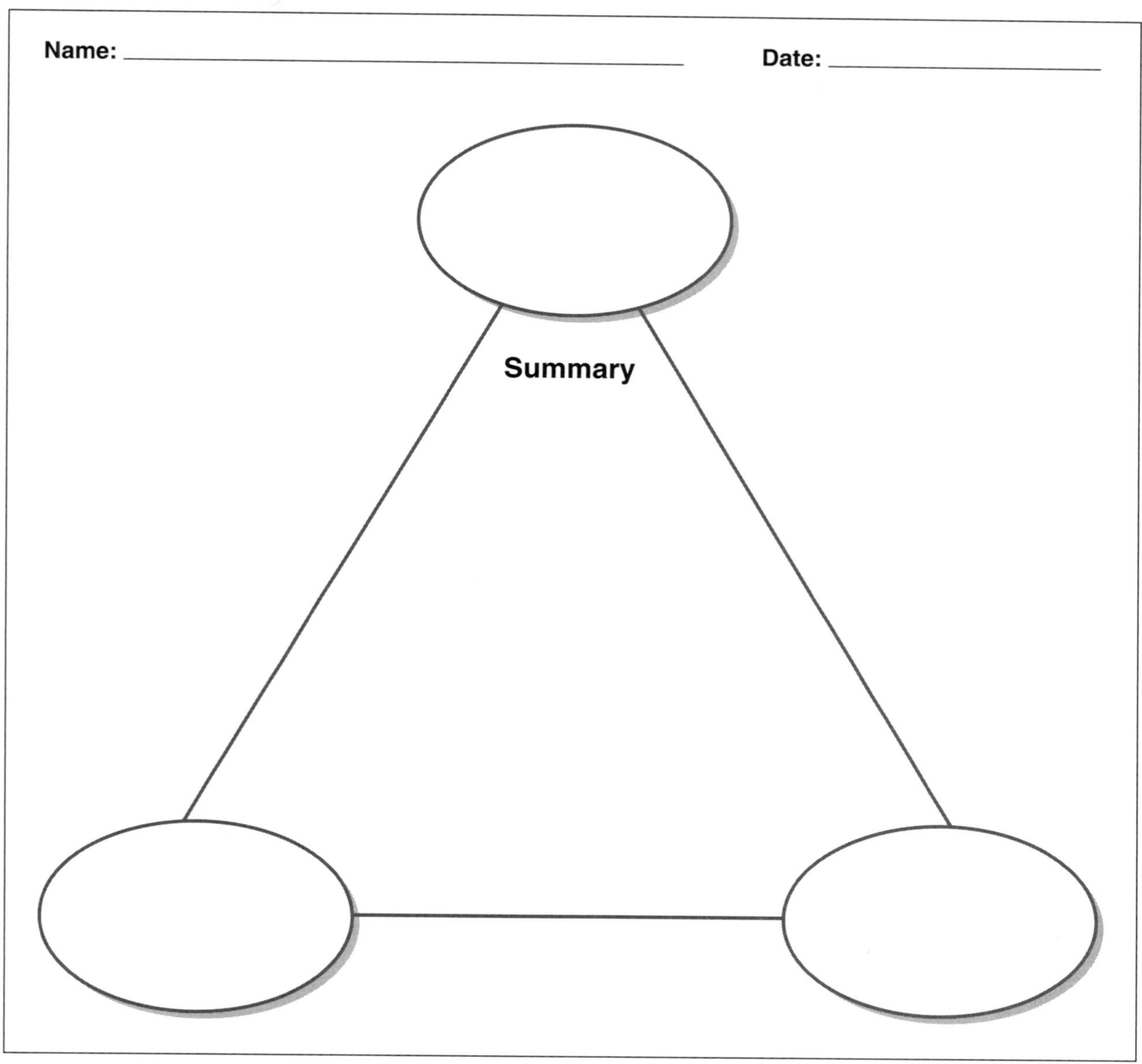

WHICH ONE DOESN'T BELONG?

Purpose

Comparison is one of the most powerful and most natural forms of human thinking. When students know how to compare a set of data, extract key similarities and differences, and then use their findings to draw conclusions, they are exhibiting the skills of first-rate thinkers. Which One Doesn't Belong? enables students to hone their powers of comparative thinking as they examine a set of data to determine what all the items—except one—have in common.

Overview

Which One Doesn't Belong? is a simple technique that nurtures sophisticated thinking. Students are presented with a set of mathematical expressions, problems, tables, graphs, etc. It is the student's job to (1) compare items; (2) look for common characteristics or properties; (3) decide which item does not belong, and (4) explain their reasoning for excluding the chosen item.

Steps

1. Identify an important characteristic or principle associated with a mathematical concept.
2. Select or develop three problems, expressions, or items that all share the identified characteristic.
3. Select or develop a fourth item that does not share the identified characteristic.
4. Ask students to analyze items, identify the exception, and explain their rationale for excluding it.
5. Over time, ask students to develop their own Which One Doesn't Belong? activities.

Examples

Which One Doesn't Belong activities fall into two categories: those in which the common characteristic is given and those in which the student must supply the common characteristic.

Examples Where the Common Characteristic Is Provided

1. Three of the following equations share a common solution. One does not. Identify the one that does not and explain why it is different from the others:

   a. $x - 3y = 2$
   b. $x - y = 6$
   c. $2x + 3y = 13$
   d. $x - 5y = 0$
   The answer is b: Only equation b does not contain the point (5, 1).

2. The dimensions of rectangular shipping containers are listed below. Identify which container doesn't belong from options a, b, c, and d.

   Common characteristic: equal volumes

   a. 12 ft. by 10 ft. by 30 ft.
   b. 20 ft. by 16 ft. by 12ft.
   c. 10 ft. by 10 ft. by 36 ft.
   d. 5 ft. by 24 ft. by 30 ft.

   The answer is b: Only b does not have a volume of 3,600 ft^3.

3. Common characteristic: equations of lines

   a. $y = \frac{x^2}{x}$
   b. $y = x$
   c. $y = 2$
   d. $x = \pi$

   The answer is a: While all are linear relations, equation a is not a line because it is missing the single point (0,0).

Examples Asking Students to Provide the Common Characteristic

1. Examine the four items below. Which one doesn't belong? Why?

   a. 2^{10}
   b. 4^5
   c. 8^4
   d. 32^2

   Common characteristic: ______________________________
   The answer is c: All are equivalent to 1,024 except option c.

2. Examine the four items below. Which one doesn't belong? Why?

   a. 11%
   b. 11
   c. 0.11
   d. $\frac{11}{100}$

   Common characteristic: ______________________________
   The answer is b: All are equivalent except option b.

3. Examine the four items below. Which one doesn't belong? Why?

   a. $xy = 10$
   b. $x^2 - y^2 = 5$
   c. $x^2 = 5 - y^2$
   d. $y^2 - x^2 = 5$

   Common characteristic: ______________________________
   The answer is c: All are hyperbolas except option c, which is a circle.

4. Examine the four items below. Which one doesn't belong? Why?

   a. $y = \cos x$
   b. $y = x^4$

c. $y = |x|$
d. $y = 4x$
Common characteristic: ________________________________
The answer is d: All are even functions except option d, which is an odd function.

YES, BUT WHY?

Purpose

Yes, $2^{-1} = \frac{1}{2}$, *but why?* Too often, students take answers to problems (and the mathematical procedures that led to those answers) for granted. Yes, But Why? is a simple probing technique that forces students to go beyond the simple recitation of answers—all the way to the principles and logic that animate mathematics.

Overview

Yes, But Why? requires students to focus their attention on the solution process rather than the answer. This emphasis on process enables students to develop their powers of mathematical explanation as they build comprehension and root out common misconceptions in their thinking. Yes, But Why? can be used in a variety of ways in any mathematics classroom. For example, you can ask students to provide specific reasons why:

- The answer to a given problem is correct.
- The steps in a procedure are valid.
- The restrictions to a particular problem are necessary.
- A particular mathematical convention is so important.
- An explanation, trigonometric identity, or mathematical induction proof is valid.

Steps

1. Have students solve a problem or provide an answer to a question. Alternately, you can provide a problem and its answer to students.
2. Ask students to focus their attention on explaining the process and justifying the answer. (Yes, but why?)
3. Allow students to share and compare the explanations they generate.

Examples

Ten Yes, But Why? Activities:

1. Yes, $10 = \dfrac{1}{1/10}$ but why?
2. Why it is true that $\dfrac{\sin^2 a + \cos^2 a}{\cos^2 a} = \sec^2 a$?

3. Write down any three-digit number between 100 and 1,000 (e.g., 502). Make a six-digit number by repeating that same number (e.g., 502,502). Your six-digit number will be divisible by each of these three prime numbers, 7, 11, and 13. Use your calculator to confirm that this is true for at least three different six-digit numbers you create using the format described above, then explain the outcome.

4. A student correctly calculated the sum of the first one hundred integers as 5,050. She showed her work as follows: 1 + 2 + 3 . . . + 98 + 99 + 100 = 50 • 101 = 5,050

Explain the relevance of the number "101" to this problem.

Explain why the product "50 • 101" is a valid shortcut to adding up all 100 numbers.

5. Charles says that a line whose equation is $2x + 3y = 5$ is perpendicular to a second line $3x - 2y = 1$. He is correct. Explain why he is correct.

6. $x^2 + 10x + 25 > 0$ for any real number x. Show why this is so.

7. The proof statements given below reveal a logical proof progression from Given to Prove. What is missing? Provide a reason for each step in the proof.

Figure 3.25 Proof Statements

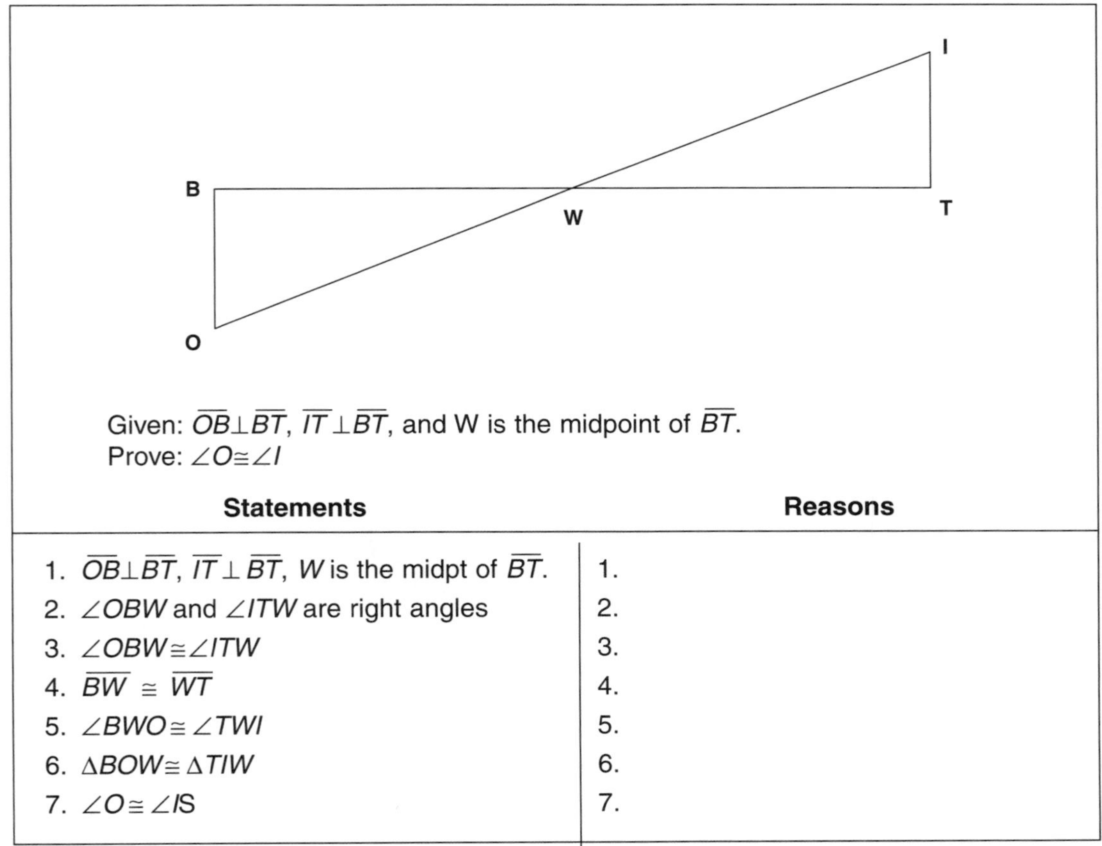

Given: $\overline{OB} \perp \overline{BT}$, $\overline{IT} \perp \overline{BT}$, and W is the midpoint of $\overline{BT}$.
Prove: $\angle O \cong \angle I$

Statements	Reasons
1. $\overline{OB} \perp \overline{BT}$, $\overline{IT} \perp \overline{BT}$, W is the midpt of $\overline{BT}$.	1.
2. $\angle OBW$ and $\angle ITW$ are right angles	2.
3. $\angle OBW \cong \angle ITW$	3.
4. $\overline{BW} \cong \overline{WT}$	4.
5. $\angle BWO \cong \angle TWI$	5.
6. $\Delta BOW \cong \Delta TIW$	6.
7. $\angle O \cong \angle IS$	7.

8. $\frac{x^2+3x+2}{x+1} = x + 2$ for $x \neq -1$.
Why does the quotient equal $x + 2$?

Why must the restriction, $x \neq -1$, be part of the answer?

9. For the function $f(x)=\frac{\sin x}{x}$, both a numeric table of values of $f(x)$ and a graph of $f(x)$ suggest that the limit of $f(x)$ as $x\to 0$ appears to be 1. Show algebraically that, in fact, $\lim_{x\to 0} f(x) = 1$.

10. Yes! The parallelogram area formula is simply base times height. Take one of the two diagrams below and explain why the diagram illustrates how the area of a parallelogram is equal to its base times height.

Figure 3.26 Area of a Parallelogram

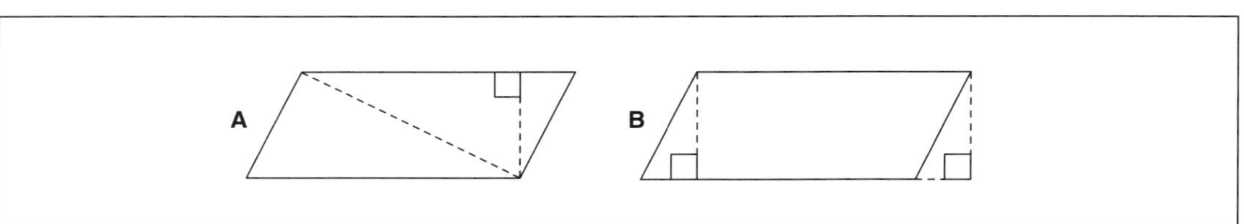

YES, BUT WHY^3?

Purpose

Ask any parent what the preferred question of an inquisitive three-year-old is, and you'll hear the same answer over and over again: Why? *"Why is the sky blue?" "Why does the wind blow?" "Why does my older brother get to ride without a car seat?"* Of course, Why? is hardly the exclusive domain of preschoolers. Scientists, mathematicians, philosophers—all of them rely on that simple but extraordinarily powerful little word: "Why?" Yes, But Why^3? challenges students to think beyond solutions and facts by inviting them to take part in a quest for larger patterns, broader generalizations, and deeper mathematical truths.

Overview

When a teacher poses a sequence of Why? questions to a class, students are asked to search for the reasons, generalizations, and principles that lie behind mathematical procedures. Students are not able to rely on their memories or computation skills alone; rather, they need to employ critical-thinking and inquiry skills to develop an argument that explains why the mathematics we all take for granted works. When using the Yes, But Why^3? technique, teachers first ask students to solve a problem or respond to a question (or teachers may elect to simply give students the answer). Once the correct answer is established, the teacher asks students "Why?" three times. This sequence of "Why?" questions opens a dialogue between teachers and students, as together they search for mathematical patterns and principles.

For example, after a mini-lesson on the Fibonacci Sequence (the famous sequence named after Italian mathematician Leonardo Fibonacci), a middle-school mathematics teacher had students figure out the pattern by completing the sequence up to the 12th term, as show in Figure 3.27 below.

Figure 3.27 The Fibonacci Sequence

TERM	1st	2nd	3rd	4th	5th	6th	7th	8th	9th	10th	11th	12th
VALUE	1	1	2	3	5	8	13	21	34	55	89	144

Then, the teacher asked these Yes, But Why^3? questions:

Teacher: Why is the 12th term in the sequence 144?

Jake: Um, well because that's the answer you get when you follow the pattern and add up the numbers.

Teacher: Yes, but why? Why is it that we can figure out any term in the sequence?

Sarah: Because, um . . . Because you can figure it out. It's pretty easy actually once you figure it out. You just add the two numbers that are next to each other to get the next number in the sequence. If you just keep on going, you can get any term in the sequence.

Teacher: Ok, so now that we've looked at a few different number sequences, why are patterns important in mathematics?

Ruben: Patterns show you how the numbers you're looking at work.

Teacher: Anyone else?

Anita: It's like a secret code. You can use the pattern to figure out what's going on.

Steps

1. Provide students with a problem, equation, or situation to consider.
2. Either reveal the correct answer or allow students time to work on and come up with the correct answer.
3. Once the correct answer is established, ask students to explain why the correct answer is, in fact, correct.
4. Depending on the response(s) given, frame and ask another "Why?" question.
5. As students provide more information, keep asking "Why?" questions to challenge their assumptions.
6. Make sure the last "Why?" question leads students to a larger and more complete understanding of the mathematical concept or procedure being discussed.

Examples

Possible sequence of Yes, But Why³? questions for *addition of fractions:*

Initial Question: What is the sum of $4\frac{1}{2} + 3\frac{3}{4}$?

First Why? Question: Why is your answer $8\frac{1}{4}$?

Second Why? Question: Why did you use fourths for your denominator instead of eighths?

Third Why? Question: Why do you need common denominators to add or subtract fractions?

Possible sequence of Yes, But Why³? questions for *calculating volume:*

Background information: A tank is made up of a cylinder with two hemispherical ends. The tank is 6 meters in diameter and 22 meters long.

First Why? Question: Why do you think the volume is approximately 565 m^3?

Second Why? Question: Why is the formula to calculate the volume of a cylinder: $V = \pi r^2 h$?

Third Why? Question: Why do cylindrical tanks containing liquids have rounded ends?

Possible sequence of Yes, But Why³? questions for *calculating rate of expansion:*

Background information: A sphere has a radius of 2 meters. Air is being forced into the sphere at a rate of 4 m^3/min.

Initial question: How fast (at what rate) is the radius of the sphere expanding when the radius is 2 meters?

First Why? Question: Why did you arrive at the answer of $\frac{1}{4\pi}$ meters per minute?

Second Why? Question: Why did you not evaluate the formula for the radius of 2 meters before differentiation?

Third Why? Question: Why are related rates important to calculus?

SHOW ME

Purpose

Show Me is a simple but powerful way for teachers and students to assess students' understanding of mathematical concepts. Students demonstrate their understanding and assess their mastery over key content using a variety of thinking styles and forms of multiple intelligence.

Overview

The power of the Show Me technique as an assessment tool lies in its ability to engage students in a variety of tasks that demonstrate comprehension. Students can be asked to display their understanding in any or all of the following four ways:

- *Identify* items that fall within a given range or that fulfill certain requirements.
- *Generate* equations, formulas, or statements to express a situation or to fulfill specific requirements.

- *Illustrate* an example, equation, formula, problem, or situation through drawing or graphing.
- *Cite* a tested example to prove or support a claim, statement, or theory; *cite* a counterexample to disprove a claim, statement, or theory.

Steps

1. Review the mathematical concept(s) that your students are studying.
2. Determine how many (and which types of) Show Me activities students will work through.
3. Instruct students to complete the Show Me activities individually.
4. Have students share and discuss their work and examples/counterexamples with a partner or within a small group.

Examples

Below you will find various Show Me activities that require students to identify, generate, illustrate, and cite examples for different mathematical concepts.

Show Me activities that ask students to identify:

1. Which of the following numbers are prime numbers?

   10, 12, 17, 21, 23, 41, 51, 99, 101, 109

2. Read the following descriptions of pairs of geometric figures and identify which pair does not belong. (*Hint: Find the area of each figure.*)
   - A $3 \times 4 \times 5$ inch right triangle and a 3×10 inch rectangle.
   - A square with a perimeter of 24 inches and a rectangle with sides of 3, 12, 3, and 12.
   - A circle with the radius of $\frac{1}{4}$ inch and a circle with the diameter of $\frac{1}{2}$ inch.
3. Correctly name each of the following quadrilaterals:

Figure 3.28 Identification of Quadrilaterals

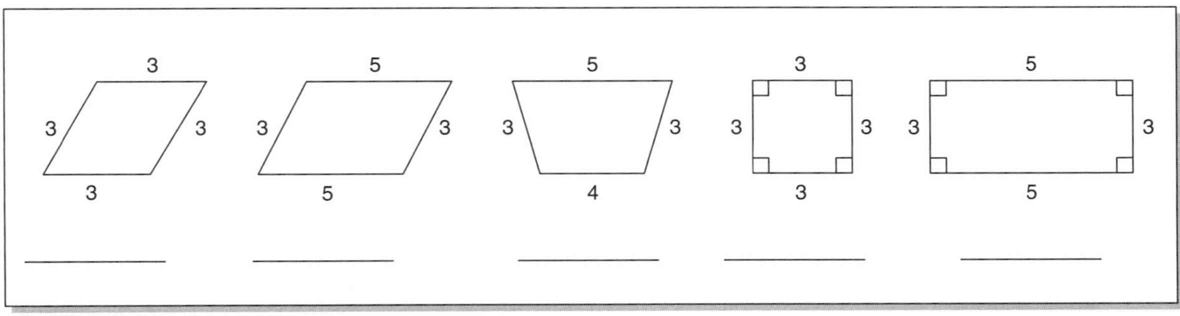

Show Me activities that ask students to generate:

1. Write five numbers, in fraction form, that exist between 0.333 and 0.667.
2. Using these numbers (1, 2, 3, 4, 5, 6, 7, 8, 9, and 10) no more than once, create a total of four fractions: two fractions in simplest form and two fractions not in simplest form.
3. Write three equations (in standard form) whose graphs would display a set of three parallel lines.

Show Me activities that ask students to illustrate:

1. Sketch three isosceles triangles; make sure that one is a right triangle, one is an acute triangle, and one is an obtuse triangle.
2. Draw four separate graphs: two different graphs that illustrate "even functions" and two different graphs that illustrate "odd functions."
3. Continuity of a function at a point does not imply differentiability of the function at that same point. Sketch the associated graphs for at least two functions that illustrate this important statement.

Show Me activities that ask students to cite:

1. Consider the statement: "The square of any positive number is larger than the original number." Essentially, this statement claims that if $x > 0$ then $x^2 > x$. Provide two examples to support this claim as well as two counterexamples to disprove this claim.
2. A student named James says that, "Only odd numbers can be prime numbers." Give three examples of prime numbers and three examples of nonprime numbers that support his statement. Now, can you think of a counterexample to show James that what he said is not always true?
3. The measurements of 3, 4, and 5 can be the lengths of the sides of a triangle. Provide two examples of other triangles that also have a perimeter of 12. Draw and label the lengths of the sides of each triangle.

4

Self-Expressive Math Tools

SELF-EXPRESSIVE MATH STUDENTS

Want to . . . use their imagination to explore mathematical ideas.

Like math problems that . . . are non-routine, project-like in nature, and that allow them to "think outside the box."

Approach problem solving . . . by visualizing the problem, generating possible solutions, and exploring among the alternatives.

May experience difficulty when . . . math instruction is focused on drill and practice and rote problem solving.

Learn best when . . . they are invited to use their imagination and engage in creative problem solving.

—Silver, Thomas, & Perini (2003)

Self-Expressive Math Tools Matrix

PAGE	MATH TOOL	NCTM PROCESS STANDARDS: Problem Solving	Reasoning and Proof	Communication	Connections	Representation
124	**Picture = 1,000 Words**—Students create images that represent mathematical concepts to make math memorable.			●	●	●
127	**3-D Approach: Algebraic, Graphical, and Numerical**—Students represent and solve problems using symbols, graphs, and tables of values.	●	●	●	●	●
129	**M + M: Math and Metaphors**—Students compare a mathematical concept to a person, place, object, or idea and explain the connection.			●	●	●
132	**Math Recipe**—Students analyze a problem, break it down into steps, and create a problem-solving "recipe."	●	●		●	
135	**Cinquains**—Students write short poems to make concepts memorable and deep-process essential questions and ideas.			●	●	●
137	**Write to Learn**—Students write about a concept, using critical vocabulary in ways that demonstrate understanding of meanings.		●	●	●	
141	**MATHEMATICS Writing Frames**—Eleven writing frames that activate a variety of math skills and develop mathematical literacy.	●	●	●	●	●
144	**Storytellers**—Students practice vocabulary, learn to think and communicate about math, and make concepts memorable through stories.			●	●	●
146	**Math Is Everywhere**—Students write a story about a life event as if it were a math problem, then discuss the role of math in the story.			●	●	●
149	**Group and Label**—Students classify related terms, make predictions, and collect evidence to support or refute their predictions.		●	●	●	
156	**And the Question Is . . .?**—A "Jeopardy!"-like game with no right answers, designed to lure out creative responses.		●	●		
158	**What If?**—Students develop variations on math problems to develop deeper and more creative understanding of mathematics.	●	●	●		
160	**Making Up Is Fun to Do**—Students generate synonyms for mathematics concepts and explain why their terms are appropriate.		●	●		●
162	**Create Your Own**—Students create their own problems and explore the implications with their peers.	●	●		●	
164	**Divergent Thinking**—Students examine a problem in groups and explore creative approaches and solutions.	●	●	●	●	●

SELF-EXPRESSIVE MATH TOOLS

EDUCATIONAL RESEARCH BASE											INSTRUCTIONAL OBJECTIVES							
Identifying similarities and differences	Summarizing and note taking	Reinforcing effort and providing recognition	Homework and practice	Nonlinguistic representations	Cooperative learning	Setting objectives and providing feedback	Generating and testing hypotheses	Questions, cues, and advance organizers	Vocabulary	Writing	Preparing	Presenting	Practicing	Processing	Problem Solving	Performing	Personalizing	MATH TOOL
				●					●		●	●		●			●	Picture = 1,000 Words
●			●	●					●				●	●	●	●	●	3-D Approach
●				●					●		●	●		●		●	●	M + M
			●					●				●	●	●	●			Math Recipe
	●								●	●				●		●	●	Cinquains
	●				●			●	●	●	●			●	●	●	●	Write to Learn
●	●						●	●	●	●	●			●	●	●	●	MATH Writing
	●								●	●				●		●	●	Storytellers
	●				●				●	●		●		●		●	●	Math Is Everywhere
●							●		●		●			●				Group and Label
								●	●		●			●			●	And the Question Is . . . ?
●							●				●			●	●	●		What If?
●									●					●			●	Making Up Is Fun to Do
					●		●	●						●	●		●	Create Your Own
●			●	●					●				●	●	●	●	●	Divergent Thinking

SOURCE: Marzano, R. J., Pickering, D. J., & Pollock, J. E. (2001). *Classroom instruction that works: Research-based strategies for increasing student achievement.* Alexandria, VA: Association for Supervision and Curriculum Development.

PICTURE = 1,000 WORDS

Purpose

Visualization is an effective and powerful way for students to enhance their understanding of often complex and abstract mathematical concepts. The Picture = 1,000 Words tool encourages students to be creative as they make meaningful connections to mathematical concepts in the form of icons, sketches, illustrations, or other visual representations.

Overview

Picture = 1,000 Words works well with any topic or level of mathematics, especially those areas of the curriculum that come with a high level of abstraction. What makes the tool work is the psychological process known as "dual coding" (Paivio, 1990). When students dual code information—that is, when they process information both linguistically and visually, they are able to turn abstract concepts into concrete images, make stronger memories, deepen their understanding, and increase their retention of mathematical concepts. What's more, the Picture = 1,000 Words tool gives students the opportunity to engage in creative thinking and self-expression. Students are invited to draw, sketch, illustrate, design, and bring mathematical concepts to life using any medium, from pencils to markers to computer software.

Steps

1. Identify a topic or concept in mathematics that you want students to explore more deeply and creatively.
2. Model possible ways in which mathematical concepts could be interpreted and represented visually. If available, show quality examples of other students' work to help explain the process.
3. Remind students that making meaningful visual representations is far more important than their artistic abilities.
4. Have students share and discuss their pictures in small groups or as a class.

Examples

Picture a Procedure

Illustrate two factoring patterns using parentheses, "+," "–," and symbols:

Figure 4.1 Student's Picture of Two Factoring Methods

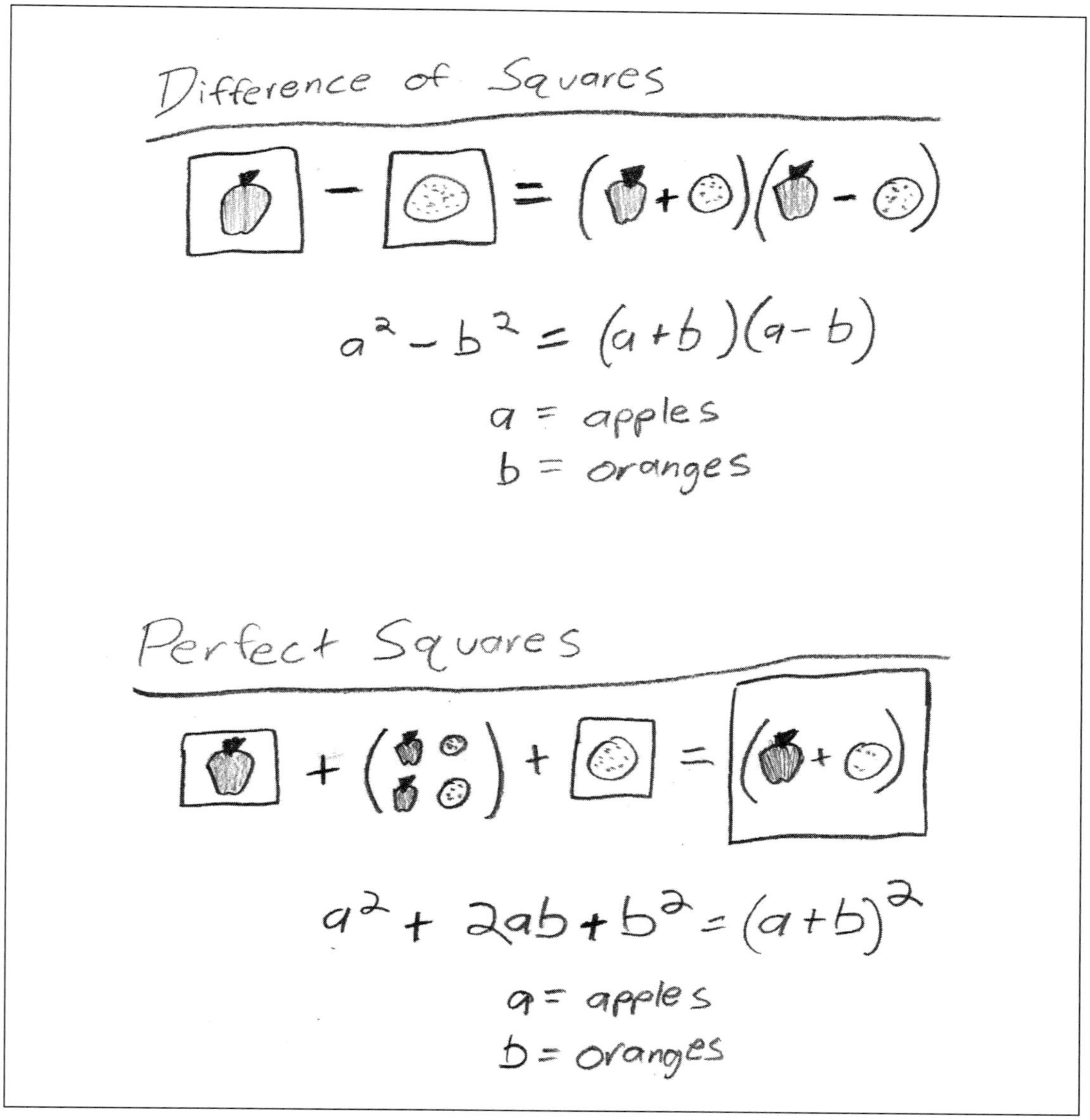

Difference of Squares

$$a^2 - b^2 = (a+b)(a-b)$$

a = apples
b = oranges

Perfect Squares

$$a^2 + 2ab + b^2 = (a+b)^2$$

a = apples
b = oranges

Illustrate a Real-World Inverse

Make an illustration of a real-world situation that has an inverse and a similar situation that does not have an inverse. For example:

Inverse: water can be frozen into ice and melted back into liquid. Not an inverse: water can be boiled in an open pot, but once the water boils away and evaporates, there is no way to get liquid water back.

Geometric Illustrations

Draw illustrations that will help you remember the following geometry theorems:

- Proving lines are parallel and the converses of those theorems
- Isosceles triangle theorem and its converse
- Perpendicular bisector theorems for segments

Go With the Flow of Prime Numbers

Create a flowchart that would help determine whether an expression is prime (or has been prime-factored). Be sure to incorporate the factoring patterns and procedures that we have studied so far.

Triangle Slideshow

Develop a computer slideshow presentation that visually links three types of triangles—acute, obtuse, and right—to the basic triangle area formula. Present each triangle, highlight one of its sides, and then reveal the respective altitude. Be sure to include the names of each type of triangle and the requisite area formulas.

Draw Conclusions

Draw a picture for a conclusion or an ending of a chapter or unit that we have studied. Create your illustration on a clean sheet of unlined, white paper so that your pictures can be put on display around the classroom.

Mathematics Crest

Form a small design team of three to five students and create a crest for a mathematics concept or a set of related concepts that you have studied. Once the crest is designed and sketched, each student in the team will select a portion of the crest to enlarge.

Illustrator

Create an illustration explaining a key concept from a unit we have studied. For example, one student created an "Ocean of Complex Numbers" (Figure 4.2) for a unit on basic number theory.

Geometry in Art and Architecture

Using the Internet, periodicals, or books, find an example of geometry enhancing the aesthetics of architecture (for example, the pyramids in the courtyard of the Louvre). Your picture must be a printout or a photocopy (do not tear out pages or illustrations from a book). With your picture, write a twenty-word caption explaining how geometry operates as an artistic device in your picture. Also, if you are confident in your abilities, you may draw, sketch, or illustrate your chosen example of architecture.

Figure 4.2 Student's "Ocean of Complex Numbers"

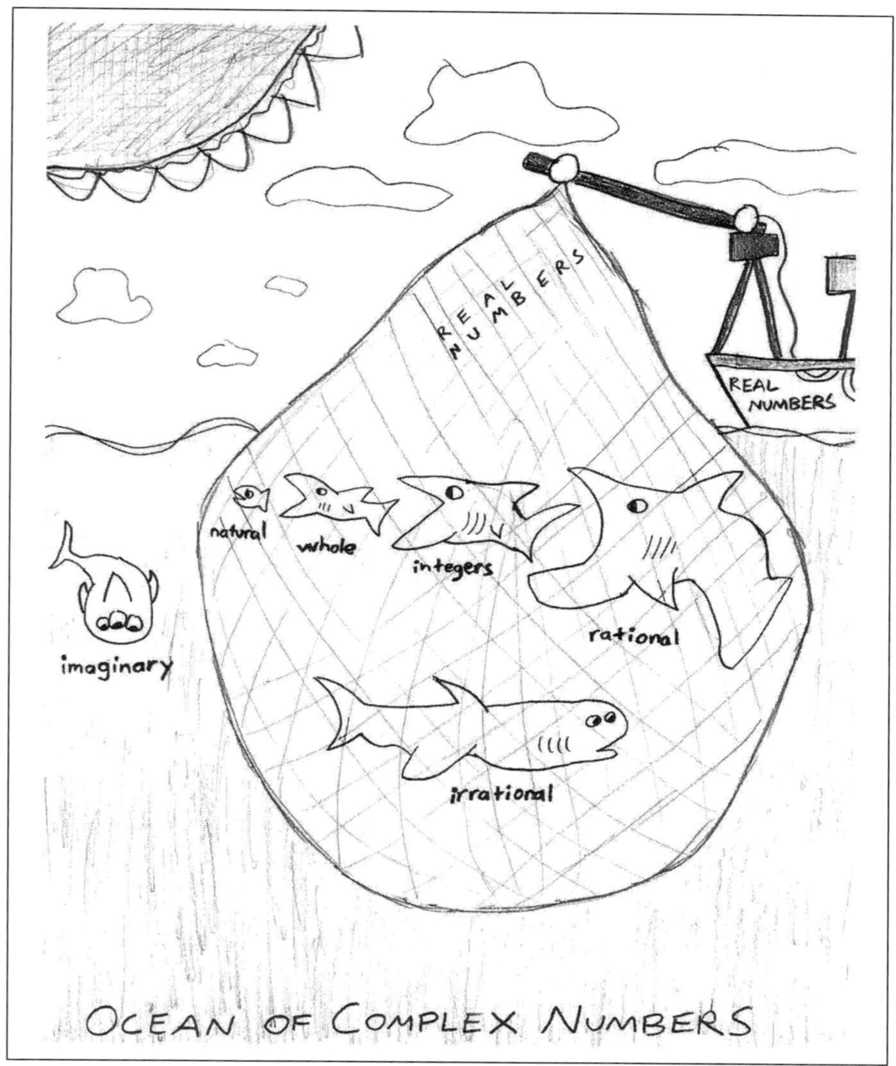

3-D APPROACH: ALGEBRAIC, GRAPHICAL, AND NUMERICAL

Purpose

The NCTM Standards stress the need for mathematics students to do more analysis in order to attain deeper conceptual understandings. A wonderful analytical practice is to view a given problem from multiple viewpoints, rather than emphasizing a single perspective, e.g., algebraic. The 3-D Approach is a reasoning technique that is designed to ensure that students do not settle for any single procedure as they consider important concepts.

Overview

The 3-D Approach requires students to represent or solve a problem algebraically (symbolically), graphically, and numerically (table of values). In this way, students conduct more and deeper analyses of the mathematics, and take greater notice of the connections between problem representations. By posing questions or problems that require this threefold thinking, teachers are able to see whether their students can use various mathematical tools to support and confirm conceptual understanding. In addition, classroom discussions that make use of 3-D Approach increase student understanding and also improve student communication skills.

Steps

1. Model the 3-D Approach tool. For example, you might show students how a vertical line can be represented graphically on a coordinate plane, algebraically as an equation ($x = 5$), and numerically as a table of values like this:

x	y
5	0
5	–3
5	2
5	7

2. Develop a question that requires students to represent their answer using the three "dimensions": algebraic, graphical, and numerical.
3. Allow students to use the necessary resources (graphing calculator, graph paper, etc.) to demonstrate their work.
4. Have students work individually or in groups to solve problems.
5. Ask students to decide which approach best contributes to their understanding of the concept (e.g., "In representing a vertical line three ways, which approach proved most helpful in explaining what a vertical line is? How do other answers let you know you are dealing with a vertical line?").
6. Lead a discussion with the class on various representations and how they show mathematical concepts.

Examples

1. Find the zeroes of the linear equation $y = 2x - 4$ in three ways: algebraically, graphically, and numerically. Which of the approaches makes the most sense to you? Why?
2. For what values of x will the expression $x^2 - 4x + 5$ have negative values? Find the set of values algebraically. Confirm your answer by showing graphical evidence. Then confirm your answer by showing numerical evidence. Which of the 3-D Approaches makes the answer the most obvious to you? Why? What are the disadvantages of the other methods?

3. The inverse of the function $f(x) = 2x + 3$ is the function $g(x) = \frac{x-3}{2}$. Confirm this graphically, numerically, and algebraically. Which of the 3-D Approaches makes the most sense to you? Why?

4. A fraction is of the form $\frac{n}{n+1}$ where n is a positive integer. Create a table showing the decimal values of the fraction for $n = (1, 2, 3, \ldots, 10)$. Graph the ordered pairs from your table of data. If n were to take on any integer value, what is the smallest value of n for which $\left|1 - \frac{n}{n+1}\right| < 0.0001$ is true? Which of the 3-D Approaches would provide the answer the fastest?

M + M: MATH AND METAPHORS

This adaptation of the Metaphorical Expression strategy (Silver, Strong, & Perini, 2007) was developed by Wendy Lee Reddy, a fifth-grade teacher from Errick Road Elementary School in North Tonawanda, New York.

Purpose

M + M engages divergent and creative forms of thinking by linking metaphorical thinking and mathematics. Students compare two seemingly unrelated concepts. By finding new and unusual parallels, students deepen their understanding of both the mathematical content and the content they are using to compare against it. The M + M technique taps into the well-known power of metaphors to increase conceptual understanding and academic performance (Cole & McLeod, 1999; Chen, 1999).

Overview

M + M extends an invitation to Self-Expressive students, who often feel constrained by mathematics and the premium it places on procedures, by allowing them to express their mathematical literacy in unique and creative ways as either metaphors or similes. Even the title of the tool suggests a metaphor: Just as the rich chocolate lies beneath the shell of an M & M's candy, so do rich mathematical insights lie beneath the surface. The idea is to get students to explore that richness through metaphors.

M + M works well as a review technique, as a tool to help students generate ideas, or as a way to invite students to access their prior knowledge before a lesson or unit. For example, a fifth-grade teacher began her year by asking students to think about this simile: *How is learning mathematics like riding a bike?* Together, the teacher and her students generated these ideas:

- Practice helps you do better in both.
- They are both difficult at first.
- An adult can help you do both.
- You can make a career out of both.
- Both occur in the real world.
- If you don't keep doing them, you will not be as good as you were before.
- Some people do not like to do either one.

- Mathematics and bikes have different parts.
- Some kids are better at both than I am.

Steps

1. Introduce (or review) the process of metaphorical thinking with your students by comparing two dissimilar concepts or objects. (Often, this is done in the form of a simile: How are parentheses in a mathematics problem like an eggshell?).
2. Review a mathematical concept with students.
3. Allow students to choose a non-mathematical concept or object to serve as a metaphorical counterpart to the mathematical concept, or provide students with a range of choices. Encourage students to explain their metaphors/similes.
4. An alternative to the basic M + M technique is to fill a box or bag up with "stuff"—random items collected from the home or classroom. Students are given a mathematics concept and then pull an item from the bag or box. They then identify as many parallels as they can.

Examples

The possibilities of metaphors in relation to mathematical content are endless. Students may develop their own metaphors and similes, or you can provide them with examples which they then have to explain. Here's a list of mathematical similes you might use:

- How are fractions like closets?
- How is multiplication like a shortcut through a neighborhood?
- How is long division like following a set of directions to a place you have never gone to before?
- How are number lines like elevators?
- How are pie charts like cakes?
- How are fractions like members of Congress?
- How is factoring like sluicing for gold in a river?
- How are linear equations like people?
- How is the Pythagorean Theorem like the Golden Gate Bridge?
- How are mean, median, and mode in mathematics like RBI, ERA, and OBP in baseball (run(s) batted in, earned-run average, and on-base percentage, respectively)?
- How is a function like a person?
- How is solving equations like digestion?
- How is doing a geometry proof like playing a basketball game?
- How is perpendicularity like a dictatorship?
- How is right triangle trigonometry like white water rafting?
- How is trigonometry like a bridge?
- How is a trigonometric identity like an octopus?
- How are permutations like the batting order for a baseball team?
- How is a discontinuous function like a family car trip?
- How is a chi-squared test similar to a doctor's diagnosis?
- Is solving a mathematics problem more like climbing a mountain or riding a bicycle? Why?

Figure 4.3 shows the way in which one student used an M + M organizer designed by her teacher to compare the mathematical procedure of measuring circumference with one of her favorite sports activities—running on a track.

Figure 4.3 Student's Metaphorical Comparison of *Circumference* and *Running Track*

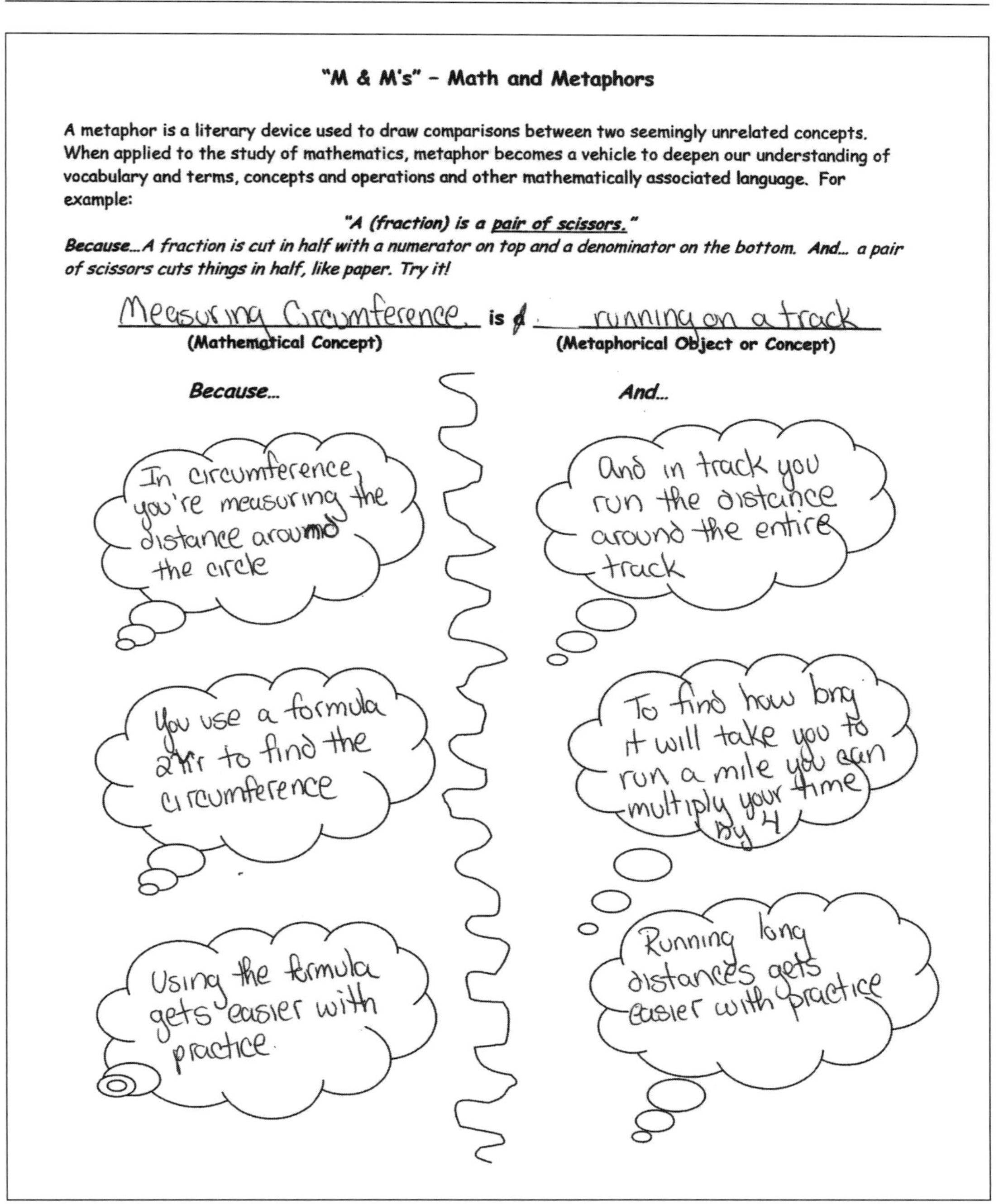

"M & M's" - Math and Metaphors

A metaphor is a literary device used to draw comparisons between two seemingly unrelated concepts. When applied to the study of mathematics, metaphor becomes a vehicle to deepen our understanding of vocabulary and terms, concepts and operations and other mathematically associated language. For example:

"A (fraction) is a pair of scissors."

Because...A fraction is cut in half with a numerator on top and a denominator on the bottom. And... a pair of scissors cuts things in half, like paper. Try it!

Measuring Circumference **is** ~~a~~ running on a track

(Mathematical Concept) **(Metaphorical Object or Concept)**

Because...

In circumference, you're measuring the distance around the circle

You use a formula $2\pi r$ to find the circumference

Using the formula gets easier with practice.

And...

And in track you run the distance around the entire track

To find how long it will take you to run a mile you can multiply your time by 4

Running long distances gets easier with practice

MATH RECIPE

Purpose

Because of the procedural nature of mathematical content, students can easily fall into the trap of "blind calculation"—following a procedure without really understanding how the steps in a process work together. Math Recipe addresses the problem of "blind calculation" through an analogy to cooking. Students fill out a recipe card that shows each step in the problem-solving procedure *and* that explains the mathematical rationale behind each step. In this way, students learn to see important mathematical procedures not as an isolated series of activities, but as an integrated process where all the "ingredients" and "steps" interact in mathematically predictable ways. The tool also provides Self-Expressive students, who often have trouble with step-by-step procedures, with a creative approach to learning new procedures.

Overview

The Math Recipe tool provides students with a clear and engaging format for organizing their thoughts and relevant information as they work through problems. Math Recipe can be used in two different ways:

Make Your Own Math Recipe

The teacher provides students with a problem and a blank Math Recipe card organizer (see Organizer 4-A). Students create a recipe for solving the problem by filling out the card step by step. For example, one student's recipe for following the order of operations is shown in Figure 4.4.

Mixed Math Recipe

For this variation, the teacher provides students with a Math Recipe card that is partially filled out (see Figure 4.5). Students must analyze the information that is given and incorporate their prior knowledge to complete the Math Recipe card correctly.

Steps

1. Select a mathematical procedure for students to practice.
2. Model how students can use Math Recipe cards to organize and clarify their thinking.
3. Provide students with a blank Math Recipe card or a partially completed Math Recipe card and have them develop the "recipe."
4. Make sure students store their completed Math Recipe cards for future reference. You may want students to create a yearlong "recipe box" in which they can collect and refer to essential "recipes."

Examples

Figure 4.4 Student's Math Recipe Card for *Order of Operations*

RECIPE: Order of Operations

SPECIAL INSTRUCTIONS/REMINDERS: multiply/divide and add/subtract from left to right

INGREDIENTS: $12 - 4 \bullet 6 + 5^3$

FIRST STEP:	exponents	TO GET:	$12 - 4 \bullet 6 + 125$
NEXT STEP:	multiplication	TO GET:	$12 - 24 + 125$
NEXT STEP:	subtraction	TO GET:	$-12 + 125$
NEXT STEP:	addition	TO GET:	113

FINAL RESULT: 113

Figure 4.5 Mixed Math Recipe Card for *Measuring a Circle*

RECIPE: ____________

SPECIAL INSTRUCTIONS/REMINDERS: $A = \pi r^2$ $C = 2\pi r$ $\pi \approx 3.14$

INGREDIENTS: diameter = 13

FIRST STEP:		TO GET:	$A = \pi r^2$
NEXT STEP:	find radius	TO GET:	
NEXT STEP:	calculate exponents	TO GET:	$6.5^2 = 42.25$
NEXT STEP:		TO GET:	$3.14 \cdot 42.25$

FINAL RESULT: ____________

Organizer 4-A Blank Math Recipe Organizer

Name: ______________________

Date: ______________________

RECIPE: ______________________

SPECIAL INSTRUCTIONS/REMINDERS: ______________________

INGREDIENTS: ______________________

____

FIRST STEP: ______________________ TO GET: ______________________

NEXT STEP: ______________________ TO GET: ______________________

NEXT STEP: ______________________ TO GET: ______________________

NEXT STEP: ______________________ TO GET: ______________________

FINAL RESULT: ______________________

CINQUAINS

Purpose

While poetry seems out of place in most mathematics classrooms, cinquains are powerful learning tools that give students a creative way to distill their understanding of important ideas and concepts. The concise, five-line format of a cinquain forces students to "think economically," to cut away all of the non-essential details and include only the most critical information.

Overview

The cinquain technique has students demonstrate their understanding of mathematical concepts, theorems, vocabulary, procedures, or topics through creative and poetic writing. While the focus of the cinquain can be anything from arithmetic to algebra, triangles to trigonometry, or polygons to pre-calculus, a successful cinquain will not only follow the poetic cinquain structure, but will also show that the student knows the critical attributes of the concept.

Figure 4.6 Cinquain Format and Successful Cinquain for *Algebra*

Cinquain Format	Successful Cinquain (Shows understanding of critical attributes)
one noun	algebra
two adjectives	simple complex
three action verbs (ending in "-ing")	ordering factoring balancing
four-word sentence or phrase	a relationship between variables
one ending or summarizing word	solution

Cinquains can inspire students in any mathematics classroom to think deeply, creatively, and with a tight focus on core concepts and big ideas. To introduce cinquains, you should explain what a cinquain is, provide effective models, and allow students to practice writing their own based on the big ideas they are studying. One option to help students get their thinking out in the open and generate more ideas and better cinquains is to supply each student with a visual organizer. (See Organizer 4-B on page 138 for a blank Cinquain Organizer.)

The students in a classroom can all write a cinquain for the same topic, or each student can select his or her own concept from a glossary or Word Wall. After students craft their cinquains, have them share their poems in small groups or with the entire class. Sharing cinquains and discussing how they were created will help students become more comfortable with the activity and reinforce the mathematical content being discussed.

Steps

1. Introduce (or review) the concept of a cinquain and the format it follows.
2. Model and provide an example of a completed cinquain. (Depending on your class's comfort or familiarity with cinquains, modeling multiple examples may be helpful for students. Make sure models focus on the critical attributes of the concept.)
3. Select a word for students to focus on or allow students to pick their own words from a textbook, glossary, or Word Wall.
4. Allow students time to review what they know about the concepts for their cinquains.
5. Have students create a cinquain in class, either individually or within a small group. (Cinquains also make for excellent homework activities.)
6. Encourage students to share and discuss their cinquains, how they were made, and the mathematical concepts they used.
7. Display exemplary cinquains for other students to see and use as models.

Examples

A cinquain for *subtraction*:

subtraction
simple useful
borrowing removing taking away
making big numbers smaller
reduce

A cinquain for a *bar graph*:

bar graph
visual colorful
describing analyzing deciding
ways to organize data
representation

You can use cinquains in a variety of ways in your classroom. To increase participation and build a sense of intrigue and play, have students withhold the title, or first line of their cinquains. Students can read each other's cinquains as if the lines are a series of clues to a riddle. Students then guess what the topic of the cinquain is. Another option is to take an "inductive" approach to cinquain-building by providing students with separate elements that they have to put together into a cohesive, correctly formatted sequence. For example, students might be asked to put the following "clues" together to form a cinquain (see page 137).

Clues

organized
graphing
factoring
procedural
necessary
basis for higher mathematics
solving
algebra

Cinquain

algebra
organized procedural
solving graphing factoring
basis for higher mathematics
necessary

WRITE TO LEARN

Purpose

Research on vocabulary comprehension is clear about this point: If you fail to give students multiple opportunities to "try out" and use new words, then you can be sure the words will never make it into their permanent memories. Write to Learn is a tool that simultaneously builds students' vocabulary development and writing skills. Students develop short written responses, descriptions of mathematical procedures, explanations of mathematical concepts, or even stories or creative writing pieces, while incorporating key vocabulary terms into their writing. The tool works especially well when combined with the vocabulary tool known as Word Walls (see pages 54–57).

Overview

Write to Learn helps teachers of mathematics answer these questions:

- How can I help students gain a deeper understanding of important mathematical ideas?
- How can I provide students with opportunities to use critical vocabulary terms meaningfully so that they learn and remember them?
- How can I incorporate more writing into my classroom?

The most important thing to remember when developing Write to Learn activities is that students are writing to *learn.* That is to say, they are using the power of writing to increase their comprehension. The object is not for students to produce multiple drafts that lead to an A+ paper. Rather, the object is for students to gain greater control over important ideas and terms by incorporating the vocabulary they have been learning into a short piece of writing.

Many different forms and formats for writing can be used. Student writing can be as basic as a description of the steps used in a mathematical process (e.g., Here's how you find the area of a *rectangle.* First, you identify the *length* and *width* of the rectangle . . .). On the other hand, student writing can also be as creative as this student's story:

> "Halt your ship!" the alien said to Commander Ziff's ship, but it was too late. The planet of Quadriladopapopalus was 2-D. Ziff's computers couldn't see it. Ziff and his pilot, Benson, couldn't stop in time. They crashed.
>
> "Commander, we're safe, but everything looks flat." Ziff looked around. Benson was right, this place was flat.

(Continued)

Organizer 4-B Blank Cinquain Organizer

Name: ______________________ **Date:** __________

Cinquain Topic: ______________________

What I Know About the Topic

Cinquain

Topic or Key Word (1 word)

Adjectives (2 words)

Action Verbs (3 words)

Sentence or Phrase (4 words)

Conclusion or Final Word (1 word)

(Continued)

"This planet is private. Leave or else . . . ," said the alien voice to Ziff's ship.

"On screen," Ziff ordered. Benson turned on the screen. The voice introduced itself.

"I am Lord Square. I am perfect. All of my angles are equal and so are all of my sides. You are completely surrounded."

Ziff really was surrounded. An army of four-sided polygons with sharp pencils and pink erasers were everywhere.

"Maybe we can work this out," Ziff said to Benson. He stepped out of his ship. "I am Ziff Spacely. I am the commander of the USS Tuna. Who are you?"

The polygons came forward and introduced themselves.

"I am a trapezoid," a shape said. "Two of my sides are parallel, but two are not. I am a servant of the square."

Another shape stepped forward. He pushed the trapezoid down. "I am a rhombus. We are totally awesome because all of our sides are equal. Pay no attention to the trapezoids."

A third shape stepped up. "We rectangles rule this land! It is so obvious! We have great symmetry! All of our sides are parallel! We have all 90 degree angles! And, best of all, our parallel sides are equal!"

Ziff knew that the shapes didn't get along. Then Lord Square came over and spoke.

"I rule this land! Look at me! I am perfect! All of my sides are parallel and equal! Now leave before I erase you!"

Ziff thought quickly. His ship was broken. He tried to talk his way out.

"You are far from perfect, Lord Square," Ziff said. The polygon drew his eraser. "Even though your sides and your angles are equal, there is no equality here. And you know what else? Squares are boring!"

Lord Square was mad. He attacked Ziff with his eraser. Ziff jumped back, and Lord Square fell on his own eraser. And just like that, he was gone. All the quadrilaterals were happy.

"You are so cool, Ziff," a rhombus said. Ziff and Benson high-fived. Ziff and Benson stayed until their ship was fixed. Then they flew home.

In all cases, the underlying expectation is that students include, in a meaningful way, at least five key vocabulary terms in their writing.

Write to Learn is a flexible tool that works well with many other tools in this book. For example, you can:

- Ask students to use vocabulary from a Word Wall (see pages 54–57) in their writing.
- Use MATHEMATICS Writing Frames (see pages 141–143) to develop a variety of prompts and assignments for Write to Learn.
- Incorporate the writing and vocabulary usage elements of Write to Learn into almost any lesson or tool, from Compare and Contrast (see pages 98–105) to Group and Label (see pages 149–155) to M + M: Math and Metaphors (see pages 129–131).

Steps

1. Select a topic or concept that you would like students to write about.
2. Post, distribute, and/or review the critical vocabulary terms associated with the topic or concept.
3. Pose a question, writing frame, or prompt for students to respond to in writing. Remind students that they must incorporate at least five vocabulary terms into their writing and that each term must be used in a meaningful context.
4. Allow students to share their writing in pairs or groups. Writing pairs/groups should focus their attention on how well the vocabulary terms were integrated into the piece and on how the writing helped them improve their comprehension of the topic or concept.

Examples

Write to Learn Prompts

1. Write an explanation of how to add two mixed numbers using at least ten of the words from the Fraction Unit Word Wall.
2. Write two paragraphs about how order of operations is like and/or unlike the order used when organizing a file drawer. Be sure to use at least eight of the words on the Word Wall in your piece.
3. Write a letter explaining the findings of your group to the owner of Handy Dandy Candy Co., who asked your group to see if there was any correlation between the mass of their chocolate peanut butter pieces and the number of chocolate peanut butter pieces in each bag. If there is a statistically significant correlation, let the owner know how much she should expect 3,000 chocolate peanut butter pieces will weigh.
4. Write a personal ad for one of the following: Rectangle, Rhombus, Square, or Isosceles trapezoid.
5. Write three paragraphs about the metric system versus the English System of Measurement. The first paragraph should explain how each was developed. The second paragraph should discuss the advantages of each system. The third paragraph should include what you think would be the two or three worst problems if the United States were to change to the metric system and whether you think that change should be made.
6. Write a creative story for the local newspaper using as many mathematics words and terms as you can from our problem solving Word Wall. Identify five vocabulary words that you used most creatively and compare your "creative" usage with the corresponding mathematical definition.
7. Develop an explanation of whether it would be more important to lower the average rate of change or the instantaneous rate of change of the velocity of a car about to be involved in an accident on an interstate highway.

MATHEMATICS WRITING FRAMES

Purpose

Both NCTM and a wide body of research stress the need for a steady regimen of writing in mathematics classrooms. Yet, many teachers of mathematics struggle to incorporate writing into their instruction. MATHEMATICS Writing Frames (see Figure 4.7 for example) provide mathematics teachers at all grade levels with a wide variety of writing activities, stems, and thinking frames that help students enhance their memories, build deeper comprehension, and develop their thinking and communication skills as they learn how to put their thoughts about mathematics into words.

Overview

But I'm not an English teacher! The truth is that writing still seems a bit foreign to many teachers of mathematics. Many mathematics teachers approach us during workshops and ask questions like: "How can we meet the NCTM Standards for writing? How can we assess the writing we assign without overwhelming our students? Or without overwhelming ourselves?" MATHEMATICS Writing Frames was designed to help teachers of mathematics answer these questions. The tool does not ask teachers of mathematics to become English teachers; nor does it ask students to write ten-page essays that go through multiple drafts. Instead, MATHEMATICS Writing Frames (so called because each letter in MATHEMATICS stands for a type of writing) provides a menu for frequent, but short writing assignments that can be used to:

- Increase student engagement.
- Help students activate their prior knowledge of mathematical content.
- Deepen comprehension through summarizing or elaboration on key ideas.
- Check understanding.
- Promote higher-order thinking.
- Build specific reasoning skills (e.g., comparison, explanation).
- Encourage reflection and metacognition.

Steps

1. Choose a frame for focusing students' thinking and writing.
2. Develop a prompt, stem, or question to spur student thinking and writing.
3. Ask students to generate a written response in their journals or Learning Logs.

Examples

Figure 4.7 MATHEMATICS Writing Frames

Make a Comparison	• What are the key similarities and differences between area and perimeter? • The Box and Whiskers plot and bar graph below show the same information. Compare the two visual models in terms of how they convey data.
Access Prior Knowledge	• Think of a time when you or someone you know used math to settle a dispute. Tell what the problem was and how math was used to solve it. • Before we begin the next section on the Pythagorean Theorem, think about what you already know about the topic. On the left side of the paper, write down everything you know or think you know about the Pythagorean Theorem. On the right side, write at least one question you have about it.
Think About Learning or Feelings	• What part of our unit on projectiles have you enjoyed the most? What has been especially difficult for you? What might you do to help address your difficulties? • Which icon best represents your understanding of proportions? Explain your selection. • How would it feel to be a remainder in a long division problem?
Hypothesize	• We have learned that when you multiply a postive number by a negative number, the product is also a negative number. What do you think happens when you multiply two negative numbers together? Why do you think that? • We no longer use Roman numerals in everyday life. Why do you believe this is the case?
Explain	• A rectangle must also be a parallelogram, but a parallelogram is not necessarily a rectangle. Why? • Any line can be written in standard form but not in slope-Intercept form (e.g., vertical lines). Why?

Make Real-World Connections	• Think of three activities or situations in which slope is an important factor. Make sure you tell how slope factors into each situation. • The Statue of Liberty's nose is approximately 4 feet, 6 inches long. How would you find the length of one of her arms?
Analyze Errors	• Here are two problems that use rounding. The solution to the first problem is correct. The solution to the second problem is incorrect. Look at the work for each problem. Then explain what went wrong in Problem 2. • Here is a sample problem from last year's SAT. Answer B is correct. Answer A is a distractor. Use what we've learned about surface area and volume to tell why A is a distractor.
Take a Position	• Was Calculus invented or discovered? Defend your position. • Imagine your friend tells you that he thinks algebra is useless outside of the classroom. (Perhaps you need new friends—just kidding.) What would you say to your friend to convince him he is wrong? • Some people say that division is really just subtraction over and over again. Do you agree or disagree? Explain.
Interpret Data	• This line graph shows the number of VHS tapes purchased over the last five years. What pattern is evident? Why do you think this is the case? • What conclusions can be drawn from this frequency curve? How do you know your conclusions are valid?
Creative Writing	• You are the number zero. Tell a story that highlights some of your unique and unusual properties. Some ideas for story structures: superhero story, love story, "fish-out-of-water" story, underdog story, mystery/crime story. • What would life be like if you woke up to discover that the U.S. was now using a "base 2 numbers" system? • How is the order of operations like a batting order in baseball?
Summarize	• In your Learning Log, write down: 3 facts you learned during today's lesson, 2 questions you have, and 1 big idea that you believe is the most important. Explain why you believe your big idea stands out. • How do you divide two mixed numbers? Tell how the process works in your own words. • What is a line of best fit? Summarize in no more than four sentences.

STORYTELLERS

Purpose

Mathematics is a discipline filled with theorems, laws, proofs, and calculations, but rarely do teachers or students tell good mathematics stories. This is unfortunate, since our brains are hardwired to receive and make up stories. The Storytellers tool is a way for students to explore and make mathematics content their own by creating short stories that use and explain mathematical vocabulary and concepts.

Overview

Storytellers is an excellent way for students to demonstrate their understanding of the specific meanings and appropriate uses of mathematical terms. Through writing, students are given the opportunity to be creative and use their imaginations to take greater control over what they are learning in mathematics.

Before writing, the teacher generates a list of mathematical terms that students will incorporate during the Storytellers activity. The teacher models the process by choosing a few words from the list and spinning them into the beginnings of a story. Students then work either on their own or in small storytelling groups to create their own mathematics tales. Students' stories can be fiction or nonfiction, and can be written as drama, comedy, tragedy, science fiction, or in any genre they choose. (It is always a good idea to expose students to various text structures and story formats to help them organize their writing.) The key requirement, however, is that the words students use are in proper mathematical context and are not simply mentioned.

Steps

1. Generate a list of mathematical terms for students to use when writing.
2. Model a sample story or an excerpt that demonstrates how mathematical terms are used in a narrative.
3. Encourage students to be creative and choose a genre or topic that is meaningful to them. Explain to students that their stories can be wacky or serious, but their stories need to be coherent.
4. Remind students that stories can be of any length (from one paragraph to two pages), so long as all of the vocabulary words are used correctly and in proper context.

Examples

In each of the following samples of student writing, the mathematical terms for the unit are listed as a table.

How I See Shapes

quadrilateral	triangle	rectangle	square	rhombus
parallelogram	pentagon	isosceles triangle	octagon	trapezoid
equilateral triangle	hexagon	right triangle	circle	

When my mom drives me to school I like to look out the window and find different shapes. On my corner is a red STOP sign, which is an *octagon*. On the next street there is a traffic light made up of a *rectangle* with one red, one green, and one yellow *circle*. The white speed limit signs are also *rectangles*. There is a red *triangle* sign where we go from the main road and a brown *square* sign that tell us that the name of the park is Brookside Park. Outside school is a yellow *pentagon* that shows people where the school crosswalk is. Our crossing guard, Mrs. Sylvan, holds a red *octagon* STOP sign, too.

Besides the many *quadrilateral* signs in store windows and traffic signs, I also see many other shapes while I ride to school each day. There is a house being built on our street, and the rafters have *right triangles* and *isosceles triangles* in them. There are *equilateral triangles* and *trapezoids* in the supports of the railroad bridge over the river. When I mentioned this assignment to my mom, I said I was missing a few shapes, which she helped me find. She pointed out a *rhombus* in the sign on the jewelry store that advertised their diamond sale. She also helped me see how the drawings of cubes in the kindergarten class windows are *hexagons* if you look at the lines of the cubes. And, finally, she helped me see the *parallelograms* that are also hidden in the support structure of the railroad bridge.

Math Versus Social Studies

sequence	finite	infinite	*n*th term	set	
Fibonacci Sequence	arithmetic sequence	geometric sequence	common difference	common ratio	Cauchy Sequence

There are a lot of *sequences* in school. There are *sequences* of dates to remember in social studies. *Sequences* in social studies are *finite* since they start at one time or place and end in another. In mathematics, there can be *finite sequences* like all of the integers between 0 and 10 and *infinite sequences* like all of the integers greater than 0. When working with *sequences,* it is important to know how to find a certain term of the *sequence*. This specific term is called the *nth term*. There are also special *sequences* like the *Fibonacci Sequence* and *Cauchy Sequence*. The *sequence* of years for World War II would be 1939, 1940, 1941, 1942, 1943, 1944,

(Continued)

(Continued)

1945, with these years making up a *set* of numbers. If you are asked what is the *n*th term of this sequence that denotes the year the United States entered the conflict, your answer should be the 3rd term. Analyzing the *terms* and looking for patterns in the *sequence* of a *set* of numbers can give you a clear answer or show you where a *sequence* is going. Since consecutive terms of this sequence of war years have a *common difference*, the sequence is an *arithmetic sequence* (as opposed to a *geometric sequence,* in which consecutive terms would have a *common ratio*).

Science Fiction

radius	diameter	circumference	chord	secant	tangent
pi	3.14	22/7	formula	calculate	

It was cold and dark in the ship as it floated in the shadow of the planet known as X22–7. It was a sphere, but from the screen, X22–7 looked like a big gray *circle*. The planet they were looking at was made of rock and ice and had a solid core. The instruments projected the *diameter* of the planet to be 18,000 km. They also showed that the *secant* line from the ship's present location to the place they needed to reach in order to radio for assistance, hit the planet in a *chord* that measured nearly 10,000 km. Unfortunately, they could not take such a path through the planet, nor even on *tangent* to the planet's atmosphere. The captain asked the science officer how far their journey would be in order to get a radio signal sent. However, the ship lost power before the computer could *calculate* the distance to the opposite side. The captain started scribbling and said, "*r* is 9,000!" "*R?*" the crew said. "*R* is for *radius!*" said the captain, "It's half the *diameter.*" Using the ancient *formula* usually programmed into computers, the captain figured out the distance around the planet, which she called the *circumference*. The captain said, "2pr = 2 • p • 9,000." The crew saw p as a hieroglyphic symbol and wondered why the captain didn't write *3.14* or $\frac{22}{7}$. The captain said that the ship needed to travel half of the *circumference* or 28,260 km. She breathed a sigh of relief. With three fuel cells left, each allowing 10,000 km of travel, the ship could make it to the far side of the planet and signal for help. They were going to make it!

MATH IS EVERYWHERE

This creative writing math tool was developed by Wendy Lee Reddy, a fifth-grade teacher from Errick Road Elementary School in North Tonawanda, New York. *Thanks, Wendy!*

Purpose

Math Is Everywhere is a highly-engaging and motivating tool that invites students to explore mathematical applications in their own lives and tap into their creativity by turning their experiences into a "Crazy Math Story." The tool uses Jon Scieszka and Lane Smith's zany children's text—*Math Curse* (1995)—as a springboard for students' own literary responses to mathematics. In that book, a teacher explains that "you can think of almost everything as a math problem." As a result, the student in the book can't stop thinking about mathematics and seeks to explain each and every episode in his life in mathematical terms.

Overview

Current research on vocabulary instruction tells us that academic terms should be actively taught, embedded throughout units, and that students need opportunities to use these terms in meaningful contexts. Math Is Everywhere is an instructional tool that focuses students' attention on the deep connections between mathematics and real life, giving students the chance to try to explain everything from their own breakfast to a favorite hobby using mathematically appropriate vocabulary.

Steps

1. Read the text, *Math Curse*, to the class.
2. Hold a discussion about how we use mathematical terms and numbers to describe and explain things. Ask students to share some examples.
3. Have students think of an important event in their life and make some notes about it.
4. Encourage students to use as many mathematical terms and numbers to describe and explain the event as they can.
5. Allow students to meet with a partner and hold a "knee-to-knee conference." Each partner reads the other's essay and tries to identify as many of the mathematical terms and numbers that the partner used.
6. Have partners make a list of all the terms used in their stories and group them into mathematical categories.
7. Hold a synthesis discussion in which students identify the different ways we use mathematics to describe and explain things: time, measurement, location, and so forth.
8. An extension of this activity is to have students make a collage of their favorite activity and then list as many mathematical concepts and numbers that are related to the activity.

Examples

The following Math Is Everywhere passage (entitled "I'm Late!!!") was written by a student from Errick Road Elementary School.

Tomorrow is the first day of school. Yesterday, my mom and I had a conference with the teacher. I was only a little afraid to go. OK, OK, I freaked out. Bobby is my next-door neighbor and she can make people feel very guilty, especially with this kind of thing. Anyway, at the conference Mr. Bambule said we were going to learn elapsed time. I pointed out that we learned that in second grade. He then asked me what 6 hours and 20 minutes before 3:35 p.m. was. My amazing response was, "I see your point." "9:15 a.m." he said cockily.

It's the next day and I can't believe that I forgot how to tell time! Maybe we'll have a pop quiz in the morning. Oh no! "MOM! How do you tell time? I forget." "Honey, it's easy to tell time. You just have to know how to count. First you see what the hour is. For instance, the mini hand is on the 9, so, it would be 9 something, then the big hand is on the 8, 8 times 5, you always do the number times 5, = 40. Oh geez, it's 9:40 on a school night, time to go to bed."

Morning! OK, first, I pack my lunch: a cookie, a banana, a PB and J sandwich, a juice box, and three carrots. Next, I have to get my school supplies: a glue stick, 10 pencils, 4 notebooks, 5 folders, a pair of scissors, a box of crayons, a pencil sharpener, a clipboard, and a gorgeous backpack. After that, I have to get dressed.

I sat with Bobby and Casey, like always, and across from this girl named Gina and her little sister Katie. The whole 15 minutes was MIND-NUMBING!! When we finally got to school though, I wished we were back on the bus. When we got to the classroom Mr. Bambule was talking, "In conclusion . . ." Yah! We missed his morning speech.

"All right, we are going to start with charts, and graphs. A chart is a list where you can organize information to make it easier to read. For example, if I needed to see what $8 \times 8 \times 6 \times 7$ equals, you can put it on a chart and figure it out one by one. A graph is if you want to compare something or see the amount of it. Everyone, draw a graph to show the percentage of you swimming, doing sports, and riding your bike during the summer. Then, make an organized chart on the same concept."

It took like a half an hour for me to do these tasks. I checked the time; most of the people were still working. I finally figured out it was 9:30. So, if it's 9:30 and special takes 1 hour and 15 minutes, then we'll be done with special by . . . 10:45! Hey, where is everybody? Oh my gosh! I'm late for special! I don't even know what we have today. Oh good, my class is right out the door. When we got to gym, our special today, the teacher said that we had 65 minutes to play kickball. Let's see, if you convert that to hours, we have . . . well I never learned that. I walked up to the gym teacher and asked her. It took her forever to explain. When she was finally done, she tapped my shoulder and pointed.

My class was gone! I was late! (Well at least I know one thing; we had 1 hour and 5 minutes to play.) I ran out the door. When I got back to the classroom Mr. Bambule was telling everyone about line graphs. He said they were the rise and fall of a company or stock, things like that. I checked the time. Of course, by the time I was done, everyone was off to lunch. I'm late! I hurried to the lunchroom; I knew the place by heart. Lunch was short and boring like always. The day surprisingly whizzed by today. (Probably because I missed everything that took forever.)

The worst part though, was not that I was late for everything, but when I got home my mom asked, "Honey, how was your day? I have a surprise that will help you tell time better!" It was a digital clock that told you the exact time. "Thanks mom, but I already know how to tell time perfect!"

GROUP AND LABEL

Purpose

Group and Label asks students to conceptualize their way to deep understanding by organizing mathematical data into meaningful categories. Students analyze a collection of mathematical information, group the items into categories, and label each category in a way that explains why the items go together. Finally, students use their labeled groups to generate a set of hypotheses or generalizations, which they revisit periodically and refine in light of new learning.

Overview

Group and Label is based on a three-phase process designed by Hilda Taba (1971). Taba found that students' proficiencies in forming generalizations, identifying big ideas, and using evidence improved dramatically when they were asked to: generate and analyze terms; categorize items and develop descriptive labels for each category; and use their categories to form hypotheses.

By applying Taba's model to mathematics instruction, students are encouraged to find relevance and make connections with a variety of mathematical terms.

The Group and Label technique starts with a collection of data—numbers, fractions, figures, symbols, or vocabulary words—that the teacher compiles for students. Before starting a unit on geometric figures, a teacher presented students with this list:

isosceles	oval	rectangle
cylinder	octagon	decagon
square	circle	pentagon
right triangle	sphere	cone
hexagon	scalene	cube
rhombus	trapezoid	pyramid

As students go through the list, they begin to group terms into categories such as: *polygons, 3-D objects, shapes with right angles, round shapes, quadrilaterals,* and so on. One student grouped and labeled terms in this way:

Figure 4.8 Student's Groups and Labels

triangles	shapes with 4 sides	shapes with more than 4 sides
isosceles	square	hexagon
scalene	rectangle	pentagon
right triangle	rhombus	octagon
	trapezoid	decagon

shapes with rounded sides	3-D shapes
oval	cube
circle	cylinder
cylinder	sphere
sphere	cone
cone	pyramid

Steps

1. Generate a collection of relevant data using terms, numbers, percentages, symbols, etc. Make sure the items are a heterogeneous mixture; students should not be making one or two groups.
2. Model the grouping and labeling process with students. Make sure students understand the difference between groups that are mathematically meaningful and those that are arbitrary. (See Figure 4.9.)

Figure 4.9 Meaningful Versus Arbitrary Groupings of *Fractions*

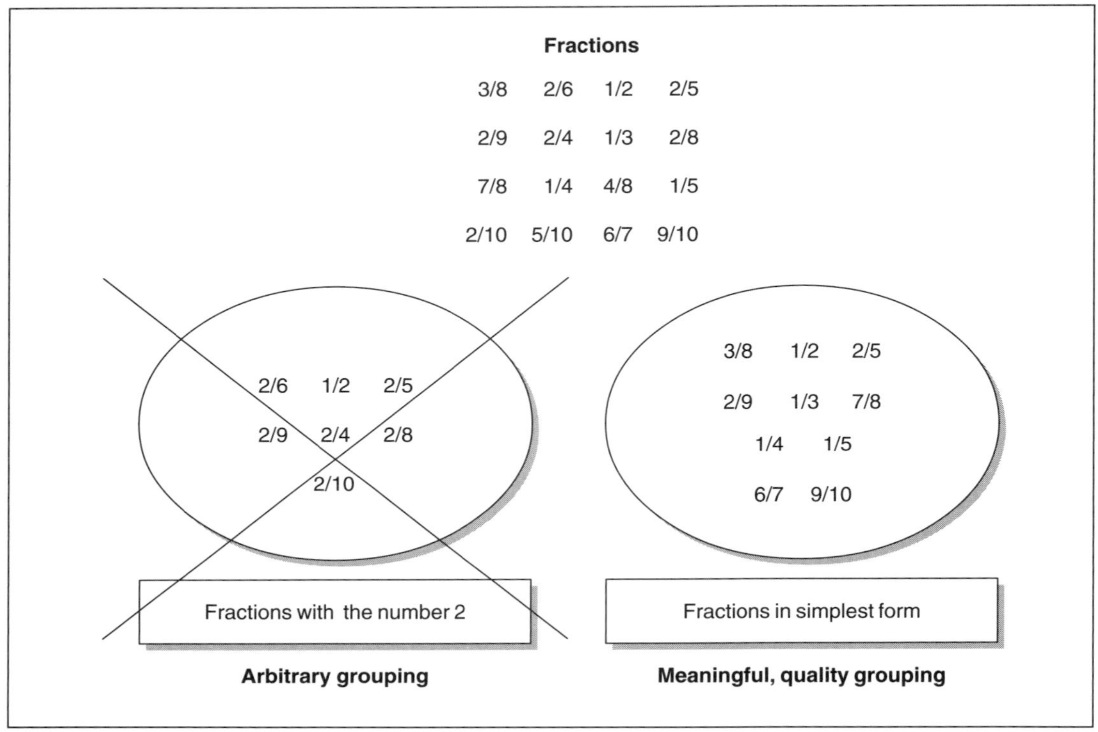

3. Have students group and label the data either in teams or individually. Be sure to specify group-and-label guidelines; e.g., data can or cannot be used in more than one group. (See Organizer 4-C for a blank Group and Label Organizer.)
4. Encourage students to think deeply by considering moves such as combining groups and looking for less obvious connections.
5. Have students use their labeled groups to record a set of predictions on a three-column Prediction Organizer (see Organizer 4-D).
6. Facilitate a classroom discussion where students share some of their groups and labels, the reasons behind their groupings, and their predictions.
7. Allow students to revisit, refine, and revise their predictions as they learn more about the content.

Examples

Money Matters

Look at the different amounts of money below. Make groups of money and numbers that you think go together, and then label your groups.

Figure 4.10 Coins and Money

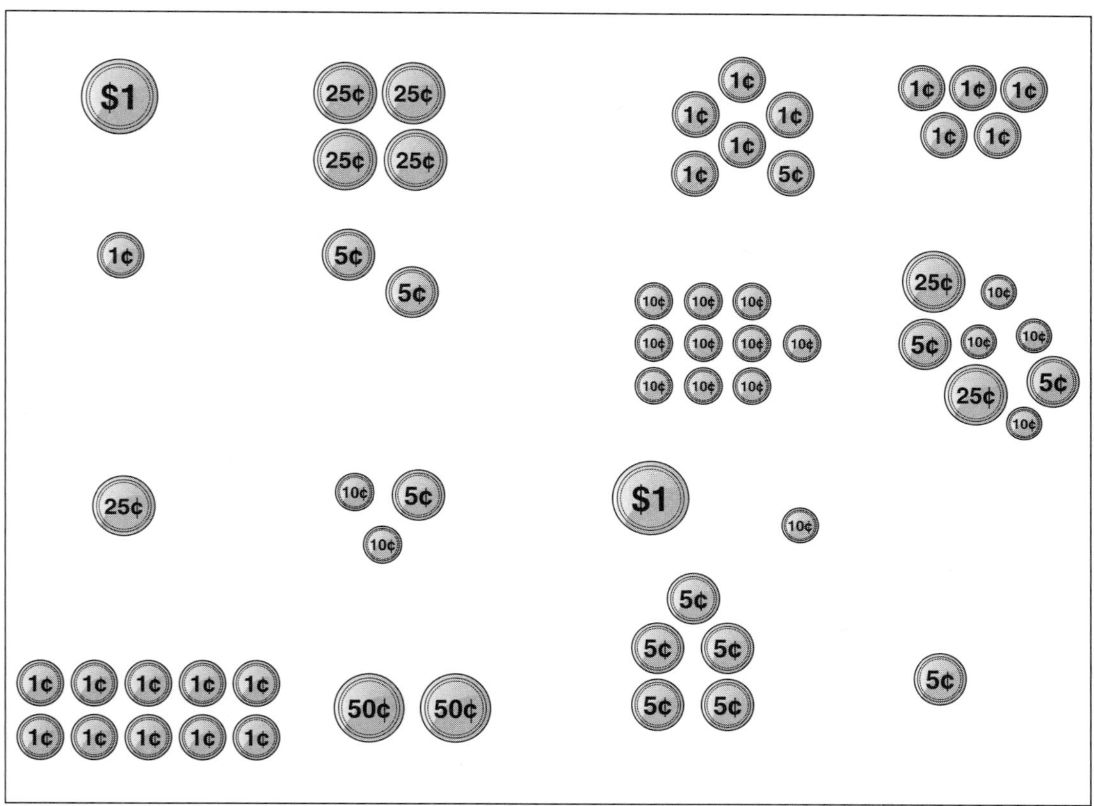

Math Words

Look over the list of common mathematical words and phrases below. Organize the items into no fewer than four labeled groups:

sum	product	times	plus	difference
reduce by	less than	diminished by	multiply	add
quotient	take away	added to	division	more than
increased by	minus	triple	ratio	double

Figure It Out

Below is a collection of geometric figures. Create groups for the figures and label them explicitly:

Figure 4.11 Assorted Geometric Figures and Shapes

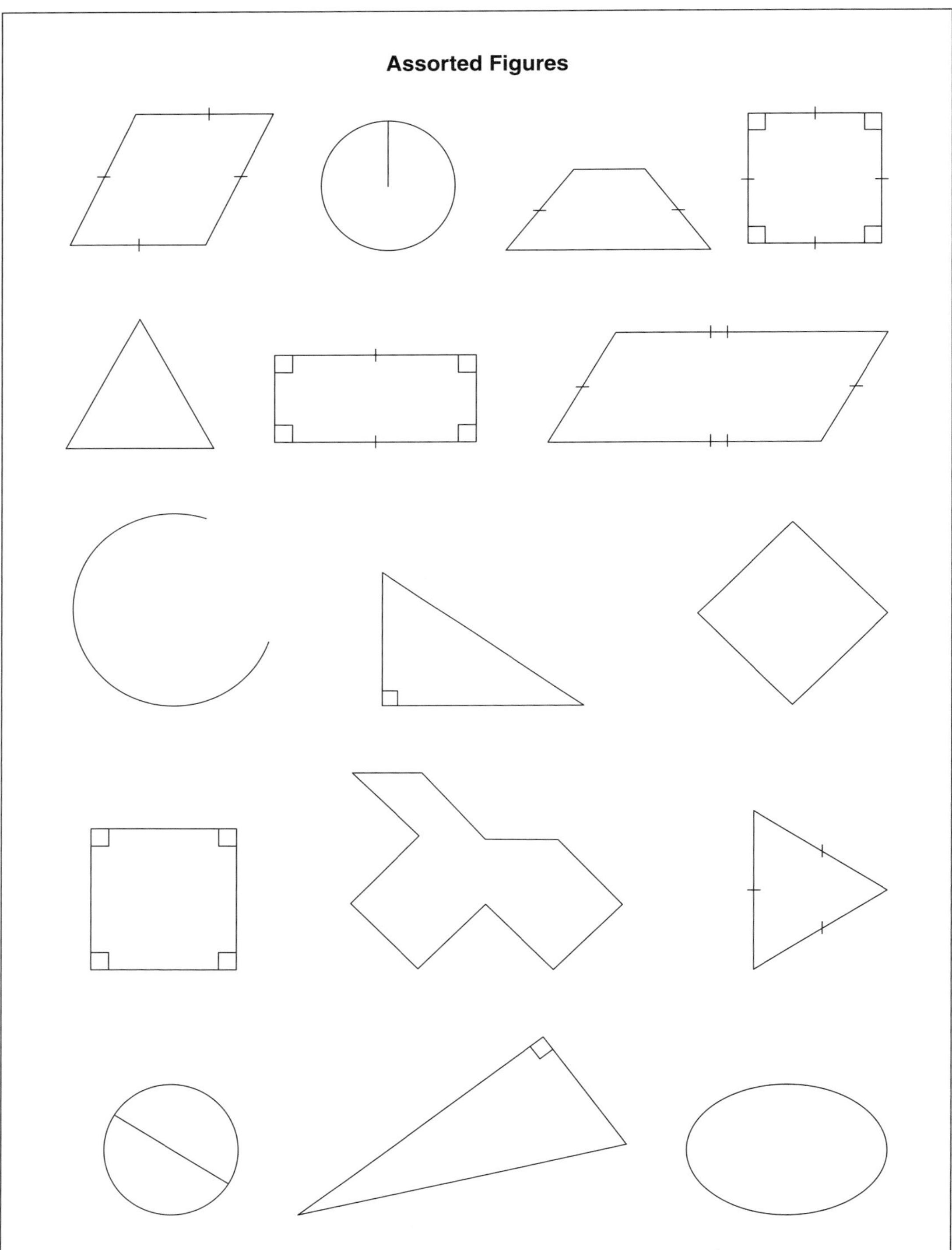

Equations

Look over the equations below and organize them into no fewer than four distinctly labeled groups:

$y = 2x - 5$	$y = 3 - 2x$	$y = 0$	$y = x - 100$
$y = 3x$	$y = 5$	$x = y$	$y = \frac{1}{2}x$
$y = 2$	$y = -x + 1$	$y = 0.5x - 2$	$y = -0.25x$
$y = x$	$y = 7x$	$x = 2$	$y = 100x$
$y = 2x$	$y = -4$	$y = 4 - 3x$	$y = 1/x$
$y = 4x - 1$	$y = 3x + 3$	$y = -3x$	$x = y - y$

Conic Sections

On the worksheet there are twenty equations (Figure 4.12), most of which are conic equations. Without graphing, using a calculator, or looking to your notes, group the equations into at least three (and no more than five) categories and label them according to type of conic section.

Figure 4.12 Conic Section Worksheet

Conic Section Worksheet

$x^2 = y$	$x^2 - y^2 = 1$	$x^2 + y^2 = 2$	$xy = 3$
$\frac{x^2}{4} + \frac{y^2}{9} = 1$	$\frac{x^2}{4} + \frac{y^2}{9} = 1$	$2x + y^2 = 0$	$25 = x^2 + y^2$
$x = y^2$	$\frac{y^2}{2} + \frac{x^2}{2} = 2$	$y^2 = x^2 - 10$	$x^2 + 4y^2 = 5$
$\frac{x}{16} + \frac{y}{16}$	$3x^2 + 9y^2 = 27$	$\frac{x}{y} = 16$	$y = \sqrt{3x}$
$y = \sqrt{3x^2}$	$x - y = 0$	$\frac{y^2}{4} + \frac{x^2}{9} = 1$	$y = \frac{1}{x}$

Organizer 4-C Group and Label Organizer

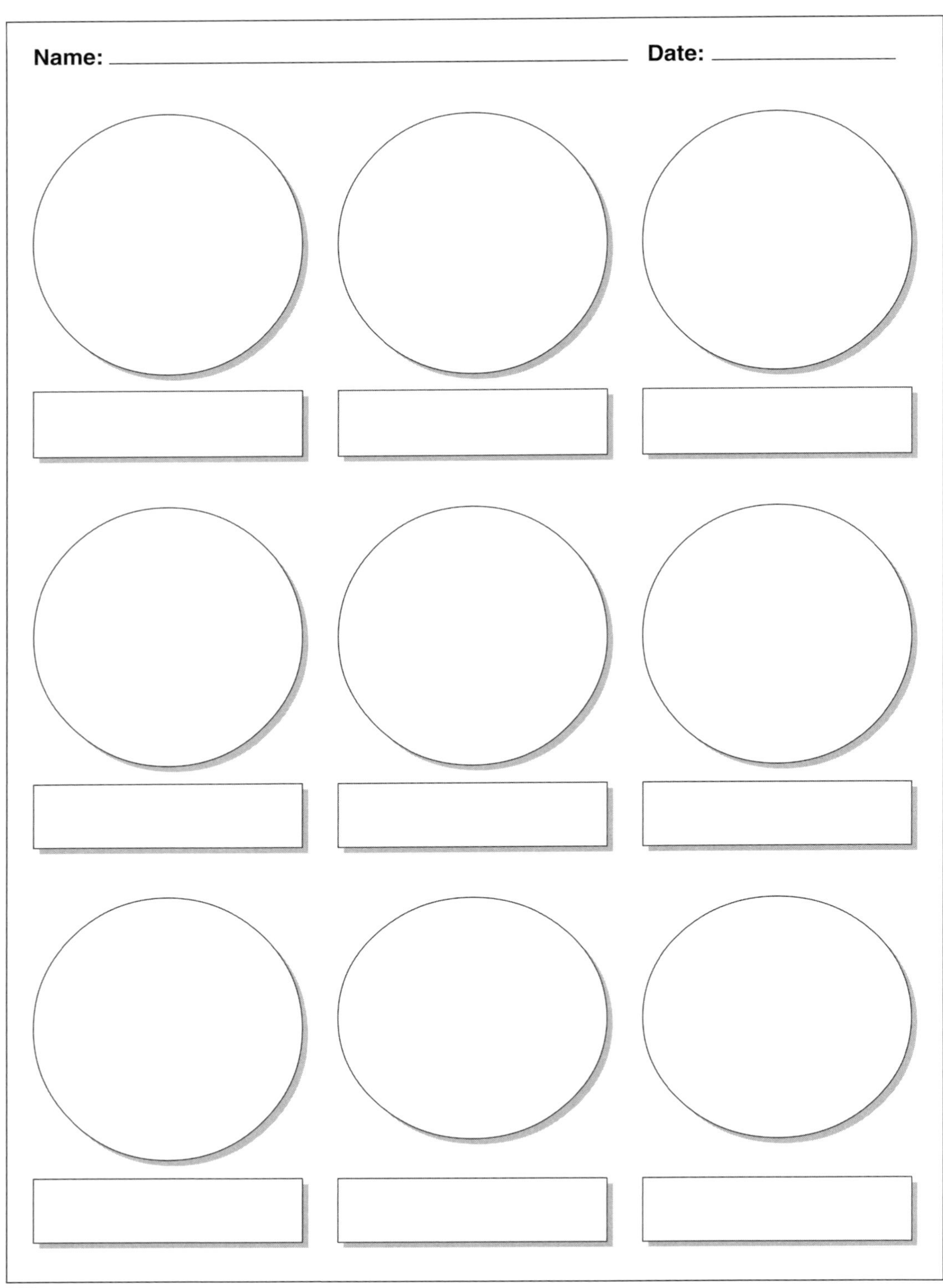

Organizer 4-D Prediction Organizer

Name: ______________________ **Date:** ______________

Supporting Statements	Predictions	Refuting Statements

AND THE QUESTION IS . . . ?

Purpose

And the Question Is . . . ? uses the format of a game to get students to think more deeply about mathematical concepts and their applications. And the Question Is . . . ? operates as both an assessment tool and an invitation to think creatively and divergently about mathematics, as students generate as many correct responses as they can in as many different ways possible.

Overview

Taking a cue from the popular game show Jeopardy!, And the Question Is . . . ? starts with the answers and asks students to compose the appropriate questions. But the tool goes deeper than Jeopardy!, which uses answers that have only one correct question. In And the Question Is . . . ?, there are multiple correct responses and students generate as many of them as they can in a limited amount of time.

After receiving the And the Question Is . . . ? answer, students are given time (usually 1 to 2 minutes) to generate as many relevant questions as they can. Once students have composed their questions (either individually or in small teams), the teacher reviews student responses to assess students' understanding of and proficiency with the mathematical concepts being studied.

Steps

1. Provide students with the answers for the And the Question Is . . . ? activity.
2. Model or review the And the Question Is . . . ? format with students.
3. Give students a limited amount of time to generate as many questions as they can.
4. Review student responses as a class.

Examples

Category: Angles

Answer: Right Angle
Student Questions:

- What kind of angle measures 90 degrees?
- What angle is opposite the hypotenuse of a right triangle?
- What angle occurs when two lines are perpendicular?
- What angles are in squares and rectangles?
- What angles are made by the diagonals of a kite or rhombus?
- What angle is neither acute nor obtuse?

Category: Triangles

Answer: Ways to Prove Triangles Congruent
Student Questions:

- What is SAS?
- What is SSS?
- What is ASA?
- What is HL?
- What is AAS?

Answer: Ways to Prove Triangles Similar
Student Questions:

- What is SAS?
- What is AA?
- What is SSS?

Answer: Ways to Prove Triangles Similar and Congruent
Student Questions:

- What is SAS?
- What is SSS?

Category: Quadratic Equations

Answer: A quadratic equation in standard form with a leading coefficient of 1 and the constant term of 8 where all coefficients are real numbers.
Student Questions:

- What is $x^2 + 9x + 8 = 0$?
- What is $x^2 - 9x + 8 = 0$?
- What is $x^2 + 6x + 8 = 0$?
- What is $x^2 - 6x + 8 = 0$?
- What is $x^2 + 4\sqrt{2}x + 8 = 0$?
- What is $x^2 - 4\sqrt{2}x + 8 = 0$?

What makes the tool especially powerful is that it invites many forms of mathematical thinking into the classroom. Suppose the teacher presents students with the answer of "Prime Numbers." Some students will generate a list of questions from "What is 3?" to "What is 101?" trying to remember or figure out as many prime numbers as they can in the allotted time. Other students may respond more conceptually, turning the definition of a prime number into a question, such as, "What is a number that is divisible only by itself and 1?" Still other students may look for more creative responses, generating questions like:

- What group of numbers contains odd numbers and the number 2?
- There are exactly 25 of these numbers between 0 and 100. What are they?

- Following Wilson's theorem, what group of numbers are greater than 1 with each number (p) having the factorial $(p - 1)! + 1$ that is divisible by p?
- If n is a positive integer greater than 1, then Bertrand's postulate says that you can always find one of which type of number between n and $2n$?

Category: Measurements of Time

Answer: 1 Hour
Student Questions:

- What is 60 minutes?
- How much time has passed when the small hand moves from 12 to 1?
- How much time goes by when the big hand makes one full trip around the clock?
- How much playing time is there in a professional football game?
- What is 3,600 seconds?
- How long does a "singing" episode of *American Idol* last?

WHAT IF?

Purpose

What If? asks students to think about familiar mathematical concepts, procedures, or topics, and then challenges them to consider "what if . . . ?" By changing the rules that govern mathematics (or by altering the context in which mathematical rules are applied) and allowing students to play and mentally experiment with mathematical ideas, the What If? technique inspires deep and creative forms of thinking. As students consider the consequences and changes that a What If? question brings about, they gain new insights and develop a more personally meaningful understanding of the content they are learning.

Overview

What If? activities invite students to revisit problems in light of changing parameters and explore familiar mathematical concepts from new perspectives. While What if? questions naturally encourage divergent and playful forms of thinking, they also lead students to survey and solidify the current state of their knowledge, since answering a What If? question requires a solid understanding of "what is." It is a good idea to introduce the technique using a What If? question that relates to a non-mathematical or everyday topic. For example, you might ask students to consider how their lives would be changed if computers didn't exist or if the United States were no longer a superpower. After students are familiar with What If? thinking, they can turn their attention and creativity to mathematics-based What If? questions.

Steps

1. Review a mathematical concept with students.
2. Pose a non-mathematical What If? question for students to answer.

3. Have students share their thinking and discuss their responses to the general What If? question.
4. Frame a What If? question or a series of What If? questions related to a mathematical topic under investigation or familiar to students.
5. Allow students time to think about the consequences of the What If? question.
6. Have students generate and share their responses to the What If? question within a small group or with the entire class.
7. Facilitate a discussion with students on how thinking hypothetically deepens learning.

Examples

What If? questions fall into two broad categories: concept-based and problem-based. We begin with concept-based What If? questions, which ask students to explore mathematical concepts in new ways and contexts. For example, after a lesson on Arabic and Roman numerals, a fourth-grade teacher asked students: "What if we still used Roman numerals?" Sample student responses included:

- The answers for math problems would be a lot longer than they are now.
- Multiplication and division problems would be really hard to do.
- There would be a lot to remember. There are the X's, V's, and I's, but what are the Roman numerals for 50, 100, 500, or really big numbers?
- Showing our work for any type of problem would not be easy because we would need to write so much more.
- How would people in other countries write Roman numerals?
- How do you use Roman numerals for decimals or fractions?
- I've seen my brother's homework and he has to do math with letters and numbers mixed together. How could he do it if there were only letters?

Here are some more examples of good concept-based What If? questions:

- What if the United States Congress passed a law saying that there must be a correlation between the size of money and the value of money? What if the international community adopted the same law for currency in all countries?
- What if the United States adopted the metric system overnight? How would your mathematics class, science class, lunch, and entire day be different?
- What if the United States stopped using the penny?
- What if zero was not a number?
- What if negative numbers didn't exist?
- What if there was no number for π?
- What if *scientific notation* was never developed?
- What if the sum of the angles of a triangle were not always 180 degrees? How would Euclidean theorems be altered?
- What if every function had to be differentiable?
- What if you lived in a two-dimensional world? How would you distinguish circles from line segments?

Problem-based What If? activities ask students a series of What If? questions about a specific situation or problem. Students need to analyze all of the provided information, review their own calculations, and think critically about the variables and parameters. The example below shows how a few What If? questions force students to think more deeply about a basic word problem.

Sample Word Problem

Two brothers want to give the exterior of their large garage a new coat of paint. The garage is only one story high with a flat roof. The front (south side) and back (north side) of the garage are each 12 ft. high and 20 ft. wide. The front has a brand new garage door that is 8 ft. high and 18 ft. wide. The west and east sides of the garage are each 12 ft. high and 28 ft. long. Both sides of the garage have three windows each, and each window measures 2 ft. by 2 ft. The back (north side) of the garage has one 2 ft. by 4 ft. window and one 7.5 ft. by 4 ft. door. What is the total surface area of the garage that the brothers have to paint (not including doors and windows)?

What If? questions that could be used to enhance the problem:

- What if the brothers had to also paint the front garage door and the back door?
- What if the entire west side of the garage was covered by ivy and did not need to be painted?
- What if each $10 gallon of paint covers 200 sq. ft. and each $4 quart covers 50 sq. ft.? What is the least amount of money the brothers will need to spend to paint the garage?
- What if the brothers installed a drop ceiling in their garage? How many pieces of 2 ft. by 4ft. sections of ceiling would they need?

MAKING UP IS FUN TO DO

Purpose

In mathematics there are many critical terms and theorems that students need to use and understand. Making Up Is Fun to Do is a technique designed to help students think about the deeper meanings of vocabulary terms. It also encourages the creation of alternative words or phrases that can yield more personally meaningful understanding. Students who like to think of alternative ways to approach conventional mathematics will enjoy this opportunity to use their imaginations. Students who normally memorize terms will find themselves applying their knowledge of the critical attributes of vocabulary in new ways.

Overview

Making Up Is Fun to Do activities ask students to consider mathematics vocabulary, names of theorems, and foundational concepts. After analyzing the critical attributes of key terms, students select a synonymous term and defend that synonym's appropriateness. For example, for the term *improper fractions*, students might generate the following terms and descriptions:

- *Top heavy fractions*—This word is better since it tells us that the top of the fraction is larger than the bottom.

- *Skyscraper fractions*—This term tells us that the fraction is so tall because the top is bigger.
- *Huge heads*—If your head is very large it would mean your body's biggest part could be the top of it. This name is funny enough that everyone would remember it better.
- *V fractions*—Because the "V" has its biggest part at the top.
- *Flag pole fractions*—Since we put the flag at the top of the pole, this name will help students remember the top is bigger than the bottom.
- *Circus fractions*—The name makes you think of a big top tent and helps you remember that the top is bigger.
- *Ice cream cone fractions*—This is a delicious way to remember fractions, since ice cream cones have bigger tops than bottoms.

Making Up Is Fun to Do is founded on educational research showing that retention and understanding increase significantly when students are exposed to new vocabulary terms multiple times and are given the opportunity to work and play with words in a variety of ways (Beck, McKeown, & Kucan, 2002; Marzano, 2004). Students who connect important mathematical terms to words or phrases that they create benefit from making these new connections to prior knowledge. Student communication skills are also sharpened, as they must explain how the critical attributes of the vocabulary are addressed by the synonym. After students present their synonyms, the class selects the best among the alternatives.

Steps

1. Develop a list of important vocabulary words for the unit.
2. Select one or more terms for the Making Up Is Fun to Do activity. Make sure students understand the critical attributes of each term.
3. Explain to students that they need to find a word or short phrase for use in place of the given word.
4. Have students write a synonym (alternate term) and an explanation of why the new word is better than—or at least as good as—the given term.
5. Have students discuss the proposed words in groups or class discussion, then select the "best of the best."

Examples

A la "Mode"

When studying simple statistics, students often find the word *mode* to be rather strange. Can you think of a more appropriate word or phrase that would be better? Identify your term and explain why it is better suited to the critical attributes of the statistical *mode.*

Numerator Versus Denominator

Numerator and *denominator* are strange words outside of the mathematics classroom. Work with your partner to come up with replacement words for *numerator* and *denominator.* Explain why your words are better than the traditional ones.

What's Wrong With Improper Fractions?

The phrase *improper fraction* seems to imply there is something wrong with a fraction. What is a better word or words (maximum of three words) that could replace the phrase *improper fraction*? How does your answer let other students know what kind of fraction you are describing?

Efficient Coefficient?

Coefficient does not seem to be a very efficient use of letters, since the term does not tell someone who does not already know the definition what the word means. Can you think of a word or two that should replace it? How would your idea make it easier for a student to remember the meaning of the word *coefficient?*

The "Right" Angle

Since a 90 degree angle is a "*right*" angle, does that make the other angles "wrong"? What word or phrase for a 90 degree angle would be less judgmental with respect to the other angles? How does your term not put the other angles down?

Asymptote?

When spoken, the word *asymptote* often evokes awkward smiles and laughs. It is also hard to spell. Your assignment is to find a different word or phrase (maximum of three words) that mathematicians should use to replace *asymptote.* Explain how your choice better illustrates the critical attributes of *asymptote.*

Mmm . . . Sandwich Theorem

In calculus, the *Sandwich Theorem* has an appetizing name that can actually distract student concentration—especially right before lunch! Come up with a different name for this theorem that still conveys its critical attributes but is not likely to cause stomachs to rumble.

CREATE YOUR OWN

Purpose

In any mathematics classroom, keeping students actively engaged is essential to learning. Quite simply, if students are not actively engaged in the learning process, then they will retain a minimum of what you teach them. Create Your Own builds student engagement by turning mathematics instruction into a creative endeavor. By allowing students to generate examples or questions of their choosing, they stay focused on learning and forge deeper and more personally meaningful connections to mathematical content.

Overview

Traditional drill and practice may be important for helping students develop their abilities to follow procedures and make calculations correctly, but a steady diet of drill and practice will turn off even the most active of minds. The Create Your Own activity gives teachers a different way for students to learn skills and concepts—a way that incorporates students' interests, personal preferences, and imaginations into the process. Rather than having all the content handed down from the teacher, students create their own problems or questions, and then explore their mathematical implications with their peers.

Steps

1. Select a topic with which students are familiar and comfortable.
2. Design a question, situation, or set of criteria to prompt and guide students' creative responses.
3. Have students generate problems or questions that are mathematically correct within the parameters given. Whenever possible, encourage creativity.
4. Allow students time to share their work in pairs or small groups. A good follow-up activity is to have students work through the problems or questions that their classmates have created.

Examples

Add and Subtract Lucky 13

Create five addition problems and five subtraction problems that all have an answer of 13.

Quadratic Regression

Use your graphing calculator's quadratic regression capabilities to create equations of two parabolas that contain points (–5, 3) and (2, –1). One of your parabolas must open upward and the other downward.

Breakfast Is Served

Create three word problems that could be solved using the following information:

A diner claims to use 5,000 eggs a week. The diner serves eggs fried, scrambled, or poached. A single hen takes an average of 24 to 26 hours to make a single egg. After laying an egg, a hen needs to rest for 1 hour before it can start producing another egg.

Operations

Use all four basic operations and every digit from 1 through 9 to create an expression that equals 99. You can use parentheses in your expression.

Shopping Spree

Pick one or more store advertisements and identify three ways that $150 could be spent meeting the conditions below.

- At least three items must be purchased.
- Sales tax and shipping must be included if applicable.
- The total sum, including sales tax and shipping, must be no less than $149.00 and no more than $151.00.

Cubic Functions

Create a cubic function that has two *distinct* real roots and *no* imaginary roots. Express your cubic function in factored form.

DIVERGENT THINKING

Purpose

Thinking divergently in the mathematics classroom is much more than a way to engage your creative, or Self-Expressive, students in the learning process. Divergent Thinking helps all students build their capacity to think flexibly and to pursue a range of mathematical options. The tool serves as an important reminder that many mathematics problems have more than one correct answer. Students who are able to try out different approaches to non-routine problems have a serious advantage over students who believe that knowing algorithms is all there is to mathematical problem solving.

Overview

The ability to think divergently is an essential skill that transcends the mathematics classroom. Students who are comfortable with "thinking outside the box" are much more likely to employ logic and experiment with alternative and innovative approaches to solving both mathematical and real-world problems. In a mathematics classroom, students may feel they need "permission" to think divergently. Using the Divergent Thinking tool and striving to create a learning environment where discussion, collaboration, and mathematical experimentation play a central role in the classroom go a long way in helping students become more divergent—that is to say, more adaptable and more powerful—thinkers.

Before using the Divergent Thinking tool, it is a good idea to hold a whole-class discussion or a modeling session in which you and your students explore a non-routine task or problem and the kinds of thinking it evokes. For example, you might ask groups of students to analyze and lay out the steps they would use to solve a non-routine problem. Then, you can ask students to share their approaches. As different approaches or perspectives emerge, you can use them to highlight the critical ideas: that there is more than one way to solve the problem; that different approaches are cause for discussion; and that knowing how to explore and discuss multiple approaches makes you a better thinker and problem solver.

Steps

1. Generate a problem, situation, or question that has multiple solutions and many ways of finding the different solutions.
2. Encourage students to imagine or view the problem from a variety of perspectives. Looking at a problem in various ways will help students to think of multiple and creative solutions.
3. Have students meet in pairs or small groups to discuss their solutions and the thinking processes behind them.
4. Discuss with students the importance of thinking divergently in mathematics and other areas as a way to find effective and innovative ways of working.

Examples

Under Pressure

As a pre-lab assignment, ask students to think about water pressure in your school's drinking fountains: *Assume that there is no direct way to measure the pressure. How would you go about determining which water fountain in your school has the greatest water pressure? Turn in a drawing and a written summary of your idea(s).*

Non-Mathematical Meanings

Given the list of our unit's twenty vocabulary words:

a. Select ten of the words that also have *non-mathematical meanings* and use each in a sentence.
b. Create a simple *non-mathematical* sentence in which you use at least three of these words.

Figure Out the Function

Given: $f(x) = x^3 - 4x^2 + 5x - 13$. Find $f(3)$ in three different ways.

Line Up

The endpoints of a line segment are (–1,5) and (3,–3). Find the midpoint of that segment in three ways—algebraically, graphically, and numerically.

Portraying Percentages

Graphically illustrate each of the following percentages: 25%, 37.5%, and 50%. Draw three different diagrams for *each* percentage. Show three different ways to demonstrate that 25% equals $\frac{1}{4}$.

Algebra Tiles

How many different ways could you arrange algebra tiles to demonstrate the answer to $(x + 3)(x + 2)$? Is there a best choice for this?

Playing With Polygons

Meet with your team. How many different polygons can you make that have the same area but different perimeters using only four unit blocks? What is the perimeter of each polygon?

Shaded Square

How many ways can you color in exactly half of the 8×8 square below?

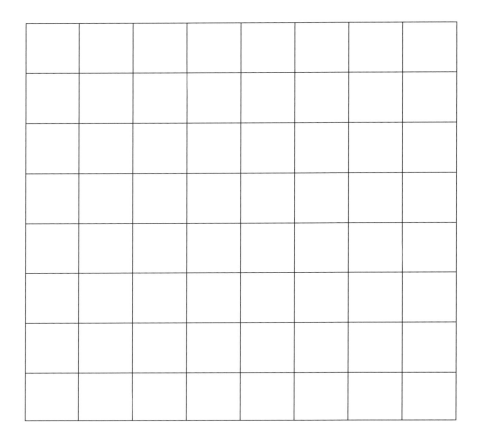

5

Interpersonal Math Tools

INTERPERSONAL MATH STUDENTS

Want to . . . learn math through dialogue, collaboration, and cooperative learning.

Like math problems that . . . focus on real-world applications and how math helps people.

Approach problem solving . . . as an open discussion among a community of problem solvers.

May experience difficulty when . . . instruction focuses on independent seat work or when what they are learning seems to lack real-world application.

Learn best when . . . their teacher pays attention to their successes and struggles in math.

—Silver, Thomas, & Perini (2003)

Interpersonal Math Tools Matrix

PAGE	MATH TOOL	Problem Solving	Reasoning and Proof	Communication	Connections	Representation
		NCTM PROCESS STANDARDS				
170	**Bring Your "A" Game**—Three tools to boost Attention, Attitude, and Aspiration.	●		●		
180	**Paired Learning**—Students work with a partner to complete a task and discuss their work with the class.	●		●		
182	**Peer Coaching**—Students work together to solve problems, with one student answering questions and the other providing coaching.	●	●	●		
188	**Where in the World?**—Students make practical connections with mathematical concepts by generating real-world examples.		●	●	●	●
190	**Real-World Connections**—Students apply classroom math to real situations—stocks, taxes, sports statistics, etc.	●	●	●	●	
193	**What's Your Favorite?**—Students' personal preferences become the foundation for their learning and problem solving.	●		●	●	
196	**Who's Right?**—Students use their analytical and debugging skills to resolve conflicts.	●	●	●		
198	**Reflective Writing**—Students reflect on learning and prior knowledge to identify strengths and confusions, and to pose new questions.		●	●		
200	**Writing About the Problem of the Day**—A writing tool that enables students to discuss how they overcame personal confusions.	●	●	●		
206	**Test Feedback**—An assesment tool that allows students to reflect on test performance (strengths, difficulties, etc.) and prepare for future tests.			●		●
208	**Range Finder**—Students select a task that best demonstrates their current level of understanding.	●		●		
212	**Math Boggle**—A "Boggle"-like review game based on mathematical concepts.			●	●	
213	**Vocabulary Games**—A collection of games that support teamwork, memory, and comprehension of math vocabulary.			●	●	
216	**Cooperative Structures for Promoting Positive Interdependence**—Learning structures that ensure group interdependence and individual accountability during group work.	●		●		

INTERPERSONAL MATH TOOLS

EDUCATIONAL RESEARCH BASE											INSTRUCTIONAL OBJECTIVES							
Identifying similarities and differences	Summarizing and note taking	Reinforcing effort and providing recognition	Homework and practice	Nonlinguistic representations	Cooperative learning	Setting objectives and providing feedback	Generating and testing hypotheses	Questions, cues, and advance organizers	Vocabulary	Writing	Preparing	Presenting	Practicing	Processing	Problem Solving	Performing	Personalizing	MATH TOOL
		●				●		●		●	●		●		●		●	Bring Your "A" Game
	●		●		●	●					●		●	●	●			Paired Learning
		●	●		●	●		●					●		●			Peer Coaching
		●					●							●		●	●	Where in the World?
					●		●								●	●		Real-World Connections
●			●								●		●		●		●	What's Your Favorite?
●							●								●			Who's Right?
	●									●	●			●			●	Reflective Writing
					●	●				●		●		●	●		●	Writing About the Problem . . .
●		●				●								●		●	●	Test Feedback
●		●	●			●					●	●	●		●	●	●	Range Finder
	●	●			●				●		●			●				Math Boggle
		●			●				●					●		●	●	Vocabulary Games
		●			●	●								●	●	●		Cooperative Structures

SOURCE: Marzano, R. J., Pickering, D. J., & Pollock, J. E. (2001). *Classroom instruction that works: Research-based strategies for increasing student achievement.* Alexandria, VA: Association for Supervision and Curriculum Development.

BRING YOUR "A" GAME

Purpose

The effort that students put into their work is greatly influenced by the three A's of learning:

- *Attention,* or their ability to focus on the tasks at hand.
- *Attitude,* or their ability to remain positive and persevere when learning becomes difficult.
- *Aspiration,* or their ability to set meaningful learning goals and strive toward excellence.

Bring Your "A" Game gives teachers and students of mathematics a trio of "brain boosters," or tools that help students put forth their best efforts in the classroom. Each tool builds one of the three A's of learning.

Overview

Each of the three tools that are a part of Bring Your "A" Game is designed to address a specific factor affecting student effort in the classroom.

- *Attention.* The competition for students' attention is fierce. It is crucial that the teacher finds ways to engage students and ensure that they are attending to the mathematical concepts and tasks at hand.
- *Attitude.* The wrong attitude can easily discourage students and disrupt a lesson, particularly lessons that involve complex or abstract mathematics. Instilling the proper attitude toward learning, including encouraging students to believe in their own abilities, dramatically improves students' understanding and enjoyment of mathematics.
- *Aspiration.* When students identify and set goals for themselves, they become more motivated and purpose-driven. This focus, in turn, makes the work of learning mathematics more manageable as students strive toward clear and meaningful targets. It also increases students' chances for success and high achievement.

Bring Your "A" Game develops each of these critical learning factors through a set of three tools.

- *Attention Monitor* is a combination of thinking and reflection activities that help students understand how they pay attention as well as what distracts them.
- *Attitude Catcher* uses two worksheets to "catch" and improve attitudes toward learning. The first gets students thinking about attitudes in general, while the second provides students with a template for analyzing their attitude toward a certain mathematical problem or concept. The tool leads to the creation of "mathitudes," which are personal affirmations that students recite to help keep them from being discouraged or frustrated while working through a problem.

- *Aspiration Goal Planner* provides students with a set of questions that help them to identify their aspirations and set personal goals for the lesson, week, or unit.

Steps

Attention Monitor

1. Ask students, "Have you ever stopped paying attention in class?" Kindle and extend the discussion by asking, "What happens when you lose your attention?"
2. Have students concentrate on a shaded black dot (4 inches in diameter) for 2 minutes. As students focus on the shape, have them take notes that describe when their attention slipped and how they regained their attention.
3. Introduce the Four C's to students for quick ways to correct a lapse in attention. The Four C's technique works like this:
   - Change Your Posture
   - Cut Away the Distractions
   - Compose or Create
   - Connect
4. To reinforce the Four C's, ask students to create an icon for each C in the technique. (Figure 5.1 shows one student's icons for each of the Four C's.)
5. Provide students with an Attention Monitor so they can reflect upon the lesson and their patterns of attention. Attention Monitors can be created by the teacher (see Figure 5.2) or by the students (see Figure 5.3).

Figure 5.1 Student's Icons For The Four C's

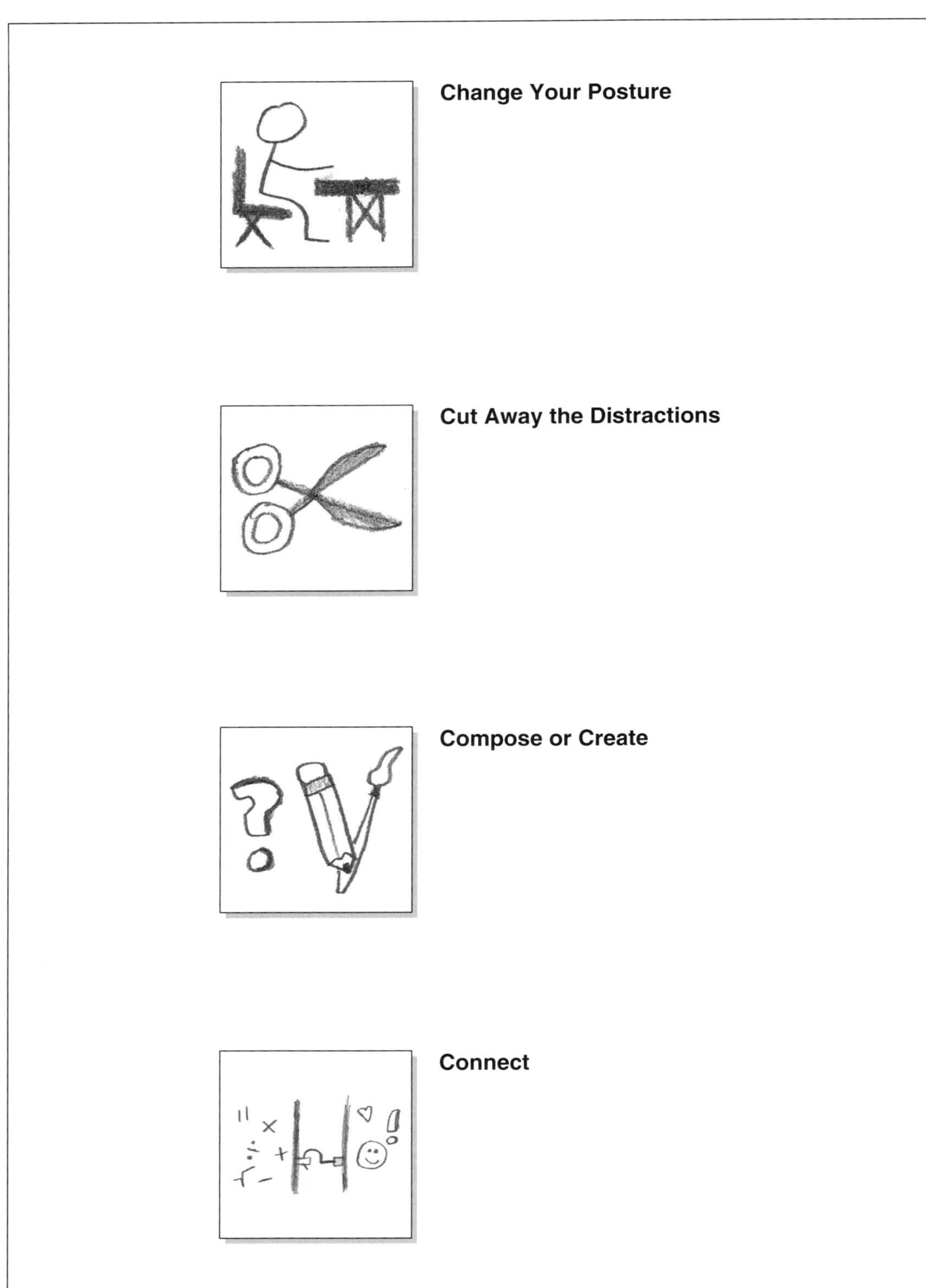

Figure 5.2 Teacher's Attention Monitor

Complete Attention	Close Attention	Good Attention	Some Attention	What Was Said?
4	3	2	1	0

Figure 5.3 Student's Attention Monitor Using Emoticons

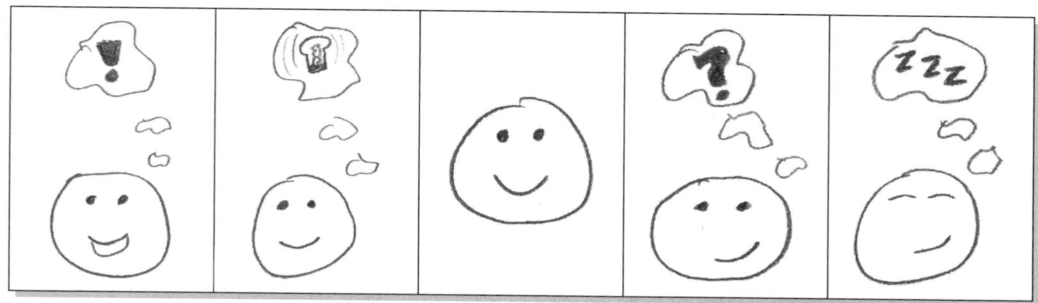

Steps

Attitude Catcher

1. Distribute an "All You Need Is Attitude" Organizer (see Organizer 5-A) to students. A completed "All You Need Is Attitude" Organizer is shown in Figure 5.4.
2. Have students read the statements about attitude. Give students time to explain why they agree or disagree with each statement.
3. Discuss with students the impact that their attitudes can have on their success, both inside and outside of the mathematics classroom.
4. Provide students with an "Attitude Catcher" Organizer (see Organizer 5-B). One student's "Attitude Catcher" Organizer is shown below in Figure 5.5.

Figure 5.4 Student's Completed "All You Need Is Attitude" Organizer

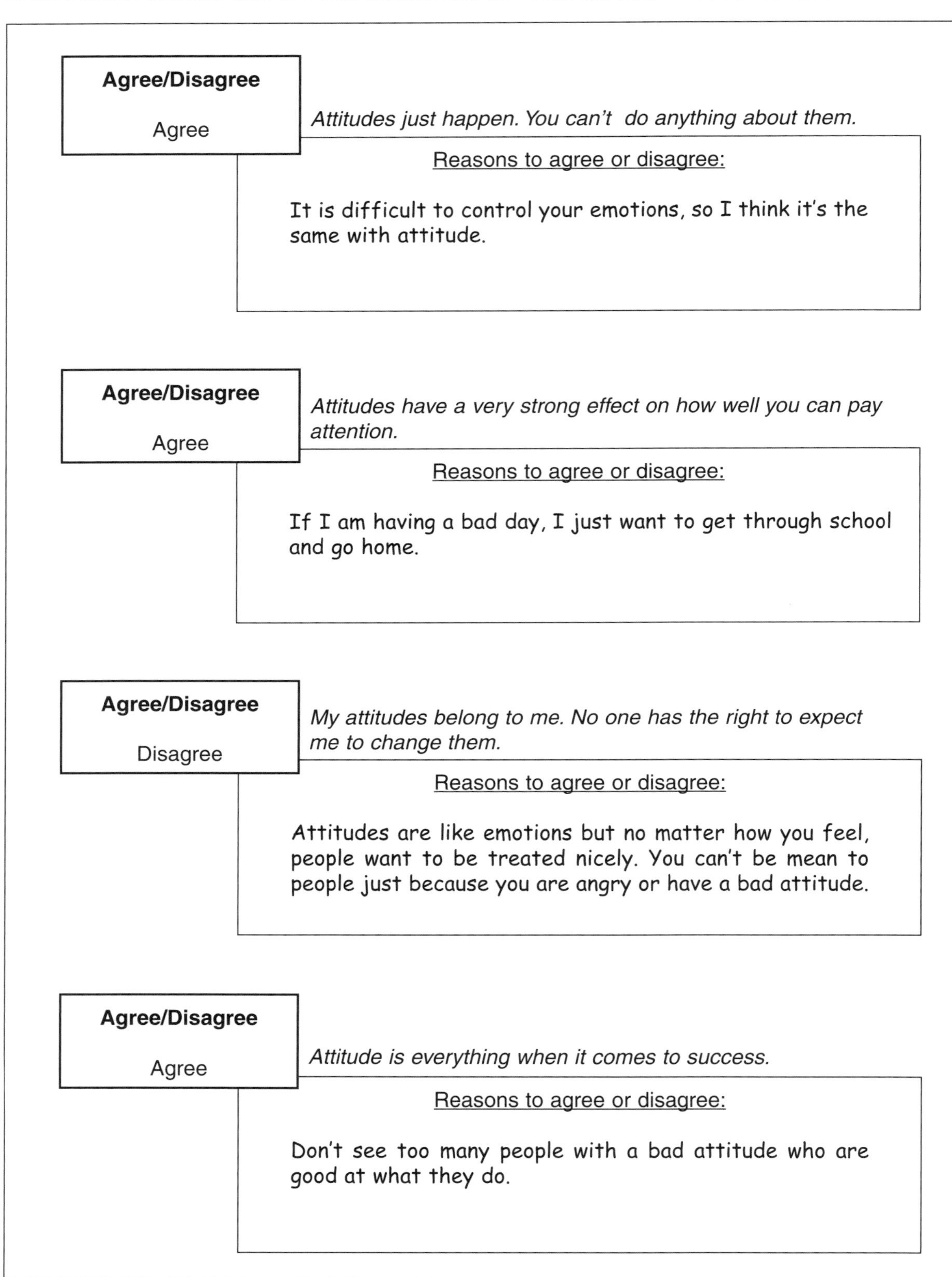

Figure 5.5 Student's "Attitude Catcher" for *Order of Operations*

Try to catch your attitude as you work. Describe your attitude. Rate your attitude on a scale of 1 to 5 in terms of how strong it is. Describe what is causing the attitude, and what you might say to yourself to improve your attitude if it is negative or sustain your attitude if it is positive.

Date: February 9, 2007

Time: 2:35 pm

Activity/Topic: order of operations

My Attitude: Don't really care

My Attitude Strength:

5 4 (3) 2 1
stronger — weaker

What is my attitude toward this activity or topic?

I'm having a bit of a hard time concentrating. My attitude is that I don't really care that much about order of operations.

Why do I have this attitude? What is causing my attitude?

I think the problem is that there are all these rules like do this first, do this second. But what does this really matter to me? I'd rather think about the basketball game I have tonight.

What could I do to improve my attitude and make it more positive than it is?

I know that I should be paying closer attention, but it's not easy. Mrs. Leonora said that order of operations are a really big deal. If you can't remember them and what they mean, you're going to have trouble in all your math classes all the way through high school. I don't want to get bad grades or anything. I'm just thinking about basketball instead of math. I can pay better attention for the next 20 minutes. Basketball can wait.

5. Give students time to reflect and complete the organizer by catching attitudes, rating the strengths of each attitude, describing causes, and considering ways to improve or sustain attitudes. Once students have completed their organizers, have them discuss their thoughts and attitudes in small groups or as a class.

6. Explain to students that optimists do better in school than pessimists because optimists have "inner cheerleaders" who say things like, "This isn't going to get me down" or "If I work at it I can get it." Remind students that talking to themselves is productive and positive.

7. Have students review the "Ten Mathitude Adjusters":
   - I can make sense of anything.
   - I am a master problem solver.
   - I am brilliant.
   - I can learn anything.
   - I am a great reader.
   - No answer is so well hidden that I can't find it.
   - I can say what I mean in front of the class.
   - Mathematics can't scare me.
   - I can write clearly and well when I make the effort.
   - 2, 4, 6, 8 . . . Math is great. *I can't wait!*

8. Encourage students to repeat one or more of the Mathitude Adjusters to themselves whenever it is productive and positive. Alternatively, you may ask students to create their own Mathitude Adjusters. For example, one class crafted the following poem and recited it before working on new mathematical problems:

   Ashes to ashes,
   Dust to dust.
   I hate to simplify you,
   but I must.
   Be cool, be calm,
   and be collected.

Steps

Aspiration Goal Planner

1. Have students reflect on their aspirations by writing a short response to the following questions:
   - What would you like to achieve in mathematics class this week? What will you do in order to achieve this goal?
   - What do you plan on doing after you get out of school? What mathematics do you need to accomplish your goals?
   - What grade in mathematics do you aspire to get this year? How can I help you reach that goal?

2. Have students write out three things they did yesterday. Then have students choose one item from their list and identify the goal they were trying to achieve.

3. Have students use the Aspiration Goal Planner (Organizer 5-C) to help them plot a goal they want to accomplish in their mathematics class.

4. Meet with students regularly to discuss goals, challenges, and learning progress.

Organizer 5-A Blank "All You Need Is Attitude" Organizer

Name: ______________________ **Date:** ____________

Agree/Disagree

Attitudes just happen. You can't do anything about them.

Reasons to agree or disagree:

Agree/Disagree

Attitudes have a very strong effect on how well you can pay attention.

Reasons to agree or disagree:

Agree/Disagree

My attitudes belong to me. No one has the right to expect me to change them.

Reasons to agree or disagree:

Agree/Disagree

Attitude is everything when it comes to success.

Reasons to agree or disagree:

Organizer 5-B Blank "Attitude Catcher" Organizer

Name: ______________________ **Date:** ______________

Try to catch your attitude as you work. Describe your attitude. Rate your attitude on a scale of 1 to 5 in terms of how strong it is. Describe what is causing the attitude, and what you might say to yourself to improve your attitude if it is negative or sustain your attitude if it is positive.

Date: ______________ **Time:** ______________ **Activity/Topic:** ______________ ______________	**My Attitude:** **My Attitude Strength:** 5 4 3 2 1 stronger weaker
What is my attitude toward this activity or topic?	**Why do I have this attitude? What is causing my attitude?**

What could I do to improve my attitude and make it more positive than it is?

Organizer 5-C Blank Aspiration Goal Planner

Name: ______________________ **Date:** ______________

My goal is to: ______________________________________

Steps:	**Schedule:**	**Possible obstacles in achieving my goals:**
		How can I prepare for obstacles?
		Some alternative or creative ways to overcome obstacles might be:

Now, meet with a group. Talk about your goals and plans. What new challenges or ideas for meeting your goals did you discover?

PAIRED LEARNING

Purpose

The Paired Learning model is an efficient and effective way to promote active learning in any mathematics classroom. Students can be paired quickly and can work together on either a short task or a more rigorous task that requires more time and more sophisticated thinking. Research has demonstrated that students benefit from working on complex tasks with a classmate (King-Sears & Bradley, 1995; Fuchs, Fuchs, Mathes, & Simmons, 1997; Butler, 1999; Hashey & Connors, 2003). In addition, most careers require the ability to work productively with others. A pair is a good configuration for working cooperatively because it is difficult for either member to be left out of the process.

Overview

Paired Learning requires asking two questions before the lesson begins:

- What type of task will students work on?
- How long will students have to complete the task?

During a Paired Learning lesson, you should move around the room to get a sense of how pairs are working together; to assess progress; and to decide if an adjustment in time will be necessary. Listening in on student partnerships also gives you the chance to hear students thinking out loud as they work to complete all kinds of challenges—from basic recall all the way to complex and non-routine problem solving. Students should never be stopped abruptly while working. Instead, announce to the groups that they have a few minutes left to complete their work.

Steps

1. Select the task you want students to work on.
2. Establish partnerships and the time needed to complete the task.
3. While pairs work, circulate around the room to monitor progress.
4. Collect student responses and lead a discussion of the work and challenges.
5. Have students reflect on the task and the quality of their learning partnership.
6. Use your observations from the lesson, student work, and follow-up discussion and reflections to decide what students still need to know and understand.

Examples

Homework Debugging

At the start of class, have students work in pairs in order to find and correct any errors on each other's homework. Post the correct answers on the board or on the overhead for everyone to see.

Answer in Pairs

Ask pairs to answer the following:

> John walks $5\frac{1}{2}$ hours every week. If he walks at the rate of $\frac{2}{3}$ of a mile every 15 minutes, how many miles does he walk each week?

After all the pairs have finished, have them switch papers with another pair and check the other pair's work and answer.

What's Your Approach?

Have your calculus students read the problem below and then discuss how they think it should be solved with their partner. Once they agree on a method, they should solve the problem individually and then check with their partner to see if they both have the same answer. If the answers are different, the pair should try to come to an agreement about the correct answer. Once they agree on an answer, each pair should check with another pair to see if they all agree on the same answer.

> The height of the radius of a right circular cylinder is twice the radius of the base. If you need to calculate the volume by using the radius measurement while having an error in volume of less than 1%, what is the greatest error allowed in the measurement of the radius expressed as a percentage of the radius, r?

Paired Reading

Have each pair of students read a section or two from a text that explores two related ideas (for example, the section on geometry containing the perpendicular bisector theorem and its converse). The first student closes her book while the other student asks questions about the perpendicular bisector theorem and its examples from the reading. Next, they switch roles and the first student asks questions about the converse of the perpendicular bisector and its examples while the second student keeps her book closed. The reading and questioning can be done during class time, or the reading can be assigned as part of the homework. If the reading is done for homework, give the students a few minutes in class to review the text and their notes before starting the activity.

Paired Notemaking and Summarizing

During the last 5 or 10 minutes of class, ask students to work in pairs. Have students check each other's notes from the day's lesson on how to create pie charts, bar charts, and line charts. Either student should make additions or changes to their partner's notes as needed.

Partners in Review

On a review day for a chapter test, have students work in pairs for 5 minutes and ask each other questions about the chapter. Then have students work for another

5 minutes to write three or four questions they have about the material that will be on the test.

PEER COACHING

Purpose

Sometimes the most effective teacher in a classroom is a student. Depending on the content and situation, students are better able to help their classmates since they know how it feels to be confused, have made similar mistakes, and can explain mathematical concepts in student-friendly ways. Peer Coaching capitalizes on the power of cooperative student learning by having pairs of students work together to solve a series of problems as both "coach" and "player." Students practice making calculations and gain valuable content knowledge by observing and assisting their partner.

Overview

Students work as a team in the Peer Coaching activity, having the opportunity to be both coach and player. Working as coaches, students guide their partners through a problem by providing feedback, making suggestions, and reviewing the calculations being made. As players, students work out the solution to a given problem with the assistance of their coach.

An essential element of the Peer Coaching activity is the worksheet. On the Peer Coaching worksheet are two sets of problems or questions with corresponding hints and answers. Students do not see the answers, hints, and suggestions for their own questions. Instead, students are given the answers, hints, and suggestions that will help them guide their partner's work.

Thinking out loud is crucial to the Peer Coaching activity. Before distributing worksheets to pairs of students, the teacher models how to solve a sample problem for the class while explaining the thinking process behind the solution.

The teacher models what good players and coaches do during the Peer Coaching activity so students know what it is to think out loud, provide constructive feedback, and work efficiently as a team. It is important for the players in each pair to express their thought processes out loud so the coaches know when it is appropriate to encourage, prompt, and direct the players.

Steps

1. Design a worksheet for students to complete in pairs. Make sure that the worksheet is constructed so that students have their questions and the hints and answers for their partner's questions.
2. Model what good players and good coaches do by working through a sample problem with the class.
3. Distribute worksheets to students in each pair. Worksheets can either be folded in half or two separate pages to ensure that students only have their questions and their partner's answers.

4. Direct the players in each pair to begin working on their problems. Encourage players to express their thinking out loud.
5. Have coaches observe and listen to the players as they work. Encourage coaches to provide hints, give feedback, and assist their partners as needed.
6. Inform students that they should reverse roles once the first player is finished. Players take a turn at coaching their partners and coaches have an opportunity to work on their problems. (For pairs who finish early, a collaborative activity may be included at the end of the worksheet.)
7. Review the problems and solutions from the worksheet with the class while paying close attention to students' thinking and coaching processes.

Examples

Figure 5.6 Order of Operations Worksheet

Worksheet A	
Student A's Problem	**Student B's Solutions and Hints**
Simplify the following: $5 \times 3 + 5(4 - 2)^3 - 9/3$	$3 \times 5 + 2(9 - 6)^2 - 8/4$ 1. What is first in Order of Operations? Parentheses . . . Simplify what's in the ( ) to get: $3 \times 5 + 2(3)^2 - 8/4$ 2. What's next? Exponents . . . $3 \times 5 + 2(9) - 8/4$ 3. What's next? Multiplication or division . . . In what order? Left to right . . . $15 + 2(9) - 8/4$ $15 + 18 - 8/4$ $15 + 18 - 2$ . . . it's OK to jump to this 4. What operation is done last? Add or subtract, left to right . . . $33 - 2$ **31 final answer**

(Continued)

Figure 5.6 (Continued)

Worksheet B	
Student B's Problem	**Student A's Solutions and Hints**
Simplify the following: $3 \times 5 + 2(9 - 6)^2 - 8/4$	$5 \times 3 + 5(4 - 2)^3 - 9/3$ 1. What is first in Order of Operations? Parentheses . . . Simplify what's in the ( ) to get: $5 \times 3 + 5(2)^3 - 9/3$ 2. What's next? Exponents . . . $5 \times 3 + 5(8) - 9/3$ 3. What's next? Multiplication or division . . . In what order? Left to right . . . $15 + 5(8) - 9/3$ $15 + 40 - 9/3$ $15 + 40 - 3$ . . . it's OK to jump to this 4. What operation is done last? Add or subtract, left to right . . . $55 - 3$ **52 final answer**

Figure 5.7 Linear Equations—Worksheet A

Linear Equations Worksheet A	
Student A's Problems	**Student B's Problems, Solutions, and Hints**
$7 + 2(x + 1) = 2x + 9$	***Hint:*** Simplify the left side $9x + 27 - 2x = 7x - 27$ (use distribute property) $7x + 27 = 7x - 27$ (add like terms) $-7x \quad = -7x$ (to get the x's on one side) $27 = -27$ ***Hint:*** When does $27 = -27$? (Answer: Never!) ***Hint:*** So, what is the answer to the original equation? **Answer:** No values of x makes this true.
$5x + 4 = 7(x + 1) - 2x$	***Hint:*** What's the first thing to do? (Eliminate "( )") $6x + 4 = 3x + 6 + 3x - 2$ (use distributive property) $6x + 4 = 6x + 4$ (add like terms on the right) $-6x \quad = -6x$ (subtract to get the x's $4 = 4$ on one side) ***Hint:*** When does $4 = 4$? (Answer: Always!) ***Hint:*** So, when is the original equation true? **Answer:** The equation is true for all values of x.
$3 + 5(x - 4) = 2(x - 7) - 3x$	***Hint:*** What's the first thing to do? (Eliminate "( )"). If they get $4(x + 4)$, remind them to use order of operations. $3x - 15 - 7x = 1 + 3x + 12$ (use distributive prop.) ***Hint:*** Next? Add like terms. $-4x - 15 = 13 + 3x$ ***Hint:*** How can you get the x's on one side? $-4x - 15 = 13 + 3x$ $-3x \quad = \quad -3x$ (subtract 3x from each side) $-7x - 15 = 13$ $+ 15 + 15$ (add 15 to each side) $\frac{-7x}{-7} = \frac{28}{-7}$ (divide by -7, don't forget the "–") **Final Answer: $x = -4$**

Figure 5.8 Linear Equations—Worksheet B

Linear Equations Worksheet B	
Student B's Problems	**Student A's Problems, Solutions, and Hints**
9(x + 3) – 2x = 7x – 27	***Hint:*** Simplify the left side. If they get 9(x + 1), remind them to use order of operations. 7 + 2x + 2 = 2x + 9 (use distribute property) 9 + 2x = 2x + 9 (add like terms on the left) –2x = –2x (subtract to get the x's on one side) 9 = 9 ***Hint:*** When does 9 = 9? (Answer: Always. No matter what the value of x.) ***Hint:*** So, when is the original equation true? **Answer:** equation is true for all values of x.
6x + 4 = 3(x + 2) + 3x – 2	***Hint:*** Simplify the right side. 5x + 4 = 7x + 7 – 2x (use distributive property) 5x + 4 = 5x + 7 (add like terms) –5x –5x (to get the x's on one side) 4 = 7 ***Hint:*** When does 4 = 7? For what value of x will 4 = 7? Answer: Never. ***Hint:*** So, what is the answer to the original equation? **Answer:** No values of x make this true.
3(x – 5) – 7x = 1 + 3(x + 4)	***Hint:*** Simplify each side. If result is 8(x – 4), remind them to use order of operations. 3 + 5x – 20 = 2x – 14 – 3x (use distributive property) ***Hint:*** Add like terms next. – 17 + 5x = –x – 14 ***Hint:*** How can you get the x's on one side? –17 + 5x = –x – 14 + x + x (add x to each side) –17 + 6x = –14 + 17 +17 (add 17 to each side) $\frac{6x}{6} = \frac{3}{6}$ (divide by 6) **Final Answer:** $\mathbf{x = \frac{1}{2}}$

Figure 5.9 Trigonometric Identities—Worksheet A

Trigonometric Identities—Worksheet A	
Student A's Problem	
$\sec y + \tan y = \dfrac{\cos y}{1 - \sin y}$	
Student B's Solution	**Student B's Hints**
tan x + cot x = (sec x) (csc x)	work on the left side (rewrite tan and cot using sin and cos)
$\dfrac{\sin x}{\cos x} + \dfrac{\cos x}{\sin x} =$	get a common denominator and add (multiply the fractions; 1st by sin/sin, 2nd by cos/cos)
$\dfrac{\sin^2 x}{(\cos x)(\sin x)} + \dfrac{\cos^2 x}{(\cos x)(\sin x)} =$	add the two fractions (what does $\sin^2 + \cos^2$ equal?)
$\dfrac{1}{(\cos x)(\sin x)} =$	break the fraction into two parts (split mult in the denom into two parts)
$\dfrac{1}{\cos x} \bullet \dfrac{1}{\sin x}$	simplify the two parts (what do 1/cos and 1/sin become?)
sec x • csc x = (sec x)(csc x)	(hooray, you've done it!)

Figure 5.10 Trigonometric Identities—Worksheet B

Trigonometric Identities—Worksheet B	
Student B's Problem	
tan x + cot x = (sec x) (csc x)	
Student A's Problem	**Student A's Solutions and Hints**
$\sec y + \tan y = \dfrac{\cos y}{1 - \sin y}$	work on the left side (rewrite each part use sin and cos)
$\dfrac{1}{\cos y} + \dfrac{\sin y}{\cos y} =$	rewrite as a single fraction (combine, since it has a common denominator)
$\dfrac{1 + \sin y}{\cos y} =$	what do you need on the top of the fraction? (multiply top and bottom by cos y)
$\dfrac{(\cos y)(1 + \sin y)}{\cos^2 y} =$	rewrite the denominator (use $\cos^2 y + \sin^2 y = 1$, so $\cos^2 y = 1 - \sin^2 y$)
$\dfrac{(\cos y)(1 + \sin y)}{(1 - \sin^2 y)}$	factor the denominator (it factors like $a^2 - b^2$)
$\dfrac{(\cos y)(1 + \sin y)}{(1 - \sin y)(1 + \sin y)} =$	simplify the fraction (what cancels or reduces?)
$\dfrac{\cos y}{(1 - \sin y)} = \dfrac{\cos y}{(1 - \sin y)}$	(hooray, you've done it!)

WHERE IN THE WORLD?

Purpose

Where in the World? encourages students to make connections to abstract concepts in mathematics by finding authentic examples of those concepts in the world outside the classroom. By empowering students to discover how, when, and where mathematical concepts are used beyond the walls at school, the Where in the World? activity deepens understanding and builds students' appreciation for the power and utility of mathematics.

Overview

Teachers of mathematics know that there are a multitude of rich, real-world examples of applied mathematics. However, this fact is often lost on students, who too often perceive the same mathematical concepts as entirely theoretical or academic and, therefore, irrelevant to them. Where in the World? activities help change this common misconception among students.

Where in the World? activities can be tailored to enhance virtually any level of mathematical content, prompting the exploration of everything from geometry in art and architecture, the importance of weight and volume in cooking, percentages in advertising, probability in children's board games, applications of algebra and calculus in physics, and measurements of time and distance (or even money) in sports, among others. As students engage in more Where in the World? activities, they soon discover that the answer to the question, "Where are these mathematical concepts used?" is quite simple: "Everywhere you look."

Steps

1. Develop a question that asks students to search for examples in the real world. Make sure that the question incorporates relevant mathematical concepts and that multiple examples can be generated.
2. Determine a way for students to report their findings. You may ask students to write an essay or report, design a poster, create an illustration, or give an oral presentation.
3. Provide students with the assignment and a reasonable time limit. If it is a lengthy project, make sure students are aware of the due date and all requirements. It will help some students if you break lengthy projects into parts with a due date for each part.
4. Set aside time for students to present (or simply submit) their work.
5. Allow students time to discuss their findings in small groups or as a class.
6. Display imaginative and exemplary work in and around the classroom for other students and classes to view.

Examples

Instructions

Students need to find a printed set of instructions for building (something) for which the order of putting things together is very important.

Presenting Data

Students need to find one example of each of the following ways to present data:

- Bar chart
- Line graph
- Pie chart
- Table of data

Stories of Central Tendency

Find three stories that include the words *mean*, *median*, and *mode*. You can receive extra credit if you can find a story that includes one or more of the terms being used incorrectly.

Percents and Purchases

One week before beginning the chapter in which students will learn about percents, including such concepts as *simple interest*, *compound interest*, *percent increases*, *percent decreases*, and *sales tax*, give the class the following Where in the World? assignment:

Working in groups, find three newspaper stories, print advertisements, or receipts from stores or restaurants (make sure any credit card information is not visible) for each of these areas:

- *Sales tax*
- *Tips or suggestions for what is an appropriate amount to tip*
- *Sales showing a percent discount*
- *Changes in costs or amounts for specific items over a certain amount of time. Find at least one increase and one decrease expressed as a percentage.*

After your group has collected the information, create a collage that will be displayed on the wall outside the classroom (names should be on the back of the collage).

Collecting Conic Sections

List all the types of conic sections that we have studied in this unit. Find three real-world examples of each type of conic section. Consider finding examples on the Internet, taking digital photographs, or scanning magazine images, and then display all pictures in a PowerPoint slideshow.

Area and Perimeter in the Community

What are three real-world examples of problems in your community that involve perimeter and three that involve area? For both area and perimeter, one of the three problems should be in your house, one problem should involve our school or campus, and the last problem should involve a part of your community that is open to the general public.

Aesthetics of Right Triangles

Identify physical examples of right triangles in architecture or art. Consider taking digital photographs or scanning magazines, and then display the images in a slideshow.

Percentages in Periodicals

Identify at least six references/uses of percentages within one edition of a newspaper or magazine of your choice.

Expressions of Exponential Growth or Decay

Find two stories, one including data, that make reference to some kind of exponential growth or decay. Use your graphing calculator and all of the data in one of the articles to calculate the exponential regression equation. Use your equation to predict the value the data will attain ten years from now. Take several different groups of three or four data pairs and calculate the corresponding regression equations and the value ten years from now. Which data points and equations would you use if you wanted to show that the values were growing or falling extremely quickly? What data points would you use if you were trying to show that the changes were not changing as fast as some people are claiming?

On-the-Spot Engineering

Choose a partner. Decide on a real-world situation for which an engineer would need to know how quickly something is changing at any given instance in time, such as during one second or maybe even over a shorter amount of time. Decide on a different real-world situation where it would be important for the person to know how quickly something was changing over a longer period of time, such as an hour, day, week, or longer. (*Teacher's Note:* This may be better to assign at the start of the year in calculus. Doing so should allow you to avoid students merely citing examples already in your text. This activity also can be used as a lead-in to the discussion of limits and how small is small enough.)

REAL-WORLD CONNECTIONS

Purpose

Often times, the rule of the day in mathematics classrooms is abstraction. Theorems, proofs, laws, and formulas all tend to be discussed and applied in ways that have little bearing on a student's everyday life. Real-World Connections activities help teachers and students cut through this abstraction by giving students the chance to learn mathematical concepts and apply mathematical operations to authentic contexts, such as solving personal problems, making good decisions, and analyzing real-world data.

Overview

When students can see how various mathematical concepts affect their lives or the lives of others, their interest in and commitment to learning mathematics grows. The intersections between mathematics and the world beyond school are everywhere. Retail, sports, finance, cooking, home building, and advertising are all saturated with mathematics. Using these real-world contexts as a base or beginning point, you can ask students to:

- Observe and identify natural or artificial phenomena in the world.
- Cite real-world examples or practical uses of specific mathematical content.
- Use data and statistics to calculate probability, generate hypotheses, or make predictions.
- Resolve conflicts using evidence, logic, and all available data.
- Analyze data and statistics to identify patterns and make decisions.

The information used to craft a Real-World Connections activity can be drawn from current events, encyclopedias, periodicals, popular culture, advertising, geography, politics, or anywhere else. Relevant and genuine information can come from *The New York Times* or your school's weekly newspaper, from *www.ESPN.com* or the statistics for the junior varsity volleyball team, from *Ranger Rick* or a local environment center. You can also turn to teachers of other subjects for content and inspiration. For example, you might ask students interdisciplinary questions about:

- Data collected on flowering plants grown in the school's laboratory.
- Geometric shapes in the abstract art they saw on a recent field trip.
- The mathematic importance of a single vote in the close U.S. Presidential Elections of 1960 and 2000.

Steps

1. Introduce (or review) the mathematical concepts you want your students to practice.
2. Generate an appropriate mathematical problem and frame it in a relevant and authentic real-world context.
3. Allow students time to discuss their work and answers with a partner or within a small group.
4. Review the problem and possible solutions with students.
5. Reinforce the point that the mathematical concepts being studied are useful and important to students outside of school.

Examples

Real-World Connections are everywhere. Here are some quick starters, or "connectors," to help you integrate the real world into your mathematics classroom:

Best Free Throw Shooter

Use our school's varsity basketball cumulative data for free throws (provided by teacher) to decide which player should shoot a game's last-second free throw. Explain your decision.

Predicting the CPI

Predict the value of the average U.S. Consumer Price Index (CPI) for both 2015 and 2050, using the data within the table found at: ftp://ftp.bls.gov/pub/special.requests/cpi/cpiai.txt. Explain your calculations. (For more information on the CPI, visit the U.S. Department of Labor, Bureau of Labor Statistics website at: www.bls.gov/cpi/.)

Common Classroom Measurements

Using units of measure of your choosing, find the area and perimeter of a:

- Student ID card.
- Mathematics textbook cover (text for this course).
- Classroom desktop.
- Classroom bulletin board (largest in the classroom).
- Floor (either a classroom or the library).
- Ceiling (either a classroom or the library).

Home Versus Road Winning Percentages

Use our school's varsity basketball scores to find the average (mean) number of points per game scored by both our team and the opposing team. Are those averages the same if you only consider our home games or only our away games?

Comparative Shopping

Look at the costs of three comparable items in four different local store advertisements. Identify and defend the best buy for each item, as well as determine which store offers the best buy for all three items.

Male and Female Students

How does the probability of being born male (or female) compare with the male/female enrollment of our class and of our school?

Height of the Class

Would you expect that the distribution of the heights of all students (in inches) in our class to be *normally* distributed? (68% within 1 S.D., 94% within 2 S.D., etc.) Are they?

Fuel Economy

Find the Environmental Protection Agency (EPA) ratings for four different vehicles in one category (choose one category of vehicles from minivan, pickup truck, sports-utility vehicle, crossover, sedan, midsize, compact, etc.). How many gallons of gas would each of the four vehicles you selected use if they were driven 0 miles, 5,000 miles, 10,000 miles, 15,000 miles, 20,000 miles, and 35,000 miles? Plot these six points on a graph and connect them. What kind of graph do you get? What does the

EPA rating tell you about your graph? How much money would be spent on fuel in a year to operate each of the four vehicles? Would you expect the graph of these values to be the same shape as your first graph? Justify your answer. What other things besides fuel costs would you need to consider in order to find the true operating cost of each of the four vehicles? If you graphed the true operating cost of each vehicle, would the graph be the same shape as the first one?

WHAT'S YOUR FAVORITE?

Purpose

A common challenge shared by many teachers of mathematics is hooking and sustaining their students' attention and interest. What's Your Favorite? is a tool designed to increase student engagement in learning by allowing them to identify personal preferences or "favorites." These personal favorites then become the "center of attention" in the classroom, as teaching and learning are designed around them.

Overview

Students can collaborate in small teams or reflect on their own to develop their "favorite" information. This information is then incorporated into the lesson, becoming a series of coordinates, collection of statistics, table of values, foundation for a word problem, or any other form of mathematical data. The inclusion of student input into classroom activities leads to increased student engagement, more focused attention, and deeper understanding of mathematical concepts and procedures.

Steps

1. Design a question (or set of questions) that requires students to input their "favorite" information. This information can consist of numbers, operations, procedures, etc., or it can be qualitative (e.g., favorite television show, favorite actor, favorite toy, favorite sport).
2. Allow students time to generate their favorite information.
3. Have students work individually or in small teams to apply their favorite information to complete a task or solve a problem.
4. Remind students to share their favorite information and solutions with the class.

Examples

Favorite Shape

1. Pick your favorite shape from the list.

Figure 5.11 What's Your Favorite Shape?

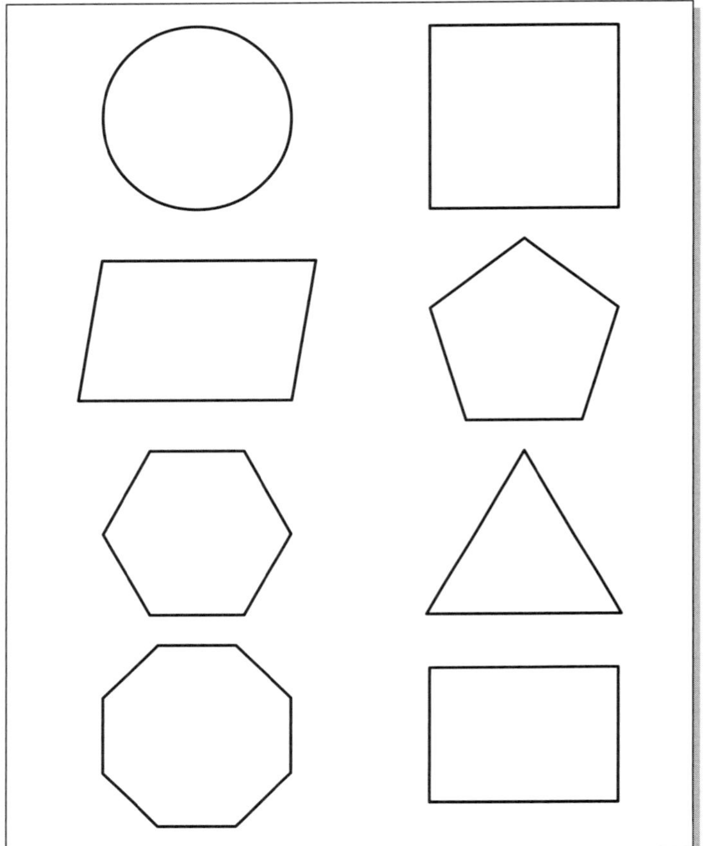

2. Draw your favorite shape and color it, using your favorite color.
3. Under your shape, tell why it is your favorite. Include at least two critical attributes of your shape in your explanation.
4. Find a student who chose a different shape. Exchange your shapes and explain in words why you chose your shape.
5. Compare and contrast your two shapes. What is similar about them? How are they different?
6. Pick one more shape from the list. Use the three shapes (your favorite, your partner's favorite, the third shape you just selected) to create a unique and interesting design.

We All Scream for Ice Cream

1. What are your two favorite flavors of ice cream? Meet in a group of three or four students. Create and label a histogram of your group's favorite ice cream flavors.
2. Collect the ice cream choices from three other groups
3. Represent the data from all four groups as a pie chart.
4. Compare your pie chart with the pie charts of groups with different data.
5. From all of the pie charts you have seen, can you tell which are our class's favorite and least favorite ice cream flavors?
6. In your original small group, compose a question that could be answered using the classroom data you have collected.
7. For homework, each member of your group should use the Internet or library to find the three most popular flavors of ice cream in the United States. How do the results from our class compare with the nation's favorite flavors?

Percentage Preference

What is your favorite percentage?

1. Write your "favorite" percentage. Don't forget to include the "%" symbol.
2. Re-write your favorite percentage as a simplified fraction and a decimal.
3. Meet with a partner and exchange simplified fractions.
4. Without help, re-write your partner's fraction as a decimal and a percentage.
5. You and your partner meet with another pair of students. As a new group of four, confirm that the decimals and fractions for each original favorite percentage are correct.

Sports and Central Tendency

1. Meet in a group with four other students.
2. If you play a sport, what is your jersey number? If you don't play a sport, what is the number of your favorite athlete? (If you are not a big sports fan, pick any two-digit number.)
3. Write your group's numbers down from smallest to largest.
4. Does your set of numbers have a mode? If so, what is it?
5. Does your set of numbers have a median? If so, what is it?
6. What is the mean of your set of numbers?
7. Assign each member of your group a letter (a, b, c, d, and e). Replace each letter with that person's number in the following equation and then solve the equation for x:

   $a + bx + c(x + d) = e$

Favorite Single-Digit Numbers

Excluding zero, what are your top three favorite single-digit numbers? From these three numbers, you can create examples, present ideas, or complete problems as in the activities below.

- Use your three numbers to find the volume and total surface area of a box with those dimensions. (geometry)
- Insert your three numbers as the values for a, h, and k in the parabolic equation $y = a(x - h)^2 + k$. Make a proper fraction using any two of the numbers and let that equal the value of a. Also, make sure that one of the numbers you use is negative. (advanced algebra)
- Your three numbers are the values a, b, and c in the equation $y = a \sin(bx) + c$. (pre-calculus)
- Create an integration problem with values including all three of your numbers. (calculus)

WHO'S RIGHT?

Purpose

Who's Right? presents students with a scenario in which two people are having difficulty reaching an agreement. At the center of the dispute is a mathematical problem, situation, or claim. By asking students to examine the situation closely and apply mathematical concepts and procedures to determine Who's Right?, the strategy engages students in deep and personal forms of thinking.

Overview

The Who's Right? activity puts a premium on student engagement by situating learning within the context of a personal dispute. The teacher presents a scenario or story in which two or more people generate competing (even contradictory) answers to a mathematical problem. After students read (or listen to) the problem, they use what they know about the situation and the mathematical concepts at work to figure out who's right. Students cite evidence—contextual clues, subjective information, their own calculations—to help explain their thinking and decision-making process.

Who's Right? can also be used to help students learn to analyze claims and use mathematics to make powerful arguments. To develop a Who's Right? activity that focuses on constructing powerful arguments, the scenario should be more qualitative in nature. The answer to the problem at hand should not yield to simple right/wrong logic. Instead, the argument might call for the student to use statistics to decide which player is most deserving of baseball's National League MVP award or to support or refute a claim such as: *If cigarettes are banned, the life expectancy of Americans would rise by more than one full year.*

Steps

1. Select or generate a problem with two or more possible solutions. Decide whether the problem will be quantitative (right/wrong answers) or qualitative (analyzing claims and developing a mathematically sound position).

2. Situate the problem inside the context of a dispute between two or more people.
3. Have students carefully read (or listen to) the scenario and study whatever positions or decisions were stated.
4. Allow students time to consider the problem and work, individually or in small groups, to determine Who's Right?
5. Facilitate a classroom discussion in which students have the opportunity to explain their choices.

Examples

Average Autumn Temperature

On the calendar below are written the high and low temperatures (in Fahrenheit) for one week in October. What is the average temperature for the week?

Figure 5.12 Calendar of Daily Average Temperatures

October						
Sunday	**Monday**	**Tuesday**	**Wednesday**	**Thursday**	**Friday**	**Saturday**
4	*5*	*6*	*7*	*8*	*9*	*10*
58	60	61	58	57	62	63
49	51	50	48	46	52	55

Three students responded to the question with three different answers. Who is right? Why do you think that student is right?

Alex's answer: 55
Carmen's answer: 56
Gina's answer: 58

Can you explain how each student might have found his or her answer?

(*Note:* The correct answer is 55; average temperature usually is found using the mean of the daily averages of highs and lows.)

Pizza Problem

On their way back from a basketball game, four brothers stop at a pizzeria for dinner. The brothers decide to order a large square pizza and share it. Terrence, the oldest brother, says that since the pizza is cut into 9 equal slices, the oldest brother should get three slices and the younger brothers should get two slices each. The second brother, James, says that he knows of a way to cut the square pizza so that each brother has an equal amount of square slices. Not wanting to lose out on any pizza, both younger brothers say James is right. Who's right—how could the square pizza be cut so that each brother gets an equal amount of square slices?

Fraction Faux Pas

Two students were racing to solve a mixed fraction problem. Allison attempted the problem using her calculator and Lauren wrote out all of her calculations. The problem is: $2\frac{1}{3} \div 5\frac{5}{6}$. Allison quickly punched in keys to come up with an answer of 0.4. Lauren wrote down the following: $\frac{3}{7} \bullet \frac{31}{6} = \frac{93}{42} = \frac{31}{14} = 2\frac{3}{14}$.

Write out the steps in Allison's calculations and compare them to Lauren's notations. Who's right?

64 the Hard Way

Three students all agree that $= \frac{16}{64} = \frac{1}{4}$, but their explanations (below) are different. Whose work is correct? Whose work is incorrect? Explain why.

Marcel's work: $\frac{16}{64} = \frac{2^4}{2^6} = 2^{4-6} = 2^{-2} = \frac{1}{4}$

Amanda's work: $\frac{16}{64} = \frac{2 \bullet 2 \bullet 2 \bullet 2}{2 \bullet 2 \bullet 2 \bullet 2 \bullet 2 \bullet 2 \bullet 2 \bullet 2} = \frac{1}{2 \bullet 2} = \frac{1}{4}$

Chris's work: Easy, cross out the 6's in $\frac{16}{64}$, and all that's left is $\frac{1}{4}$.

REFLECTIVE WRITING

Purpose

The pressures associated with "covering the content" often lead to mathematics classrooms where students have little time to reflect. But reflection, as memory expert Marilee Sprenger (2005) tells us, is not some luxury to be squeezed in a few times a year; reflection—or the process of looking back on your learning to see what you know, how you think, where you need to go next—is a requirement for learning. Reflection can and must be taught. The question is: What do good reflective practices look like in the mathematics classroom?

Overview

Reflection can take place at any time during the lesson. At the beginning of a lesson, students may be asked to think about what they already know about a particular topic and to identify what they hope to learn. During a lesson, reflection activities can be used to facilitate processing. Students are given time to think about the content they are learning, generate questions, determine "trouble spots," and seek clarification. At the end of a lesson, students should reflect on their comfort level with the content, their personal reactions and feelings, and how they can make use of their new learning.

Steps

1. Discuss with students the value of reflection for learning.
2. Model the reflection process for students.
3. Prior to the lesson, identify where you will use reflection questions and what you will sask your students to reflect upon.
4. Pose the reflection question and have your students record their thoughts in their personal journals or Learning Logs.
5. Encourage your students to use their journals to reflect upon their learning regularly.
6. Assess how well your students are able to reflect. Be sure to consider the quality of their ideas as well as the sincerity of their thoughts.

Examples

The following Reflective Writing activities fall into four categories: content-specific reflections, personal-preference reflections, general mathematics reflections, and reflections on students' feelings and levels of comfort:

Content-specific reflections:

- Having completed our lesson on percent word problems, react to at least two of the following:
  - Today, I learned . . .
  - Now, I understand . . .
  - I still wonder about . . .
  - I appreciate how we . . .
- Tomorrow is our test on fractions; take out your Learning Log and answer the three questions below:
  - What type of fraction problem gave you the most trouble to learn? (Cite an example.)
  - What made it harder than the other types of problems?
  - What questions do you have about it so that you can better prepare for the test?
- How would you explain the concept of *slope* (or *long division, internal tangents, circular permutations, limits, outliers,* or many other concepts, depending on the course) to a friend?
- Which theorem in this unit was originally, or is now, the most unclear to you? What makes it hard to understand?

- How did studying the chapter on probability change your view on the use of mathematics in the real world?
- Our calculus class just concluded the *Rates of Change* unit. Identify one unit concept that you feel you know well. Give three specific suggestions that you would make to help someone who was struggling with that same concept.

Personal-preference reflections:

- Would you rather be an odd number or an even number? Explain why.
- Would you characterize your school year so far as an equation or an expression? Explain why.
- Which type of triangle is most representative of your personality? Explain why.
- Do you see yourself as differentiable or non-differentiable? Why?

General mathematics reflections:

- Think about all that you did in class today. Take out your personal Learning Log and, in your own words, write: *What you believe was the most important thing that I wanted you to learn today.* Do you feel that you learned it? (Yes or No.) If we were to begin class tomorrow with a review, what should we discuss that is still somewhat unclear to you? What did this unit *add* to your understanding of mathematics?
- You have been asked to solve many word problems. Think about the things that you do when you confront a word problem. Write down steps/advice that might help someone who really struggles with word problems.
- What is mathematics? What do you like most about it? What do you like least?

Reflections about students' feelings/level of comfort:

Select one of the following emoticons to express how you feel about today's (or this week's) lesson. Tell why you chose it.

WRITING ABOUT THE PROBLEM OF THE DAY

This writing-based approach to analyzing one's own problem-solving abilities was developed by Wendy Lee Reddy, a fifth-grade teacher from Errick Road Elementary School in North Tonawanda, New York. *Thank you again, Wendy.*

Purpose

While challenging students to solve a mathematical "problem-of-the-day" may be a common activity in today's mathematics classrooms, using a problem-solving model that makes covert thinking processes visible may not. Writing About the Problem of the Day encourages students to explain their mathematical thinking in writing, providing a reflective tool for the student and assessment data for the teacher to drive instruction. In this model, student focus is shifted away from simply producing algorithmically correct answers. Instead, students must provide "evidence in writing" that shows they know or can plan mathematical approaches to problem-solving. And perhaps most important of all, this tool grants permission for students to be "stuck." This is critical to student growth since the recognition that getting stuck is normal allows students to zero in on difficulties and overcome them.

Overview

Writing About the Problem of the Day uses a thinking and brainstorming organizer (see Organizer 5-D) that provides students with an organized, sequential means to communicate their mathematical thinking, pose questions, hypothesize, and "try out" their theories in a safe, non-threatening context. The organizer is divided into three sections. The first asks students to explain what they think the problem means or is asking them to do. The second section asks students to provide a written hypothesis or plan for solving the problem. For the final section, students either solve the problem or explain where they are "stuck" in the process. This safety net builds confidence and curiosity because students know that the end goal is not necessarily to formulate one, correct answer. It is often more academically profitable to explore the possibilities and identify personal obstacles.

Steps

1. Introduce the tool, Writing About the Problem of the Day, providing an overview of its central tenets that writing is thinking and that it's okay to be stuck in mathematics.
2. At the start of a lesson, present a puzzling mathematical problem (e.g., on a white board, overhead projector, student worksheet).
3. Allow students time to think and work through the problem using the organizer (see Organizer 5-D for a blank template). After students work independently, follow up with small group sharing in which students exchange ideas and problem-solving strategies.
4. Remind students that the idea is to postulate ideas and plan strategies for solving mathematical problems in writing, although numbers, figures and symbols can certainly be used.
5. Students may use the last section of the organizer to indicate where they are "stuck." Conversely, they may provide a solution to the problem along with a written explanation.
6. Circulate around the classroom to facilitate learning. You may want to select students as expert tutors to provide one-to-one instruction for the "stuck" learners, or you may elect to review the problem in small-group or whole-class formats.

Examples

Processing Problems Through Writing

Below are examples of how two different students approached and processed their "Problem of the Day."

Figure 5.13 Processing the Problem of the Day: *Feeding Pets*

Processing the Problem of the Day Using Write to Learn

What I think the math problem means in my own words...

Gerbils are fed every 2nd day
Fish are fed every 3rd day
Snakes are fed every 4th day
All fed today
How many days until all fed again?

Here's what I think I need to do to solve the problem... I think I need to make a matrix to solve the problem.

S	M	T	W	T	F	S
	all		g	F	gs	
gF		gs	F	g		(gsF)
	gF		sgF	F	g	
gsF		g		Fgs		g
F	gs		gF		gs	F
g		Fgs		g	F	gs
	gF		sg	F	g	

12 days

Key
g-gerbils
F-fish
S-snakes

This is what I don't get (Help, I'm stuck!) OR...I do get it and here's my solution in words and numbers!

I made a matrix & I counted how many days until each animal was fed. Then, when there were three letters in the closest square, I counted how many spaces there were until I got to the circled square. 12 days after today, all animals will be fed.

The stratagy I did (a matrix) helped me organize my work.

Figure 5.14 Processing the Problem of the Day: *Measuring a Yard*

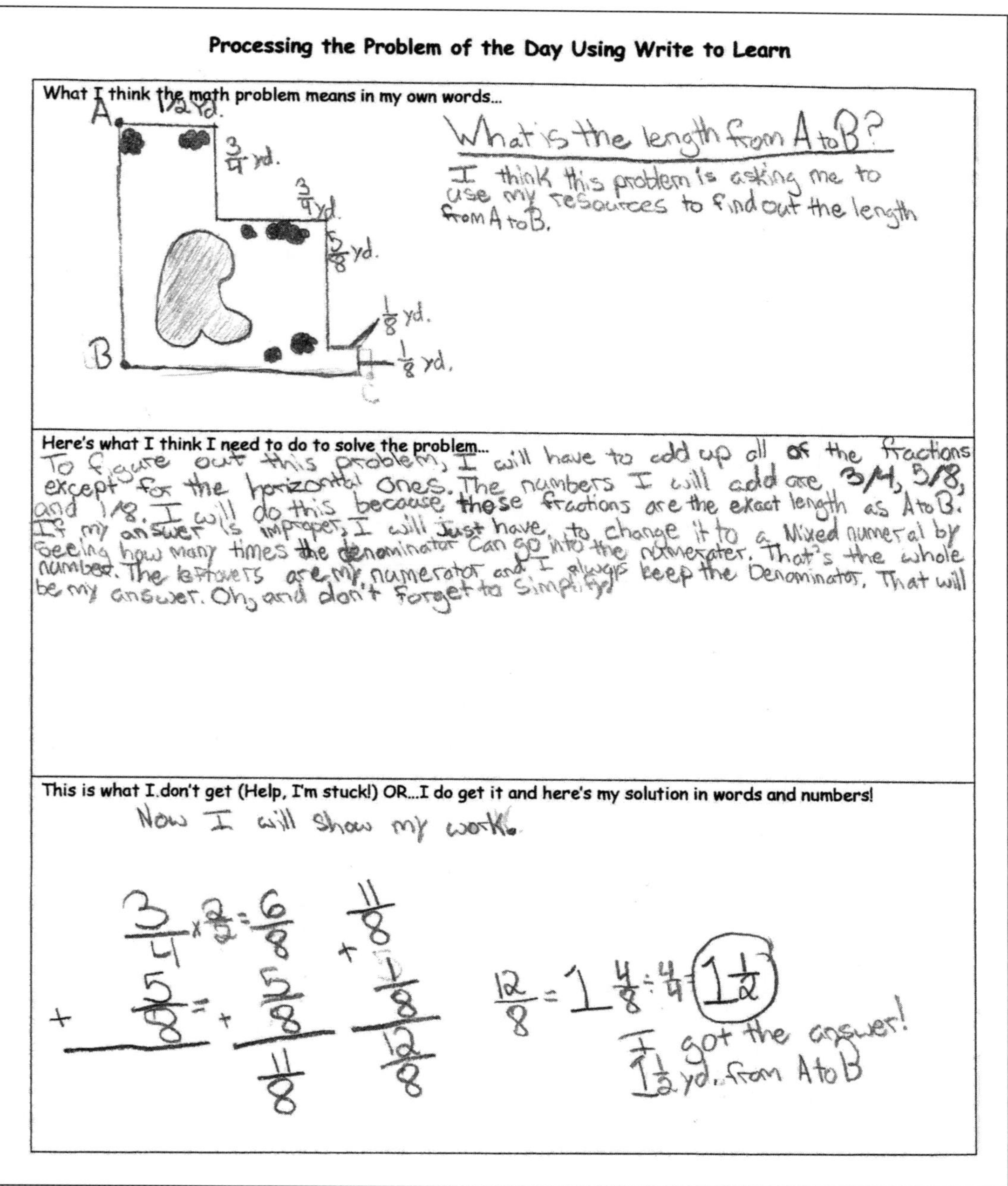

Processing the Problem of the Day Using Write to Learn

What I think the math problem means in my own words...

What is the length from A to B?

I think this problem is asking me to use my resources to find out the length from A to B.

Here's what I think I need to do to solve the problem...

To figure out this problem, I will have to add up all of the fractions except for the horizontal ones. The numbers I will add are 3/4, 5/8, and 1/8. I will do this because these fractions are the exact length as A to B. If my answer is improper, I will just have to change it to a mixed numeral by seeing how many times the denominator can go into the numerater. That's the whole number. The leftovers are my numerator and I always keep the Denominator. That will be my answer. Oh, and don't forget to simplify!

This is what I don't get (Help, I'm stuck!) OR...I do get it and here's my solution in words and numbers!

Now I will show my work.

$\frac{3}{4} \times \frac{2}{2} = \frac{6}{8}$

$+ \frac{5}{8} = + \frac{5}{8}$

$\frac{11}{8}$

$\frac{11}{8} + \frac{1}{8} = \frac{12}{8}$

$\frac{12}{8} = 1\frac{4}{8} \div \frac{4}{4} = 1\frac{1}{2}$

I got the answer! $1\frac{1}{2}$ yd. from A to B

Writing Your Way Out of Being Stuck

In the following alternative organizer, a student analyzes a problem, writes about why she was stuck, and then explains how she worked her way through the problem.

Figure 5.15 Why I Was Stuck With *Common Denominators*

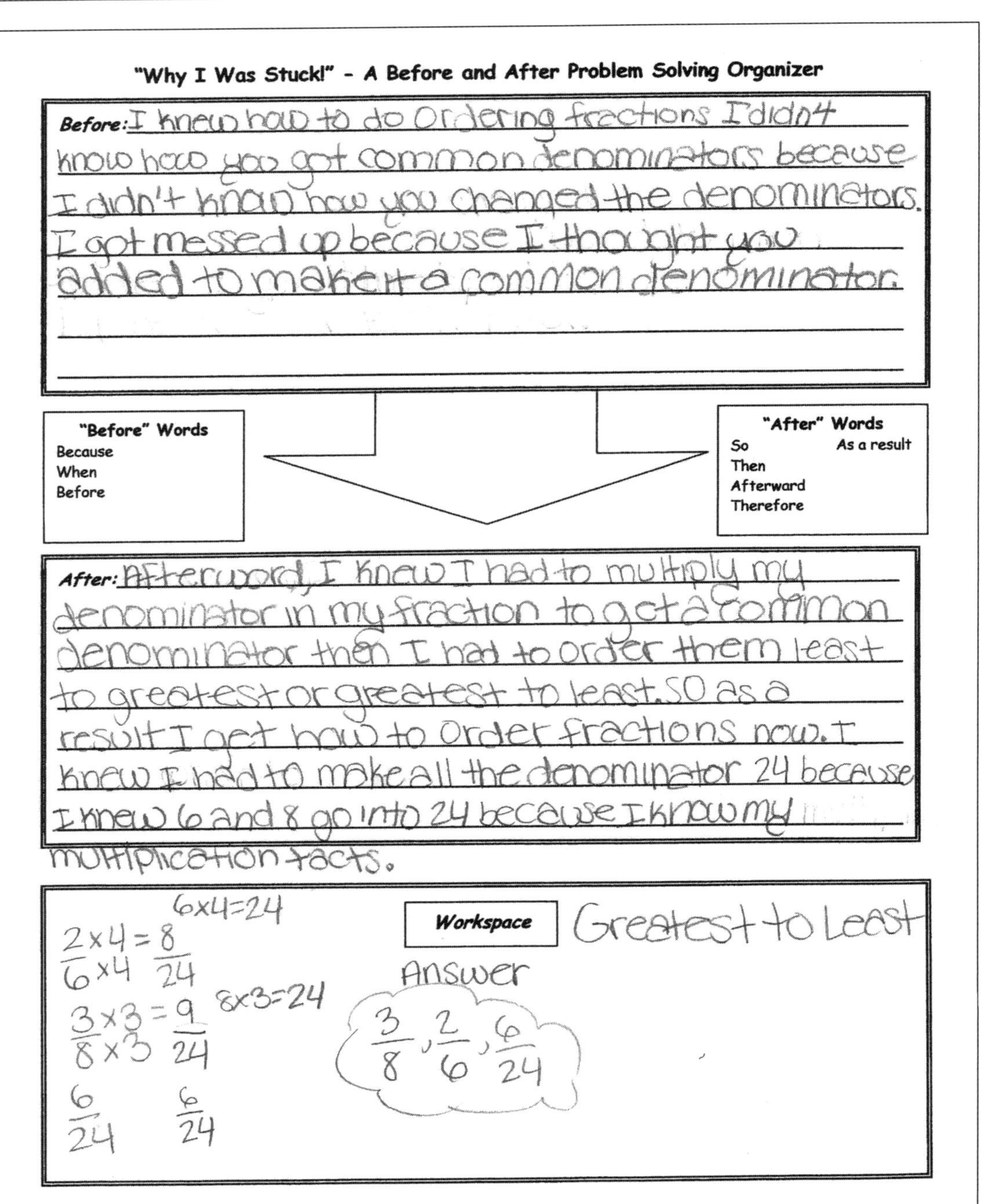

"Why I Was Stuck!" - A Before and After Problem Solving Organizer

Before: I knew how to do Ordering fractions I didn't know how you got common denominators because I didn't know how you changed the denominators. I got messed up because I thought you added to make it a common denominator.

"Before" Words
Because
When
Before

"After" Words
So
As a result
Then
Afterward
Therefore

After: Afterword, I knew I had to multiply my denominator in my fraction to get a common denominator then I had to order them least to greatest or greatest to least. So as a result I get how to order fractions now. I knew I had to make all the denominator 24 because I knew 6 and 8 go into 24 because I know my multiplication facts.

Workspace Greatest to Least

$6 \times 4 = 24$

$\frac{2 \times 4}{6 \times 4} = \frac{8}{24}$

$8 \times 3 = 24$

$\frac{3 \times 3}{8 \times 3} = \frac{9}{24}$

$\frac{6}{24}$ $\frac{6}{24}$

Answer

$\frac{3}{8}, \frac{2}{6}, \frac{6}{24}$

Organizer 5-D Blank Problem of the Day Organizer

Writing About the Problem of the Day **Name:** ______________________ **Date:** ______________
What I think the math problem means in my own words . . .
Here's what I think I need to do to solve the problem . . .
This is what I don't get (Help, I'm stuck!) or . . . I do get it and here's my solution in words and numbers!

TEST FEEDBACK

Purpose

Too often, teachers and students see the test as the end of learning. (The test is taken, the grade received, and the next unit is under way.) This is especially problematic in mathematics, since new learning is built on students' prior knowledge of mathematical concepts and procedures. Test Feedback (Silver, Strong, & Perini, 2001) is a reflection tool that helps students assess their performance on a test, retain more information, and take an active approach to learning in which test-taking is part of continuous learning.

Overview

Cramming instead of studying may enable students to pass a test, but it does nothing to deepen their understanding or to increase their retention of information. But with so much of students' present and future academic success riding on tests, it is critical to teach students how to reflect on their study skills, test-taking routines, and the quality of their learning once the test is over. Test Feedback is a metacognitive tool that prompts students to look back on:

- The structure and content of the test;
- Their performance on the test; and
- How well they prepared for the test.

After a period of guided reflection using a Test Feedback form (see Figure 5.16 for an example), the teacher leads a discussion to help expose classwide patterns, identify common areas of difficulty, and explore ideas for preparing more effectively for the next test.

Another significant benefit of Test Feedback is the insight it provides to teachers about how well their students understand their own levels of comprehension. For instance, some students, who have done poorly on a test, may feel that they have done well. This mismatch between performance and self-evaluation is often a sign that the student misunderstands or has improperly applied a core concept affecting the entire test (for example, the cross multiplication procedure on a percentage test). On the other hand, when students perform well but evaluate their performance harshly, it is often an indication of "knowing without understanding." The student can plug information into the procedures but has little conceptual understanding of how the mathematics works or what it means. Armed with this kind of data about students' self-perceptions, the teacher can make better decisions about test design (e.g., does it assess deeper understanding or just procedural competence?) and how to help individual learners target areas needing improvement.

Steps

1. Generate a Test Feedback form and provide it to students after they have completed a test.
2. Allow students time to reflect and fill out the form.
3. Encourage students to think about the test, how they prepared for the test, and which mathematical concepts were clear or challenging.
4. Lead a discussion in which students share their responses and explore questions about the test specifically or the mathematics concepts in general.

Examples

Figure 5.16 Test Feedback Worksheet—*Place Value and Rounding*

Name: ____________________ Date: ____________________

Test Feedback Worksheet

How do you feel about your performance on this test? (circle one)

Great! Good OK Not sure . . . Uh oh!

Do you think your performance on this test is a good indicator of what you know about place value and rounding? Why or why not?

Was this test more like . . .

. . . rounding up (rounding from 1.6 up to 2)?

. . . rounding down (rounding 1.4 down to 1)?

. . . staying the same (keeping 1.0 as 1)?

How much time did you spend studying for this test?

I spent about

☐ WEEKS ☐ DAYS ☐ HOURS ☐ MINUTES

studying for this test.

How well did the classroom activities prepare you for the test? (circle one)

0	1	2	3	4	5

not at all … very well

What else would you like to add to demonstrate your knowledge and understanding of place values and rounding?

RANGE FINDER

Purpose

As William Glasser's *Choice Theory* (1998) has shown, the freedom to make choices is one of the most intrinsically motivating activities for a human brain. Range Finder gives students the opportunity to select their own learning path, to examine a set of mathematical activities, and to decide which activity best suits their current levels of comfort and skill. Aside from its motivational benefits to students, Range Finder also serves as an instant assessment tool for teachers. The choices students make and their ability to complete their chosen tasks provides a snapshot of information:

- How well do students understand the content?
- How well can students apply mathematical procedures?
- How comfortable are students with the concepts?

Overview

To initiate Range Finder in any classroom, the teacher selects an appropriate topic and generates three activities of varying levels of difficulty. Students are then given the freedom to choose the activity they want to complete. The goal for teacher and students is to help each student take a "Goldilocks" approach to decision making by surveying all three activities and finding the one that's "just right." After students have made their selection and as they work through their respective activities, the teacher monitors student progress. The teacher can quickly get a sense of students' confidence and proficiency with the mathematical concepts by looking at what students are working on and how well they are doing. Often, Range Finder is employed at the start of a lesson or unit to gauge students' prior knowledge and retention, as well as to help the teacher design and plan classroom activities for the lesson or unit.

Steps

1. Identify the mathematical concepts and skills you want to assess.
2. Generate a set of three activities, each at a different level of difficulty.
3. Allow students to choose an activity to complete. Students should be encouraged to attempt the most difficult activity they are comfortable with.
4. Give students time to work through the activity they selected.
5. Walk around the room to identify which activities students chose and to monitor student performance.
6. Use your observations to help make decisions with your students about future learning opportunities.
7. Have students share and discuss their work in small groups or as a class.

Examples

Percentages

Select one of the lists below and convert each item on the list into a percentage.

Figure 5.17 Calculating Percentages

List 1	List 2	List 3
1/2 =	4/5 =	3 out of a dozen =
9/10 =	8/9 =	20 minutes of an hour =
25 out of 25 =	19 out of 20 =	5 inches of 1 yard =
4/10 =	150/100 =	999 out of 1,000 =
3/5 =	16/96 =	5/750 =
1 out of 100 =	2/1 =	20/21 =
7/21 =	13 out of 52 =	0 out of 10 =
1/4 =	15/60 =	1 day of a week =
3/5 =	5/250 =	5 months of 1 year =
91/100 =	11 out of 99 =	31/35 =

Surface Area of Three-Dimensional Figures

Calculate the surface area for one of the three-dimensional figures below.

Figure 5.18 Surface Area of Three-Dimensional Figures

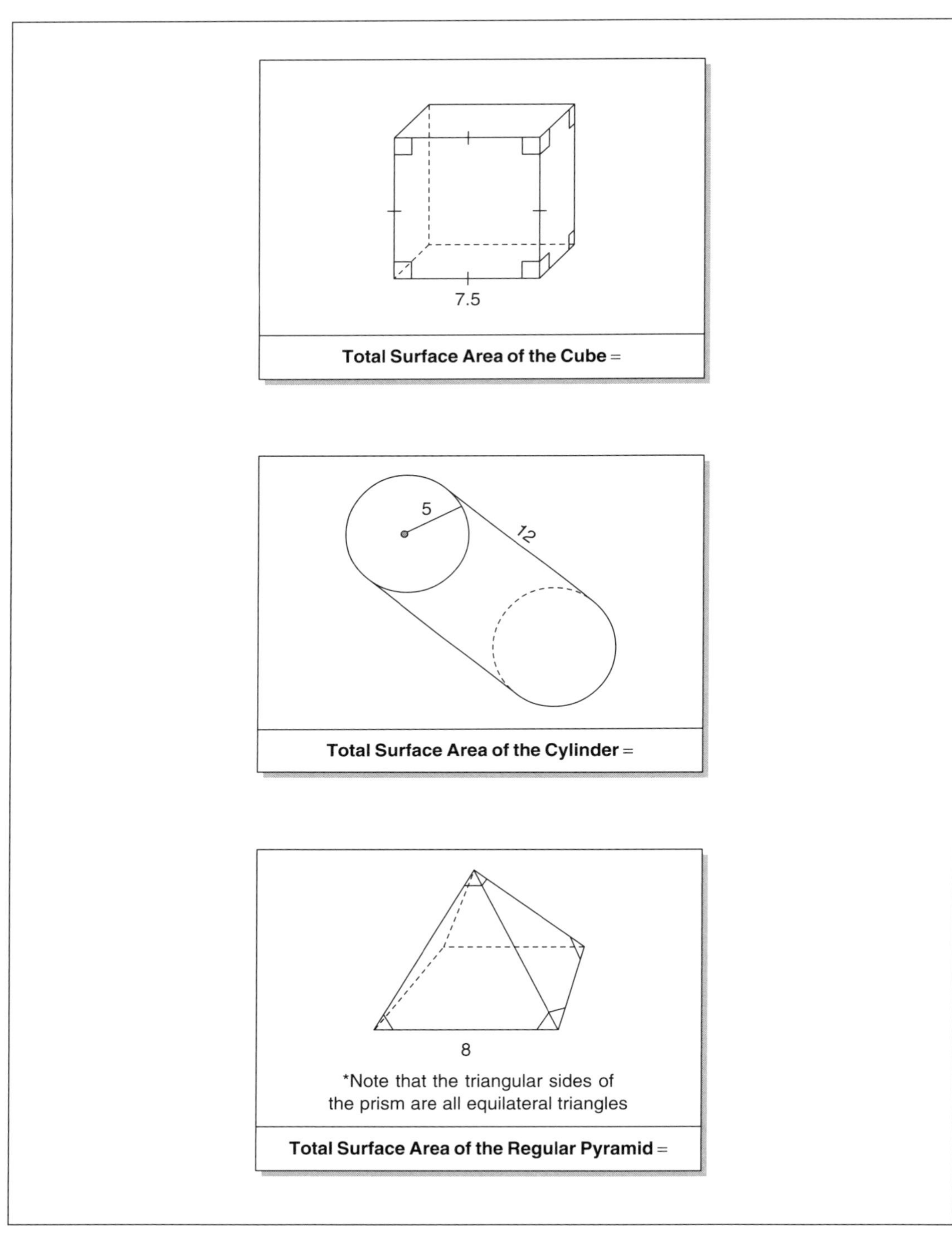

Distance Word Problems

Solve one of the word problems below by sketching the situation and making the necessary calculations.

Figure 5.19 Distance Word Problems

	Your neighbor is standing at the top of a 14 foot tall ladder, which is leaning against your neighbor's house. The base of the ladder is 4 feet from the house. How far off the ground is your neighbor?
	You are on a calm lake fishing from a small boat. You anchor your boat and while fishing, you end up floating 25 feet to the east. If your anchor rope is 35 feet long, how deep is the lake at the spot you dropped anchor?
	You are going skydiving, and your plane is cruising at 180 mph at an altitude of 11,000 feet. You jump from the plane and freefall for 45 seconds before deploying your parachute at 3,000 feet. After deploying your parachute, you float safely to the ground. If the plane you jumped from continues at the same speed and altitude, approximately how far away will you be from the plane at the moment you deploy your parachute? (You may ignore glide ratio and assume your freefall toward earth followed a straight path.)

MATH BOGGLE

Purpose

Board games like Boggle, Outburst, and Scattergories, to name a few, are popular because they are competitive, fun, and relatively simple to play. The Math Boggle tool (which borrows its name from the popular board game Boggle), engages students in a competitive review game in which their knowledge of mathematical concepts earns them points.

Overview

Math Boggle offers students an opportunity to review and study mathematical concepts in a way that is fun, exciting, and memorable. The teacher selects a topic, lesson, or concept(s) that will be the focus of the game. After presenting or reviewing the content for Math Boggle, students are given time to review their notes and pick out big ideas, important details, and key concepts. The teacher then has students set their notebooks and textbooks aside. With nothing but their memories to assist them, students are given 3 to 5 minutes to jot down as much information as they can retrieve on a blank sheet of paper. Students then gather in small teams (three to four students) to discuss their lists, share ideas, and add information that they did not think of themselves. It is critical that students work together to make sure all team members have as much information as possible since they will need it for the competitive round that follows.

For the competitive round of Math Boggle, students leave their teams to play against other students one-on-one (or in groups of three). Students "boggle" or compare their lists against the list(s) of their opponent(s). One point is scored for each item that appears on the student's own list that does not also appear on an opponent's list. Students return to their initial teams to total their points. Together, the teacher and the class review the content—especially those items that earned teams the most points.

While Math Boggle is an effective classroom activity on its own, it is especially powerful when combined with both the Memory Box (see pages 23–25) and Most Valuable Point (see pages 25–27) tools. By having students complete Memory Boxes, determine and explain their Most Valuable Point, and then use Math Boggle to review and compete, you help them build strong and long-lasting memories of key content.

Steps

1. Present (or review) key mathematical concepts with students.
2. Allow students time to review their notes (3 to 5 minutes).
3. Have students generate a list of as many related ideas as they can remember (three to five minutes). Students should work from memory without help from their notebooks or textbooks.
4. Organize students into small teams (three or four students) so they can share, discuss, and collect more information.
5. Pair students up and have them "boggle" for 3 minutes. Students score a point for every idea on their list that is not on their opponent's list.

6. Have students rejoin their original teams and tally their scores.
7. Review all of the ideas generated during the activity, paying particular attention to those items that earned students points.

Examples

Measuring Area

Take the next few minutes to look over your notes on the two methods we have learned for finding the area of a rectangle: the Counting Squares Method and the $A = l \bullet w$ formula. Now, close your notebooks and make sure your textbooks are put away. In the next 2 minutes, write down as much as you can remember about these two methods. Feel free to draw diagrams to help you remember key points. Once you are done, join a small study group and review your answers. Make sure you add any information that you may have missed; having a complete list will improve your chances to score points. Now we're ready to play Math Boggle!

VOCABULARY GAMES

Purpose

Many students who find mathematics difficult become excited and engaged when they get to learn with their classmates and when learning has an element of play to it. Vocabulary Games help students build command of critical terms by playing games with other students to reinforce their knowledge of mathematical terms, concepts, or theorems.

Overview

Games are naturally motivating and serve as one of the most effective ways to review and reinforce key vocabulary terms in preparation for a test. In using the games outlined in this section, you should emphasize the importance of learning together—of working with other students on fun activities that will improve students' mathematical vocabulary. At the same time, you should de-emphasize competition among students or groups of students, which can lead to a winner-takes-all mentality and dejection on the part of losing students or groups.

Steps

1. Decide how much time to commit to the game, what you want to accomplish during the game, and when the game will be played.
2. Select a game that meets your objectives.
3. Provide clear directions on how the game is played. De-emphasize competition by reminding students that the game represents a chance to learn together and have fun.
4. Once the game is over, allow students to review what they know well and what they still need to review before the test or next lesson.

Examples

Word Search Puzzle

Give students a word search puzzle and have the definitions of mathematical vocabulary terms be the clues instead of a simple list of words that are in the word search.

Math Bingo

Give students a list of twenty-four or more vocabulary terms. Have students place twenty-four of the terms and one "Free Space" on a 5 by 5 grid. (This gets students to create unique Bingo cards with no extra preparation time needed on the teacher's part.) Show the definitions for the terms on an overhead projector or computer one at a time. (Keep track of which definitions have been called out.) Students cross off the words matching the definitions called until someone has five in a row.

Classic Game Variations

Play variations of classic games like Jeopardy!, Battleship, Hangman, or Concentration using definitions or critical attributes of mathematical vocabulary. Visit the Quia website (*www.quia.com*) for game ideas and formats created by other teachers, or register and use the interactive website to create your own instructional activities and games.

Flash Card Challenge

Have students play Flash Card Challenge in pairs or small groups of three. In addition to generic mathematics flash cards, this game works very well with student-generated Knowledge Cards (see pages 20–22).

- *Two-student version:* Students take turns showing each other the front of the flash card. A point is awarded for each correct answer that a student gives. Students can either draw from the same deck of flash cards or divide one set in half.
- *Three-student version:* One student serves as the "dealer" for the two other students. The dealer reads or shows a flash card to the other two players. Whoever gives the correct answer first scores a point.

Crossword Puzzle

Give students a crossword puzzle using the definitions of mathematical vocabulary terms and theorems as the clues. These puzzles can be created by the teacher, by the students, or by using puzzle-generating freeware. You might use the definitions of vocabulary words from a textbook chapter or unit to create a crossword puzzle. Whether the mathematical vocabulary words and definitions you use are from a textbook chapter, glossary, or another source, the clues should reflect the critical attributes of the vocabulary words.

20 Questions

Make 20 Questions interactive by placing a mathematical vocabulary term or theorem on the back of each student. Have students ask as many as twenty questions as can be answered with either a "Yes" or a "No" to try to determine what concept is on their backs.

Math Tic-Tac-Toe

Select any nine tools or activities from this book that will help students deepen their comprehension of the mathematical vocabulary they are studying. Look through the matrices that open Chapters 2 through 5 (see pages 18–19, 64–65, 122–123, and 168–169) for an overview of the various vocabulary-oriented math tools that can be incorporated into your tic-tac-toe game. Across a 3 by 3 tic-tac-toe grid, distribute the nine math tools you selected (or any activities that you have designed). In order to "win" tic-tac-toe, students must complete any three of the nine activities to create a horizontal, vertical, or diagonal line of three in a row.

The comprehensive Geometry Tic-Tac-Toe game that follows was developed by Renee Watkins, a high-school mathematics teacher from Bowling Green, Kentucky.

Figure 5.20 Geometry Tic-Tac-Toe

Create Your Own	**Picture = 1,000 Words**	**Cinquains**
Create a game or puzzle that would help students review the definitions of vocabulary words for this unit.	Create a scrapbook or collage of pictures that illustrate twelve of the vocabulary words for this unit.	Choose two vocabulary words from this unit. Compose a cinquain (five-line poem) for each of the words. Each cinquain should include: 1 title word 2 adjectives 3 action verbs a 4-word phrase 1-word conclusion
Compare and Contrast	**Glossaries**	**Three-Way Tie**
Choose two vocabulary words from this unit. Describe each word seperately, then use their descriptions to draw out the similarities and differences between the words. Decide if the two concepts are more alike or more different, and explain your reasoning.	For each vocabulary word in this unit, create your own glossary definition. Make a diagram, sketch a picture, or write a description for each word and then make a connection to the word that will help you remember it.	Select three related vocabulary words from this unit and write them at the vertices of a triangle. Write a sentence along each side of the triangle connecting each pair of words. In the middle of the triangle, write a summary incorporating the words and your sentences.
Group and Label	**Write to Learn**	**Show Me**
Review the vocabulary words from this unit and place all of the words into groups based on their common attributes. Make sure you include a descriptive label for each group that you create.	Write a paragraph that describes either a man-made object or a natural phenomena that illustrates some of the geometric concepts we have been studying. As part of your writing, make sure you correctly use at least five vocabulary words in a meaningful way.	Choose two related vocabulary words from this unit. Identify the critical attributes of each word, then generate two examples and two non-examples for each word.

COOPERATIVE STRUCTURES FOR PROMOTING POSITIVE INTERDEPENDENCE

Purpose

A wide body of research demonstrates that students benefit when they learn in cooperation with their classmates. In addition, the NCTM Standards stress the importance of having students work in cooperative settings. Two questions that teachers ask in implementing cooperative learning activities in their classrooms include:

- How do I make sure that students recognize the importance of interdependence for group success?
- How do I discourage students from "slacking off" during group work? How do I ensure students are individually accountable for the work the group produces?

Overview

Cooperative Structures are founded on a simple idea: a product developed collaboratively is almost always superior to one produced alone. The six structures outlined below help mathematics teachers make the most of the cooperative learning tasks and activities they use in their classrooms. While each structure makes it nearly impossible for students to work separately, each structure also promotes a high level of individual accountability. By achieving this important balance between interdependence and personal responsibility, the six structures create an optimal cooperative learning atmosphere—one conducive to serious collaboration.

Steps

1. Discuss the values of cooperative learning and the importance of interdependence and individual accountability when working cooperatively.
2. Determine the structure that is best suited for achieving your lesson's goals.
3. Make sure students fully understand their role in each structure. Model roles if needed.
4. After groups complete their work, have them share their work.
5. Allow students to reflect on the cooperative process and how the particular structure affected their learning and group dynamics.

Examples

The following six Cooperative Structures are from *Tools for Promoting Active, In-Depth Learning* (Silver, Strong, & Perini, 2001).

United We Stand

In this technique, each group is required to produce one product that compiles each member's best work. For example, each group would develop one set of answers, one chart, one essay, one poem, one illustration, one graph, one diagram, one lab report, etc. Students understand that the group's product should be the result of everyone's efforts and that they will receive a shared grade.

- Organize students into groups of four and assign a geometric proof to each group. Have each group put their geometric proof on the board and present it to the class. Each student in the group will receive the same grade and each student will be responsible for one of the following tasks:
  - Draw and label the figure; write what is given and what needs to be proven.
  - Write out the statements and reasons for the proof.
  - Explain the proof to the class.
  - Answer any questions from the class or teacher (if there are no student questions, then the teacher will ask a couple of questions).
- Have all students respond to the following question as a pre-lab homework activity: How would you decide which water fountain in the school has the best water pressure, assuming you cannot use a water pressure gauge?

The next day, have small groups of students meet and decide which of their ideas would be the best method of measuring a fountain's water pressure. Before submitting their ideas to the teacher, students can elaborate on the one idea they agree is the best method. All of the students' ideas from each group are handed in; the one idea the group selected as being the best is listed first and marked with a star.

Different Strokes

With this technique, each group member is expected to provide an individual product after conferring with team members. This technique promotes divergent thinking since students are expected to look for many varied responses to the question. A problem or question is posed and, after group discussion, each student must formulate a unique and correct answer. Students are given credit for every correct group response that is different.

- Organize students into groups so they can review the concepts of area and perimeter. After allowing some time for review, give students two minutes to sketch as many different polygons as they can that have an area greater than the perimeter.
- Have students work in groups to come up with as many equations for parabolas as they can in $y = a(x - h)^2 + b$ form. Each of their parabolas must have integral zeroes and a vertex in the second quadrant.

Each to His Own

Group members first discuss and combine ideas. Then, each member of the group is required to produce an individual product. The group members then check with each other to compare answers. Credit is given for correct and matching responses.

- Have students discuss how to change decimals to fractions in their groups. Then, give each student the following list of decimals to convert into simplified fractions or mixed numbers. Once each student has completed converting the decimals on his or her own, students meet with their groups to compare their answers.

0.1	0.25	0.67	0.36
0.5	0.333	2.125	5.05
0.7575	2.84	0.001	5.55

• Give students a chance to meet in small groups to discuss how they can find exponential regression equations on their calculators given data points. After the discussion, assign students a small set of word problems from the textbook that involve exponential regression. The next day in class, students meet with their groups to check their homework.

Pick 'Em at Random

Students work together in a group, making sure that all members of the group have the same answer and can explain how they acquired the answer. The teacher then randomly calls on one student to represent the group and share the group's answer. A shared grade is given to each group member.

• Give students time to talk with their groups about adding and subtracting decimals. Then, have each student answer the following:

a. 0.37 + 3.07 =	d. 73.75 – 3.75 =
b. 0.003 + 3.42 =	e. 0.823 – 0.32 =
c. 457.7 – 4.577 =	f. 0.003 + 300.3 =

Once students have finished their calculations and conferred with their group, randomly call upon students to put their work on the board.

• Assign a research project about the use of statistics in journalism to groups of four students. Students are responsible for finding articles that discuss at least two of these terms: *mean*, *median*, or *mode*. Students must determine whether the terms were used correctly and can select an article from one of these sources. Each article should also include at least one graph or chart for students to analyze.

- Local newspaper
- National newspaper
- Magazine
- Internet (not from a newspaper or magazine website)

Allow students time during class to meet with their groups and discuss their findings. In their groups, students review the work each of them has done and make suggestions about how each group member could improve his or her project. All group members turn in their projects, but only one of the projects, selected randomly from each group, is graded.

Sign Off

This technique ensures student cooperation and accountability within the group structure. Each group member must sign all work that is submitted, but all members must agree that each student has done appropriate work before the signature is allowed. This technique promotes high levels of cooperation because the signature guarantees that all students have worked on the question, that they understand the answer, and that they can explain and defend the group's position if asked to do so.

- As a culminating project for a unit on decimals, have students create a poster showcasing at least sixteen careers that use decimals. Organize students into groups of four, with each group responsible for one poster and each student responsible for finding four careers. Each student should sign off on the careers that the group has found, as well as the illustrations, pictures, or graphics that were used for the poster. Also, each student should be able to present his or her careers to the class.

- Select a set of mathematical concepts or vocabulary terms for a group activity. Organize students into groups of four. With each group, have students complete one of the following tasks for each item. Students sign off on the work they completed for every concept or term on the list.
  - Draw a picture or symbol representing each concept or term;
  - Write a definition or summary for each concept or term;
  - Ask a question or create a problem incorporating each concept or term; and
  - Answer the question or solve the problem created for each concept or term.

Divided Resources

This technique limits resources given to each group member so that the members of the group must share materials and work cooperatively. The teacher may give each member of the group different documents or clues needed to solve a mystery or a puzzle. The teacher also might provide each group with one worksheet containing the questions, one map from which to work, one copy of directions, one pen that must be shared, etc. Each method ensures that students work together.

- Organize students into groups of three. Each group is responsible for drawing pie charts for a series of problems taken from the textbook. One student is allowed to have a textbook open to see the values outlined in the problem. Another student is allowed to use a calculator. The final student has a protractor and a worksheet with blank circles on it. After students have solved a problem, they pass their materials to the left and switch roles. Students work together in this way to compose a pie chart for each of the problems.

- Organize students into groups of four. Assign each group a geometric proof. Each student in the group is responsible for one of the following roles:
  - *Student A:* information on what is given and what needs to be proved
  - *Student B:* a diagram for the proof
  - *Student C:* a series of clues and hints for the proof in mixed-up order
  - *Student D:* writing out the steps in the proof using ideas from Student A and Student B

The four students in each group work together to write out the steps in the proof, include any additional information, and complete the proof using the diagram, given information, and hints.

6

Designing Lessons, Assessments, and Units in All Four Styles

So far, we have explored sixty tools for mathematical instruction. These tools all support different kinds, or styles, of thinking. Specifically, we have learned how:

- *Mastery tools* increase retention of critical terms and concepts and improve students' computation and practice skills;
- *Understanding tools* challenge students to take an analytical approach to mathematics by thinking their way through complex problems and searching for patterns and principles;
- *Self-Expressive tools* allow students to use their creativity and imagination to explore mathematical ideas and experiment with a variety of problem-solving approaches; and
- *Interpersonal tools* draw out the personal and social aspects of mathematics through real-world connections and the development of meaningful classroom relationships.

Our goal in this final chapter is different. We do not seek to add more tools to our repertoire. Instead, we will explore four strategies and structures for combining tools to create more powerful and truly differentiated lesson plans, assessment designs, and units of study.

At the heart of this chapter is a strategy known as Task Rotation, which uses a four-style quadrant to link four separate tools together into a unified instructional plan or assessment design. Because Task Rotations include tasks in all four styles, they naturally accommodate and challenge all the learners in a mathematics classroom. Students get the chance to work in their preferred styles and are encouraged to stretch and grow as learners by working in styles they tend to avoid.

The three remaining strategies that follow are all cousins to Task Rotation. That is, they all incorporate the same general principle that students of mathematics need to be encouraged to think and learn in all four styles. The three strategies that follow Task Rotation are:

- *Assessment Menus* combine the four styles of Task Rotation with levels of performance to create a choice-based approach to assessment.
- *A Test Worth Taking* puts the power of style-based differentiation to work in test design.
- *The Seven P's* is a comprehensive approach to lesson and unit design that allows teachers to select tools to meet specific lesson objectives such as preparing students for learning, presenting new information, and allowing students to practice new skills.

TASK ROTATION

Purpose

In his recent investigation into mathematics instruction, famed psychologist and Professor of Education at Yale University, Robert Sternberg (1999) found that one of the most significant reasons behind student underachievement in mathematics is the failure of teachers to recognize students' learning styles. It's easy to see why. Sooner or later, students whose preferred styles of thinking and learning are never addressed in the classroom will come to the conclusion that mathematics is not for them—that they are not and cannot be good at it. As more and more students reach similar conclusions, teachers of mathematics are faced with ever greater numbers of disengaged and disillusioned students. This situation may well be the root cause of our so-called "math crisis."

Enter Task Rotation. Task Rotation is a strategy that allows all students to explore mathematics in their preferred styles while also building the core skills of mathematicians: computation, reasoning, non-routine problem solving, and real-world application.

Overview

A good Task Rotation begins with the standards you are trying to address. Whether you are using the NCTM Standards or standards laid out by your state, you should know which ones you and your students will focus attention on meeting before designing tasks for your Task Rotation. For example, Kentucky mathematics teacher Joely McNamara wanted to create a Task Rotation to help her high-school students master the core concepts and skills embedded in her mini-unit on graphing linear equations and inequalities. She identified the following standards using the

Kentucky Department of Education's Combined Curriculum Document (CCD). The following academic expectations and content standards have been developed by the Kentucky Department of Education (www.education.ky.gov).

Kentucky Academic Expectations

- *1.5–1.9:* Students use mathematical ideas and procedures to communicate, reason, and solve problems.
- *2.9:* Students understand space and dimensionality concepts and use them appropriately and accurately.

Core Content Standards

- *MA-HS-5.3.1:* Students will model, solve and graph first degree, single variable equations and inequalities, including absolute value, based in real-world and mathematical problems and graph the solutions on a number line.
- *MA-HS-5.3.2:* Students will solve for a specified variable in a multivariable equation.
- *MA-HS-5.3.3:* Students will model, solve and graph first degree, two-variable equations and inequalities in real-world and mathematical problems.
- *MA-HS-5.3.4:* Students will model, solve and graph systems of two linear equations in real-world and mathematical problems.
- *MA-HS-5.3.5:* Students will write, graph, and solve systems of two linear inequalities based on real-world or mathematical problems and interpret the solution.
- *MA-HS-5.3.6:* Students will model, solve and graph quadratic equations in real-world and mathematical problems.

Once you have identified your standards, you are ready to think your way through the tasks you want students to complete. For each of the four learning styles, ask yourself: What do I want students to be able to do in order to demonstrate that they can meet our standards? In other words . . .

Figure 6.1 The Standards-Style Connection

Mastery What skills, procedures, and key terms do I want students to master?	**Interpersonal** How will students make personal connections or discover the social relevance of mathematics?
Understanding What core concepts, patterns, or principles do I want students to understand deeply?	**Self-Expressive** How will students explore, visualize, experiment, or apply new concepts and skills?

For each style-based goal you set for yourself and your students, select a tool that will help you achieve that goal. Let's listen in as Joely McNamara sets out her goals in each style, chooses a tool to help her achieve each goal, and designs the four tasks that make up a Task Rotation:

I think I'll start at the Interpersonal position. Working together seems to engage my students, and it will definitely help them to firm up their grip on the graphing and algebraic procedures that are central to this little unit. Using the Paired Learning tool (pages 180–182), I'll ask students to complete the following highly collaborative task:

> Work with a partner. Partner A will choose one linear equation from Set I. Partner B will choose the other. Using transparency markers, both partners will sketch their graphs on coordinate grids applied to separate transparencies. When finished, superimpose the transparencies and visually determine the point of intersection. Repeat the process for Set II and determine the region of intersection. Finally, verify your graphical solutions for both sets; verify Set I algebraically and verify Set II numerically.
>
> Set I: $y = 0.4x + 2$ and $2x + y = 6$
>
> Set II: $y > 2$ and $y < -x$

Next, I'll go to the Mastery position to make sure students can solve and graph the kinds of problems associated with this unit with complete accuracy. The Convergence Mastery tool (pages 40–44) is perfect for meeting this purpose. Here's what the first mini-quiz will look like:

Figure 6.2 Sample Convergence Mastery Quiz

For each problem, sketch the graph that represents the solution to the equation, inequality, or system.

1. $4x + 2y = 4\frac{1}{2}$
2. $5(x - 2y) > 1$
3. $y > x + 2$ and $y > -x + 2$

Given two points or the slope and one point, find the equation of the line.

4. (2.4, 4) and (–4, 0)
5. (–4, 2) and (6, 2)
6. (2, 5) and $m = -\frac{1}{2}$

The remaining four quizzes will be similar. Only the values will change. Students who score 100 percent on a quiz will be dismissed from taking further quizzes and will serve as coaches and study partners for students who have yet to score 100 percent.

In the Understanding position, I want to assess students' insight into the deeper relationships among three core concepts from this unit: linear equations, systems of inequalities, and domain restrictions. A good tool to help students discover and explain these deeper connections is Three-Way Tie (page 108–111). Students will be asked to write a sentence or two along each line that explains the relationship between each pair of terms. Then, in the middle of the triangle, they'll write a brief summary that incorporates all three terms (see Figure 6.3).

Figure 6.3 Three-Way Tie

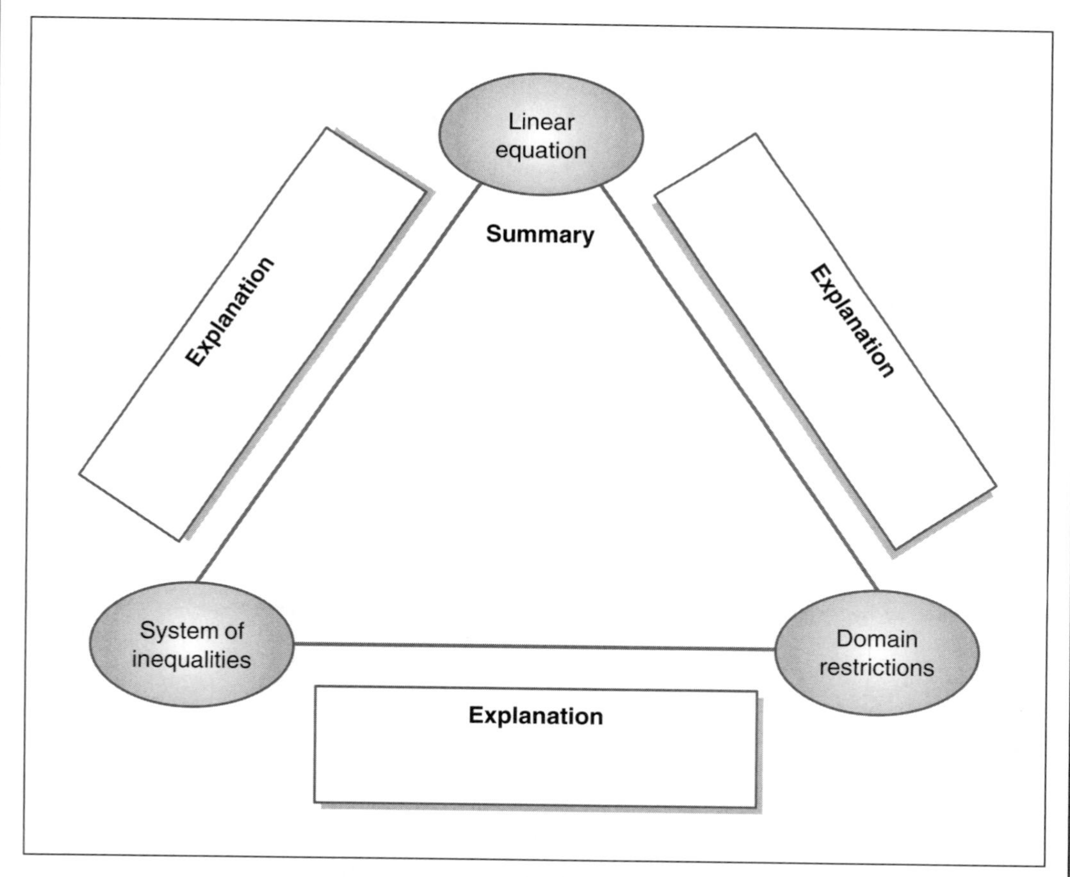

(Continued)

(Continued)

Finally, I'll use the Self-Expressive position to give students the opportunity to apply critical skills and concepts in a creative, but mathematically productive way. Here's a good Create Your Own (pages 162–164) task that does the job:

> Systems of inequalities with thoughtful restrictions on domains can represent plane figures and their interiors. Linear equations with domain restrictions can generate line segments. Create a set of linear equations and systems of inequalities whose graphs generate an interesting picture.

When designing a Task Rotation, it is always a good idea to create a "hook" or an engaging point of entry into your Task Rotation. A hook can be an activity, a discussion based on a provocative question related to the topic, or a narrative that orients students to the Task Rotation to come. For her Task Rotation on graphing linear equations and inequalities, Joely McNamara conducted a classwide discussion based on the questions in this hook:

While we live in a three-dimensional world, pictures in books, on television, and on computer screens are two-dimensional representations of objects, which consist only of points on a plane. But how can a two-dimensional picture represent a three-dimensional object? What are some other examples where the impression of three dimensions is created in only two dimensions? Are all two-dimensional pictures designed to represent three-dimensional objects? Let's continue our investigation of linear equations and inequalities to help us get a better understanding of how they work mathematically, how they're graphed, and how they can be used to create images of common shapes and pictures.

Steps

1. Identify the standards you want to address.
2. Connect your standards to the four learning styles by asking:
   - What skills, procedures, and key terms do I want students to master?
   - What core concepts, patterns, or principles do I want students to understand deeply?
   - How will students explore, visualize, experiment, or apply new concepts and skills?
   - How will students make personal connections or discover the social relevance of mathematics?

3. Select a tool from each style that will help you and your students address your standards and your four style-based goals.
4. Use the selected tools to design four tasks or learning episodes—one in each style.
5. Decide how you and your students will work through the Task Rotation. Will you:
   - Use the Task Rotation primarily for assessment (i.e., as a culminating task that asks students to demonstrate what they have already learned)?
   - Use the Task Rotation primarily for instruction (i.e., does completing each task become a goal of instruction)? Do you need to provide instruction that will develop the skills and content knowledge students will need to complete each task?
   - Ask students to complete all of the tasks, allow them to choose the tasks they wish to complete, or combine both choice and assignment?
   - Have students work in groups, independently, or both depending on the demands of each task?
6. Design a hook that will pique students' interest, activate their prior knowledge, and help them connect that prior knowledge to the Task Rotation.

Examples

Task Rotation is truly a mighty vessel. It can be used in a variety of ways to diversify instruction, or assessment, or both. What follows (Figures 6.4–6.13) is a potpourri of mathematical Task Rotations. These Task Rotations were developed by elementary, middle-school, and high-school teachers of mathematics, but all of them incorporate the tools found in this book. Which of these Task Rotations are your favorites? Why? Which of them are closest to what you already do in your classroom? Which seem least like your classroom?

(Text continues on page 239)

Figure 6.4 What an Animal

MASTERY

MATHEMATICAL SUMMARIES

The class uses the average weight data to create a bar graph showing the range of weights associated with their favorite animals. The students then create a sentence that describes the data.

INTERPERSONAL

WHAT'S YOUR FAVORITE?

Each student brings to class a picture of their favorite animal and its average weight. The students then sit in a circle, identify the animal, share their data, and tell the group why this animal is their favorite. (The teacher records types of animals and facts on chart paper for later use.)

COMPARE AND CONTRAST

Students are asked to figure out which animals could make good pets and which should live in the wild. Students should consider animal weight when making their decisions and record their evaluations in a chart.

Possible Pets	Remain in the Wild

UNDERSTANDING

CREATE YOUR OWN

Students are to create and solve a mathematical problem using the animal information gathered, graphed, and charted.

Students might create problems that ask:

What's the difference in weight between your favorite animal and you?

How many of the smallest favorite animal would it take to equal the weight of the heaviest favorite animal?

SELF-EXPRESSIVE

Figure 6.5 Personal Percentages

MASTERY	INTERPERSONAL
SHOW ME Look at the list of fractions below. Show each fraction as a percentage. Make sure you show all of the steps in converting each fraction into a percentage. $\frac{3}{4}$ $\frac{1}{3}$ $\frac{4}{8}$ $\frac{7}{10}$ $\frac{2}{5}$	**REAL-WORLD CONNECTIONS** Think about a typical day or an average week. What percent of your time do you spend doing the following activities: Going to school? Watching TV? Doing homework? Practicing/playing a sport? Practicing/playing an instrument? Reading books/magazines? Doing chores? Sending e-mail/instant messages? Listening to music/MP3s? Other activities? Convert the percentages into fractions and create a pie chart illustrating the data. Share and discuss your pie chart with a classmate.
COMPARE AND CONTRAST Think about the relationship between fractions and percentages. Explain how fractions and percentages are both similar and different. When is one more useful than the other? Make sure you explain your reasons.	**DIVERGENT THINKING** Consider the percentage 50%. Come up with five different and creative ways to show or represent 50%. You can use numbers, writing, and sketches.
UNDERSTANDING	SELF-EXPRESSIVE

Figure 6.6 Fraction Action

MASTERY	INTERPERSONAL
GLOSSARIES In your notebooks, create a glossary of the vocabulary terms listed below. You can use words, icons, numbers, and examples to define or illustrate each vocabulary term. fraction numerator denominator divisor part whole	**REAL-WORLD CONNECTIONS** Every day we use fractions whether we think about them or not. A professional football game has four 15 minute quarters, 2 halves, and a 15 minute halftime. Imagine what would happen to the athletes and the game if there were no breaks and no halftime? Think about what would happen if there were no fractions. Create a collage or draw a situation showing at least five fractions used in your favorite sport or hobby. Afterwards, illustrate how the same sport or hobby would change if there were no fractions.
SUPPORT OR REFUTE Your friend Cathy tells you that fractions confuse her. She doesn't understand how half of one thing can be smaller than a quarter of another thing when halves are supposed to be bigger than quarters. Help Cathy better understand fractions by responding to this statement. Half of something is always more than a quarter of something. Either support or refute the statement above and explain your thoughts and reasons.	**CINQUAINS** Create a cinquain (a special five-line poem) to explain what a fraction is. Follow the formula below to write your poem. 1st Line: One-word title - *fractions.* 2nd Line: Two adjectives that describe *fractions.* 3rd Line: Three action verbs related to *fractions.* 4th Line: Four-word sentence or phrase describing *fractions.* 5th Line: One-word ending that relates to *fractions.*
UNDERSTANDING	**SELF-EXPRESSIVE**

Figure 6.7 Greatest Common Factor (GCF)

MASTERY	INTERPERSONAL
MEMORY BOX Think about the different ways you have learned how to find the Greatest Common Factor (GCF) of two numbers. Without using your notebook or textbook, make a Memory Box for how to find the GCF. Greatest Common Factor	**WHO'S RIGHT?** What is the Greatest Common Factor of 72 and 540? Alex says that the GCF of 72 and 540 is 12. She came up with this answer since the two numbers factor into $2^3 \bullet 3^2$ and $3^3 \bullet 2^2 \bullet 5$, so for her the GCF is $3 \bullet 2^2$ or 12. Natasha thinks that the GCF of 72 and 540 is 6, but she didn't write down any work. Who's right? Explain any errors that either (or both) of the girls made. What is the GCF of 72 and 540?
THREE-WAY TIE Look at the triangle below. Write a sentence along each side of the triangle that connects the word or phrase at each angle of the triangle. Greatest Common Factor Least Common Multiple Fractions	**M + M: MATH AND METAPHORS** Is finding the Greatest Common Factor (GCF) of two numbers like building a house? Like putting together a jigsaw puzzle? Or perhaps like panning for gold? Describe one similarity between finding the GCF and each of the actions above. 1. 2. 3.
UNDERSTANDING	SELF-EXPRESSIVE

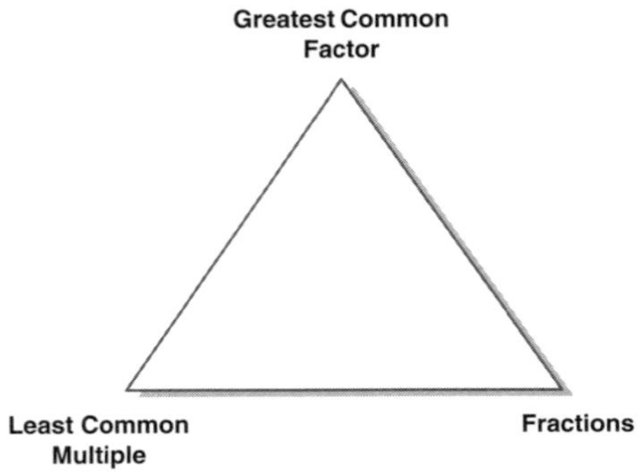

Figure 6.8 First Degree Equations

MASTERY	INTERPERSONAL
WHAT'S WRONG? Look at the student work below. Find and correct any errors. What is the correct answer? $-2(4 - 3y) = 3 + 9(y - 1)$ $8 - 6y = 12(y - 1)$ $8 - 6y = 12y - 12$ $-12y \quad -12y$ $8 - 6y = -12$ $-8 \quad -8$ $-6y = -20$ $y = \frac{-20}{6}$ $y = \frac{10}{3}$	**PAIRED LEARNING** Work with a partner to create a set of hints that could be used to help coach someone working on the following problem: $3 - 5(2x - 7) = 5 - (4 - 2x)$ Each partner should solve the equation on his or her own before working together to generate a list of helpful hints.
LEARNING FROM CLUES Below you will find all of the work required to solve a linear equation. However, the work is in pieces. You must piece the clues together and write the work in the correct order. What is the original equation? What is the correct answer? $\frac{5x}{5} = \frac{15}{5}$ $2 + 5x - 10 = 7$ $x = \frac{15}{5}$ $5x - 8 = 7$ $x = 3$ $2 + 5(x - 2) = 7$ $5x = 15$	**CREATE YOUR OWN** Keep in mind that the solution is $x = 4$. Create two different first degree equations that each fulfill the following characteristics: 1. $x = 4$ is the only solution. 2. Variables are on each side of the equals sign. 3. Solution steps to the equation use the distributive property. 4. The equation contains at least two sets of parentheses. Show all of the work and steps used to generate each equation.
UNDERSTANDING	SELF-EXPRESSIVE

Figure 6.9 Task Rotation-Factoring

MASTERY

SHOW ME

Look at the chart below. Complete the third column with the two numbers that can fulfill the requirements of both the first and second columns.

When Added =	When Multiplied =	Two Numbers
0	–25	
0	–1	
0	–100	
0	–49	
0	–4	

INTERPERSONAL

WHAT'S YOUR FAVORITE?

Write down your favorite prime number, even number, positive number, and negative number.

Use two of your numbers to fill in and solve each set of multiplication problems below. A number (#) cannot be used more than once in any single problem.

$(x + \#)\ (x + \#) =$
$(x - \#)\ (x + \#) =$
$(x - \#)\ (x - \#) =$
$(2x)(x + \#)\ (x + \#) =$
$-\ (x - \#)\ (x + \#) =$

Exchange problems with a partner to check your work. Factor out your partner's problems. If you do not come up with the same numbers, check to make sure both the multiplication and factoring are correct.

YES, BUT WHY³?

Complete each problem below using multiplication.

1. $(x - 3)(x + 3) = ?$
2. $(x + 8)(x - 8) = ?$
3. $(x - 5)(x + 5) = ?$

After you have calculated your answers, respond to the following questions:

Why is there no middle term in any of the three answers?

Why would $(x + y)(x - y)$ have no middle term?

Why are patterns like these useful in algebra?

UNDERSTANDING

GROUP AND LABEL

Carefully look at the list of problems below. Organize the problems into groups based on common characteristics. Each group should contain at least three problems. Make sure you give each group an appropriate and descriptive label.

$x^2 - 9$	$x^2 + 6x + 8$	$4x^2 + 20x + 25$
$x^2 - 8x + 16$	$9x^2 + 24x + 16$	$y^2 - 6y + 9$
$z^2 - 16z + 64$	$1 - 144k^4$	$w^2 + 8w + 15$
$p^2 + r^2$	$a^2 - 2a + 1$	$x^2 + 100$
$y^2 + 7y + 6$	$25 - 4x^2$	$4a^2 + 12ab + 9b^2$
$p^2 + 16p + 63$	$49m^2 - 16$	$16m^2 + 56mn + 49n^2$
$y^2 - 49z^2$	$9a^2 + 49b^4$	$e^2 - 22e + 121$

Bonus: Once you have grouped all of the problems above, look at the list again. Try to create a group of at least five problems that no one else will think to create.

SELF-EXPRESSIVE

Figure 6.10 Similar and Congruent Triangles

MASTERY	INTERPERSONAL
FIST LISTS AND SPIDERS Make a Fist List for each of the following concepts: Congruent Triangles Pinky: Ring: Middle: Index: Thumb: Similar Triangles Thumb: Index: Middle: Ring: Pinky:	**PERSONAL REFLECTION** Think about similar and congruent triangles, then respond to this question: Would you rather date someone whose beliefs and personality are congruent to yours, similar to yours, or some combination of both? Describe at least three uses of congruent and similar things outside of the classroom.
ALWAYS-SOMETIMES-NEVER Mark each of the following statements as being always true (A), sometimes true (S), or never true (N). Explain each selection. 1. Two congruent shapes are similar. 2. Two similar shapes are congruent. 3. Two shapes that are neither congruent nor similar have the same perimeter. 4. SAS, SSS, and AA are three ways to prove that triangles are congruent. 5. In two congruent shapes, the ratio of the areas of the two shapes is 1:1. 6. In two similar, but non-congruent shapes, the ratio of the perimeters of the two shapes is 1:1. 7. Similar shapes have congruent angles.	**CINQUAINS** Write a cinquain for either similar triangles or for congruent triangles. Follow the cinquain formula below. Make sure that each line of your cinquain is about similar triangles or congruent triangles, and not simply about triangles in general. 1st Line:(title/focus) 2nd Line: (two descriptive adjectives) 3rd Line: (three action verbs) 4th Line: (four-word phrase) 5th Line (one-word conclusion)
UNDERSTANDING	SELF-EXPRESSIVE

Figure 6.11 Quadratic Functions

MASTERY

PRACTICE MAKES PERFECT

Sketch the graph of $y = x^2 - 2x - 3$. Find the coordinates of the vertex, identify domain, range, x- and y-intercepts, axis of symmetry, and state whether the graph has a maximum or minimum.

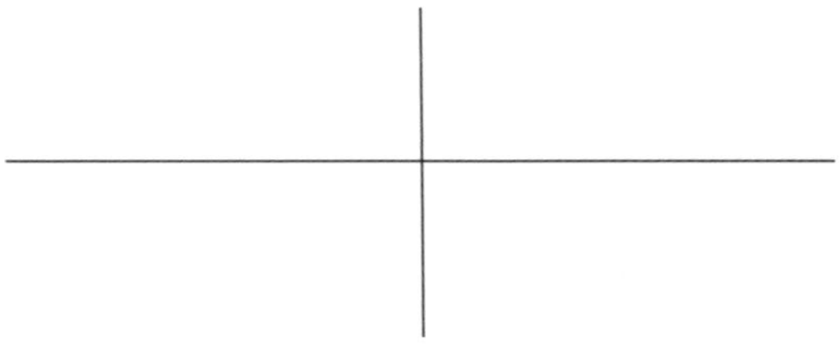

Vertex: __________

Domain: __________ Range: ____________

x-intercept(s): ________ y-intercept: ________

Axis of symmetry equation: ______________

Maximum or Minimum: ______ Value: _____

INTERPERSONAL

REAL-WORLD CONNECTIONS

Your company has promoted you to vice president in charge of the electronics division. A brand new facility is set to open outside of Vancouver that can produce either DVD players (v) or cellular phones (c). The financial advisers for the Pacific North America region created the following projected profit formulas:

$P(v) = -v^2 + 100v - 900$

$P(c) = -c^2 + 80c - 100$

Graph each profit formula to decide which product to produce and in what quantity in order to maximize monthly profits. Make sure that you explain your decision in detail.

COMPARE AND CONTRAST

The functions $y = (x - 3)^2$ and $y = (x + 5)^2$ are graphed below and labeled A and B.

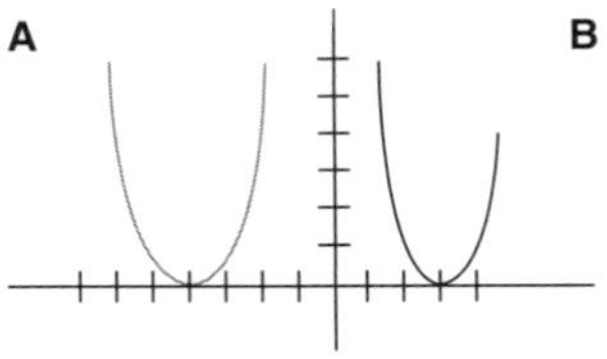

A B

Identify and compare the graphs of A and B.

	A: $y =$ _____	B: $y =$ _____
Direction		
Shape		
Vertex		

Explain how the graph of $y = x^2$ must be transformed to obtain:

the graph of A: ____________________________

the graph of B: ____________________________

UNDERSTANDING

3-D APPROACH

In the space below, sketch the graph of:

$f(x) = x^2 + 3x - 18$

(Remember to note the scale of your graph.)

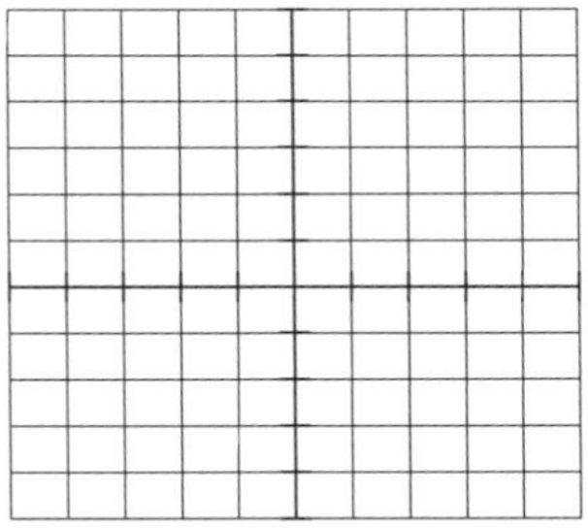

Identify and confirm the zeros of the function graphically, algebraically, and numerically.

SELF-EXPRESSIVE

Figure 6.12 Calculus

MASTERY	INTERPERSONAL
KNOWLEDGE CARDS Create Knowledge Cards for each term on the list below. Write one term on the front of each card. On the back of each card, include the value of the first or second derivative for the function for each condition to occur. Inflection Point Relative maximum Relative minimum Concave up Concave down Linear functions	**COOPERATIVE STRUCTURES** Work together in groups. Check over each person's Knowledge Cards, graphs, and explanations of which types of graphs do not belong. All of the papers from each group will be collected; however, only one of each activity will be graded. The activity to be graded will be selected at random, and any one student's work will not be graded more than once. Homework credit will be awarded if and only if all three activites selected at random are completely correct.
WHICH ONE DOESN'T BELONG? Two of the following types of graphs do not fit with the others. Which ones do not belong? Explain your choices. 1. linear functions 2. absolute value functions 3. parabolic functions 4. sine functions 5. step functions 6. exponential functions	**PICTURE = 1,000 WORDS** Draw a graph based on the following information: A continuous function that is concave up, but decreasing from $x = -10$ to $x = -5$, where there is an inflection point. It is concave down between $x = -5$ and -3. There is a relative minimum at $x = -3$. A second inflection point occurs at $x = 0$, and the graph then decreases linearly from $x = 1$ until $x = 5$. The graph is non-differentiable at $x = 5$, and slowly increases exponentially thereafter.
UNDERSTANDING	SELF-EXPRESSIVE

Figure 6.13 Go Fly a Kite!—Task Rotation and Pythagorean Kite Contest

MASTERY	INTERPERSONAL
MATHEMATICAL SUMMARIES Research the Pythagorean Theorem. Find at least three ways to prove the Pythagorean Theorem without using the proof in your textbook. Summarize your research on proofs with writing, calculations, or diagrams. Compose your summaries so that other students can easily understand and use your findings.	**WHERE IN THE WORLD?** Each member of your group must find at least four examples of right triangles being used outside of the classroom or the field of mathematics. Look for right triangles in art, architecture, advertising, or anywhere else that right triangles can be applied. Whether examples come from a book, magazine, website, or other form of media, each group member is responsible for properly citing each source of information. Meet back as a group to review the examples that everyone has found. Put together a catalog of your group's ten best examples. This catalog of ten examples will be the basis for your group's grade. Make sure that there is a reference or citation for each of the ten examples and that at least two examples from each member is included.
YES, BUT WHY? Look at all of the proofs that your group has collected and summarized. Which one would your group use to explain the Pythagorean Theorem to a group of fifth graders? Why did you choose this proof? Why didn't you choose the other proofs? Explain the reasons for your selection.	**MAKING UP IS FUN TO DO** The government of Greece is planning to honor Pythagoras and his contributions to mathematics on the 2 500th anniversary of his death. As part of the celebration, the Greek government is sponsoring an international Pythagorean Kite Contest for students of mathematics. Work with your group to design a kite for this contest. Instructions and guideleines for the Pythagorean Kite contest can be found on the accompanying page. Each group will design and construct one kite. Each group's grade will be based on how well the kite meets the contest guidlines. Creativity, originality, and functionality (flight) will also contribute to the group's final grade for the kite project.
UNDERSTANDING	**SELF-EXPRESSIVE**

(*Continued*)

Figure 6.13 (Continued)

PYTHAGOREAN KITE CONTEST

All kites must be constucted using a 30-inch long diagonal that is intersected by a shorter, 24-inch long diagonal. (See sample diagram to the right.)

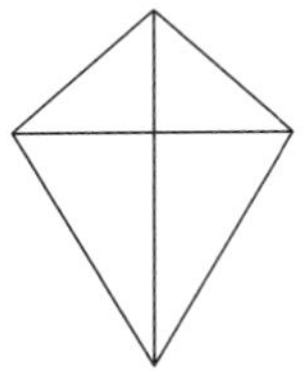

Kite Information

One side of the kite must contain the following:

~ lengths of all three sides of all of the triangles (there will be more than four triangles)

~ area of each triangle

~ measure of each acute angle in the four right triangles

~ the exact perimeter of the kite (simple radical form)

~ area of the entire kite rounded to the nearest thousandth of an inch

Kite Graphics

The opposite side of the kite must contain the following:

~ at least six sketches of right triangles

~ illustrations of both the Pythagorean Theorem and its converse

~ at least three Pythagorean triples

~ sketches of two "special" right triangles

~ any graphics or drawings of your own creation related to Pythagoras or right triangles

Kite Construction

~ Kites will be constructed following all of the above parameters.

~ Kites should be constructed for both presentation and function.

~ When constructing your kite, use only materials that will enable the kite to be flown.

Kite Presentation

~ All completed kites will be displayed indoors by your teacher.

~ Kites may also be included in an outdoor demonstration (weather and school permitting) where groups will have an opportunity to fly their kites. All kites that sustain flight will receive points, with the kites achieving the highest and longest flights receiving extra points.

ASSESSMENT MENUS

Purpose

One of the biggest challenges we face when it comes to assessing what our students know and can do is providing an equal opportunity for all students to succeed. Our students of mathematics represent a full range of learning styles and abilities, meaning that not all our students can perform at the same level or are motivated by the same activities. Clearly, a one-size fits-all approach to assessment will not do the job of helping all our students achieve at high levels.

An Assessment Menu is a variation on Task Rotation. As with a Task Rotation, an Assessment Menu includes tasks in all four styles. What distinguishes an Assessment Menu from a Task Rotation can be summed up in two bullets.

- Assessment Menus present twelve tasks instead of four. For each of the four styles, the teacher designs three tasks at three different levels of challenge or difficulty.
- Assessment Menus are truly menus, which means that students select the tasks that they wish to complete.

Overview

Assessment Menus are an ideal strategy for differentiating assessment. Students get to develop their own portfolio of activities as a way to demonstrate their growing base of knowledge and skills. What's more, the strategy naturally taps into the power of choice, which is one of the most significant motivational practices at any teacher's disposal. Yet in most mathematics classrooms, student choice gets almost no attention.

For a typical Assessment Menu, students are asked to complete four tasks. And while student choice is wired into the process, there are a few ground rules to ensure that students are not simply completing the tasks that they find easiest. Students must complete at least one task from all three levels of challenge and from all four styles.

Figure 6.14 provides a set of guidelines for differentiating tasks by learning style and level of difficulty. In each box you'll find a set of task-starters—words or brief descriptions of the kinds of products or performances associated with each style at each level.

Figure 6.14 Guidelines for Differentiating Tasks by Styles and Difficulty

Guidelines for Differentiating Tasks by Style and Difficulty

DIFFICULTY LEVEL	MASTERY	UNDERSTANDING	SELF-EXPRESSIVE	INTERPERSONAL
1	**Gathering Information** • Collect • Describe • Measure • Rank • Identify • Find • Define	**Examining Data** • Compare and Contrast • Group and Label • Map • Visually organize	**Generating Ideas** • Associations • Brainstorming • Divergent thinking • Webbing	**Expressing Feelings** • Preferences • Likes and dislikes • Prioritizing
2	**Organizing Information** • Chart • Diagram • Graph • Sequence • Label	**Interpreting Data** • Support or Refute • Yes, But Why? • Cause and effect • Formulate analogies	**Reorganizing Ideas** • Hypothesize • Speculate • Metaphoric expression • Direct analogy • Personal analogy • Compressed conflict • Transform ideas • Predict	**Understanding Feelings** • Empathizing • Personification • Reflective writing • Personal journal • Discussion
3	**Presenting Information** • Timeline • Realistic product • Demonstration • Construction • Report	**Extrapolating Data** • Draw conclusions • Propose solutions • Debate ideas • Original research	**Creating Original Work** • Design original work • Compose original work • Create original work • Invent a solution	**Acting on Feelings** • Decision making • Goal setting • Editorial • Take a position • Community action

Steps

1. Begin by following the steps in designing a Task Rotation (see pages 222–227): Identify standards, connect standards to styles, and look for tools that will help you achieve your goals.
2. Create a 4×3 grid or use Organizer 6-A (page 243).
3. Develop three tasks in each style with each task at one of three distinct levels of performance.
4. Explain the menu-based approach to assessment to students. Allow them to choose four tasks to complete. Remind students that they must choose one task in each style and at all three levels of performance.
5. Encourage students to create and present a portfolio of completed tasks that show what they know and how they have grown as learners and problem solvers.

Figure 6.15 Sample Assessment Menu—*Conic Sections*

Conic Section Assessment Menu

Directions: Complete four activities for this unit. Choose one activity from each difficulty level for a total of three. Then, choose your fourth activity from whatever difficulty level you want. Remember, each one of your choices must be from a different learning style.

DIFFICULTY LEVEL	MASTERY	UNDERSTANDING	SELF-EXPRESSIVE	INTERPERSONAL
1	Draw a picture of all of the conic sections. Label each one.	A circle is very similar to an ellipse, yet it does not have a major or minor axis. Why?	Using a flashlight, create a "shadow show" for your classmates demonstrating your knowledge of conic sections. (Could you make the image of a circle on the wall? What about a parabola?)	For each conic section put a ☺ (I feel good) or a ☹ (I have a question). Your teacher can help you answer your questions. Work until you can put a ☺ next to each conic section. If you have a ☺ next to each conic section at the start, you should choose a Level 2 or Level 3 activity instead.
2	Make a list of eight important terms to know from this unit. Define each term.	Compare and contrast the equations for conic sections. Create a list of ten "masterful tips" that could help a classmate tell the equations apart and memorize them easier.	Write a short, one-scene play with a cast that includes: Mr./Ms. Circle Mr./Ms. Ellipse Mr./Ms. Parabola Mr./Ms. Hyperbola Be sure that each character describes him- or herself.	Select the conic section that best illustrates how you feel. Draw your conic section, explain why you chose it, and relate it to how you feel.
3	Sketch the following conic sections: $\frac{x^2}{25} + \frac{y^2}{9} = 1$ $y = \frac{1}{8}x^2$ $\frac{x^2}{16} + \frac{y^2}{9} = 1$ Label each sketch.	Find a physics textbook and look up the topic *projectile motion.* What conic section is involved in projectile motion? How? Write a paragraph that shares what you learned.	Create lyrics for an original song in any genre of music: pop, rock, rap, country, etc. Your song must include two or more formulas that describe conic sections.	Play the "Art Game" with a partner. This time, play each role at least twice and make sure that you submit your art when you are done.

Organizer 6-A Blank Assessment Menu Organizer

	Mastery	Understanding	Self-Expressive	Interpersonal
Level One				
Level Two				
Level Three				

A TEST WORTH TAKING

Purpose

Who says learning has to end with the test? Who says tests can only be used to audit factual knowledge or procedural competence? Why can't a test be something that teachers and students actually look forward to—something worth taking? The answer to the first two questions is, "Not us!" The answer to the third question is this: With a little bit of rethinking and a four-style approach to differentiation, tests can inspire students, provide a rich field of assessment data for teachers, and fuel serious learning for both teachers and students alike.

Overview

In developing tests that incorporated motivational research and all four learning styles, Claudia Geocaris and Maria Ross (1999) came up with A Test Worth Taking. Disappointed with their students' attitude toward testing and the way tests seemed to signal the end of learning rather than serving as part of an ongoing learning process, Geocaris and Ross devised a set of principles for developing learning-driven tests. What Geocaris and Ross found is that when they used these principles to craft tests for their high school science classrooms, the dynamic of testing changed dramatically. Students stopped focusing on grades and began attending to the riches of the content in a way their teachers had never seen before. Some students went so far as to ask when the next test would be given because they enjoyed it so much.

So what are the principles behind A Test Worth Taking? By adapting Geocaris and Ross's work in the science classroom to the study of mathematics, we have identified six principles for designing learning-driven math tests. A test should:

- Begin with a purpose that outlines expectations, helps students activate their prior knowledge, and connects the test to future topics.
- Include clear directions.
- Allow students to explain what they have learned in their own words.
- Offer students choices of activities to complete.
- Include questions and activities in all four styles.
- Allow students to reflect on the test, their performance, and how they might improve their performance on the next test.

In designing A Test Worth Taking, a simple way to begin is to review a past test and to look for ways to adapt and modify it to integrate style and incorporate the other key principles described above (and demonstrated in the example that follows). By becoming comfortable with this test-improvement process, you will have an easier time developing Tests Worth Taking from scratch.

Steps

1. Review a test you have given students in the past.
2. Examine the test in light of the six principles of A Test Worth Taking:
   - Is the purpose clear and does it help students activate their prior knowledge?

- Are the directions clear?
- Are students encouraged to explain big ideas in their own words?
- Do the students get to choose the activities they want to complete?
- Are the questions written to accommodate all four styles?
- Is there an opportunity for students to reflect on their performance?

3. Modify your test in light of these principles. Or design a new test that incorporates these principles.

4. Be sure to introduce this new take on testing to students. Remind them that this test is about continuing the learning journey, not about "getting done with one thing and on to the next."

Example

Beginning on the following page is a sample Test Worth Taking on multiplying and dividing integers. Designed by a fourth-grade teacher, this test incorporates various mathematical activities in all four of the styles, and includes elements of student choice, self-expression, and reflection. This test serves as a quality example of A Test Worth Taking that can be easily adapted to accommodate mathematics content at the elementary, middle-school, and high-school levels. Because this Test Worth Taking is a sample, it has been formatted to fit on the following pages. The structure of this Test Worth Taking is as follows:

Section	*Total Points Available*	*Math Style*
I.	30	Mastery
II.	25	Mastery
III.	15	Understanding
IV.	25	Self-Expressive/Interpersonal
V.	5	All Styles/Reflection

A SAMPLE FOURTH-GRADE TEST WORTH TAKING

Multiplication and Division With Integers

Mathematics—Fourth Grade

Welcome to our Test Worth Taking! Because multiplication and division are everywhere, understanding how and when to use these operations will increase your confidence and ability in the classroom and the world beyond it! In this test, you will have the opportunity to show what you know about:

- Multiplying and dividing with integers.
- Defining important vocabulary.
- Identifying and correcting errors made by others.
- Applying the appropriate mathematical operations to real-world problems.

Before we begin, let's take three minutes to activate our prior knowledge so we can make use of it for the test. In the space below, write down everything you can remember about multiplying and dividing integers.

____

____

____

____

____

Great! Now let's talk about the test. This test is worth 100 points, and you will not be doing all of the problems on the test. Instead, a few of the sections allow you to choose which problem you want to complete. Be sure to read and follow all of the directions carefully, and look for the sections where you can select the problems you would like to complete. For many of these problems you can receive partial credit, so make sure that you show all of your work. But remember, calculators are not allowed on this test. If you have any questions along the way, feel free to ask me.

Have fun and good luck!

Mastery Questions

In this unit you practiced multiplication and division by doing many problems. Show me that you have mastered these operations by doing all ten problems. Show your work in the space provided.

Section I

Solve *all* problems 1–10. **10 problems @ 3 pts each = 30 pts**

Show your work.

1. 19 • 15
2. 123 • 34
3. 101 • 55
4. 258 • 499
5. $2.97 • 71
6. 91 ÷ 7
7. 255 ÷ 5
8. 256 ÷ 16
9. 505 ÷ 7
10. 330 ÷ 25

Section II

CHOICE: Solve *any three* of the five problems 11–15. 3 problems @ 5 pts each = 15 pts

Show your work and box in your answers. Circle the three problems that you *chose* to do.

11. A grocery store receives seven cases of beans, and in each case there are 12 cans. How many cans of beans are there in all?

12. Our school is collecting labels from soup cans to help raise money for a new school flag—600 labels are needed. Labels are to be collected and counted by classrooms. If each of the 23 classrooms is asked to collect the same number of labels, what goal represents the smallest number of labels saved per classroom?

13. A box of 50 blank CDs is being sold for $24. What would be the cost of a single CD?

14. Each school day John walks 6 blocks to school and then walks the same distance home in the afternoon. In a full week of school, Monday through Friday, his travels from home to school will cover how many total blocks?

15. Sherrie is saving money for her birthday. She has a babysitting job that pays $9 per week. If her birthday is eight weeks away and she wants to save $40 by her birthday, how much does she need to save each week?

Solve *both* problems 16 and 17. **2 problems @ 5 pts each = 10 pts**

16. Mathematics is a language. In any language knowing the vocabulary is essential to communication. Two of the unit vocabulary terms in your glossary are *product* and *remainder.* Write a definition for each term.

____

____

____

17. Think about the process of *long division.* Using the Fist List organizer below, fill in a word or phrase corresponding to each finger and the thumb for *long division.*

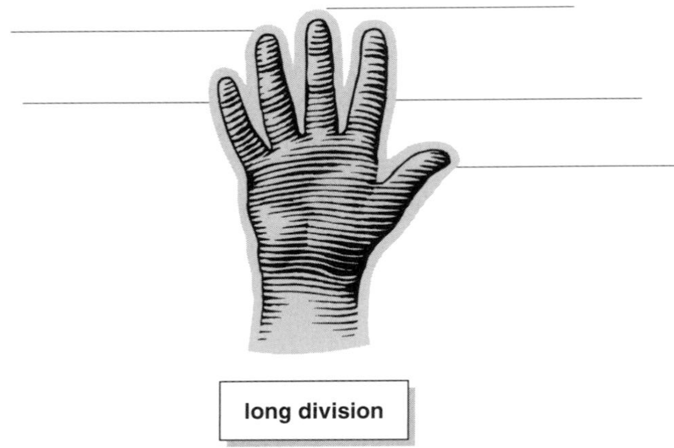

long division

Understanding Questions

Section III

CHOICE: Solve *one* of the problems, either 18 or 19. **1 problem @ 5 pts = 5 pts**

18. Estimation is a useful skill. One of the four problems below has an obviously incorrect answer. Using your estimation skills, identify the problem with the incorrect answer and explain your thinking.

a. 4 • $3.20 = $76.80

b. 1.38 • 46 = $26.38

c. 4 • $21.70 = $86.80

d. $31.75 • 22 = $698.50

The answer to problem __________ (a, b, c, d) above is obviously incorrect because____

____

19. Mathematical patterns are often beautiful and helpful! Observe the patterns in the first three multiplication problems below to determine the final missing answer. In the blanks below, write the correct answer and describe the helpful pattern you observed.

3.45 • 10 = 34.5

3.45 • 100 = 345

3.45 • 1,000 = 3,450

3.45 • 10,000 = ______________________

The pattern I noticed in the sequence of problems above, which I used to answer the last problem, is______________________________________

____

CHOICE: Solve *one* of the problems, either 20 or 21. 1 problem @ 5 pts = 5 pts

Just because something is said, that does not always make it true! Each statement below describes an operation that could be performed with many, many different combinations of numbers. Each statement promises that a certain thing WILL be true. Select one of the two problems; fill in **A**, **S**, or **N** to indicate that the statement is **A**lways true, **S**ometimes true, or **N**ever true. Give examples or counter examples to explain your A-S-N decision.

Always true? Sometimes true? Never true?

20. The product of a single-digit number times a two-digit number is a two-digit number.

_____________ (A, S, or N) because______________________________

____.

21. Divide any whole number by the number 3, and the remainder will equal 4.

_____________ (A, S, or N) because______________________________

____.

Solve problem 22. 1 problem @ 5 pts = 5 pts

22. In Section I of this test you worked with multiplication and division computations. Look back at the work involved in those problems. Compare the work involved with the multiplication problems to the work involved with the division problems by filling in the organizer below.

Multiplication Problems	*Comparison Criteria*	*Division Problems*
	Use of the operations of addition and subtraction	
	Use of multiplication	
	Use of "carrying" when adding numbers	

Self-Expressive Questions

Section IV

CHOICE: Solve *one* of the problems, either 23 or 24. 1 problem @ 5 pts = 5 pts

Show me how creative you can be with mathematics!

23. Create two problems. One must be a multiplication problem and the other a division problem. The answer for the multiplication problem must be 66. The answer for the division problem must be 6 with a remainder of 6.

24. Write a cinquain about "long division with money."

One-word Topic: ______________________
Two Adjectives: ______________________
Three Action Verbs: ______________________
Four-word Phrase: ______________________
One Final Word: ______________________

Solve problem 25. 1 problem @ 5 pts = 5 pts

25. Mathematical terms are often strange to us. They can be hard to spell and hard to remember. Six vocabulary terms (*dividend, divisor, quotient, factor, product,* and *remainder*) are shown and linked below. Select just one of the six terms and come up with a replacement word that would be a better word for us to use. Make sure you explain your thinking.

dividend ÷ divisor = quotient (+ remainder) ***factor • factor = product***

The word I picked to replace is __________________.

I think that a better, easier word for us to use in mathematics class would be __________________.

My new vocabulary word is better because__________________________

____.

Interpersonal Questions

Section IV

Solve problem 26. 1 problem @ 10 pts = 10 pts

26. Your friend showed you this homework problem and asked for your help. Help your friend by finding and correcting all of the mistakes in the following multiplication problem:

```
    224
  × 173
    662
  1,448
  224
 36,442
```

Describe the type of error that your friend keeps making:

____

____

Write out some suggestions or hints that would help your friend avoid making the same errors in the future. How could you avoid making this type of mistake?

____

____

____

CHOICE: Solve *one* of the problems, either 27 or 28. 1 problem @ 5 pts = 5 pts

27. You and four of your good friends find a small bag filled with money in the park. Inside the bag there are five hundred dollars and four coins—three quarters and a nickel. You and your friends turn all of the money over to the police. The owner comes forward to claim the bag, and she is so relieved that she gives you a reward of the four coins plus fifty dollars. If all of the reward money is shared equally by you and your friends, how much should each one of you receive?

28. Create a real-world problem involving money and the operations of multiplication *or* division. Explain how your problem is a good example of the use of computation.

Reflection

Section V

CHOICE: Answer *one* of the three problems: 29, 30, or 31. 1 problem @ 5 pts = 5 pts

29. Between learning the process of long division and multiplying two- or three-digit numbers together, which was the more difficult process for you to learn?

____

____

30. What changed in your thinking or understanding to help you become more confident to do the computation accurately?

____

____

31. How well do you think you did on the test today? Circle one of the three symbols and explain why you feel that way.

☺ 😐 ☹

____

____

Extra Credit: Tell me something that you know about multiplication or division of numbers that was not already asked on this test. Make sure that you include examples that will illustrate your knowledge of the content.

____

____

____

____

THE SEVEN P'S

Purpose

When we design lessons or units in mathematics, learning styles may not be our first concern. Often, the questions we ask ourselves during lesson and unit planning reflect much more concrete objectives. For example:

1. How will I **p**repare students for new learning?
2. How will I **p**resent new content in a way that is engaging?
3. How will students **p**ractice new skills effectively?
4. How will students **p**rocess new content deeply?
5. How will I engage students in meaningful **p**roblem solving?
6. How will students demonstrate or **p**erform what they know and understand?
7. How will students **p**ersonalize their learning so that it is meaningful to them?

Each of these questions represents one of the Seven P's of lesson and unit design. In using The Seven P's model, teachers decide which objectives (or P's) are most important to their lesson or unit and then select tools that will help them address their objectives.

Overview

A significant number of educational heavyweights, from Madeline Hunter to Grant Wiggins and Jay McTighe to Robert Marzano, have concerned themselves with the question of what powerful lessons and units look like in the classroom. What unites the work of all of these researchers is the idea that successful lessons and units are made up of distinct components and that each component meets a specific kind of instructional purpose. In synthesizing this research and applying it to mathematics instruction, we have developed The Seven P's.

The various tools in this book offer teachers of mathematics a wealth of techniques for meeting the objectives inherent in The Seven P's. You will find tools for:

- *Preparing students to learn.* Students are not ready to learn at the drop of a hat. Preparing tools help teachers prime the engine of learning by capturing students' interest, activating their prior knowledge, and connecting what students already know to what they are about to learn.
- *Presenting new content.* If lecturing and textbook reading are the only ways your students get new information, then you can be sure that they are not actively engaged in the content. Presentation tools provide teachers with a variety of techniques for developing more dynamic and memorable presentations.
- *Practicing new skills.* Mathematics is full of procedures and techniques. If we expect students to master the skills associated with mathematical thinking, then we will need to give them time to practice and refine these skills. Practice tools are designed to maximize the effectiveness of practice sessions.
- *Processing concepts.* As teachers of mathematics, we use terms like *fractions, equations, prime' numbers, polynomials,* and *functions* all the time without thinking twice about how complex, how difficult, or how foreign these concepts may be to our students. Processing tools help students get a firm grip on new mathematical concepts.
- *Problem solving.* Solving problems is the very essence of mathematical thinking. Problem-solving tools help teachers and students analyze problems, explore

solutions, discuss various problem-solving approaches, and develop new problems of their own.

- *Performing.* If traditional tests are the lone assessment tool, if mathematical skills and concepts are never applied in any meaningful or authentic way, then students' learning will be at best superficial and at worst forgotten entirely. Performance tools give students the opportunity to apply mathematical concepts and procedures by asking them to perform—that is, to create a product, demonstrate a skill, or develop and present a solution to a complicated problem.
- *Personalizing learning.* Personalizing tools enable students to make learning their own by asking them to reflect or develop a personal perspective on new learning.

Of course, not all lessons or units need to address all Seven P's. Sometimes, lessons will have a tight focus on only one or two P's. In another case, you may develop a comprehensive unit that calls for all seven types of tools. The idea is not necessarily to hit all the P's, but rather to use the P's to help you clarify your lesson and unit goals and select appropriate tools. As with Task Rotation (see pages 222–227), it is a good idea to begin with your standards and let them guide your work in lesson or unit design.

If you refer to the four Math Tools Matrices that begin Chapters 2 through 5 you'll see that the last set of columns on each matrix is reserved for The Seven P's. Use these matrices to help you identify which tools are best suited to meeting your objectives.

Steps

1. Begin with your standards. What do you want students to know and understand in this lesson or unit? What skills do you want them to develop?
2. Ask yourself the Seven P questions:
   - How will I **p**repare students for new learning?
   - How will I **p**resent new content in a way that is engaging?
   - How will students **p**ractice new skills effectively?
   - How will students **p**rocess new content deeply?
   - How will I engage students in meaningful **p**roblem solving?
   - How will students demonstrate or **p**erform what they know and understand?
   - How will students **p**ersonalize their learning so that it is meaningful to them?
3. Decide which P's are critical to your lesson/unit.
4. Refer to the Math Tools Matrices that begin Chapters 2 through 5 to help you select tools for each P.
5. Lay out your lesson or unit design on The Seven P's Organizer (Organizer 6-B).

Examples

The Seven P's Organizer (Figure 6.16) represents a seventh-grade mathematics teacher's plan for a group inquiry lesson based on three critical concepts: accuracy, precision, and strength. In designing this plan, the teacher set out to address these NCTM Standards:

NCTM Content Standards	*NCTM Process Standards*
Geometry	Problem Solving
Measurement	Reasoning and Proof
Data Analysis	Communication
	Connections

Organizer 6-B Blank Seven P's Organizer

How will I . . .	Description	Tool(s) and Style(s)
Prepare students for learning?		
Present new information?		
Help students Practice new skills?		
Help students Process new content?		
Engage students in Problem solving?		
Have students Perform or apply their learning?		
Help students Personalize their learning?		

Figure 6.16 The Seven P's

How will I . . .	Description	Tool(s) and Style(s)
Prepare students for learning?	Pose questions: What is accuracy? What is precision? Why are they important? What kinds of situations require accuracy and precision? Give students three minutes to write in their math journals before discussion. Connect to lesson: "Today we're going to look for accurate and precise ways to measure the strength of paper tubes."	Tool(s): MATHEMATICS Writing Frames (Real-World Connections) Style(s): Self-Expressive (Also Interpersonal because of real-world connections)
Present new information?	Ask students to create a Fist List of five things they associate with concept "strength." Work with students to develop a definition of "strength." Hold up a piece of paper. Present three essential questions to students: • How strong is the paper? • How can they measure the paper's strength? • How could they increase the paper's strength?	Tool(s): Fist Lists Style(s): Mastery
Help students Practice new skills?		Tool(s): Style(s):
Help students Process new content?	Introduce Essential Question Notes (as a way to record information that helps answer each essential question).	Tool(s): Essential Question Notes Style(s): Understanding
Engage students in Problem solving?	Break students into cooperative groups. Provide paper, scissors, glue, tape, string, paper cups, weight sets. Students test the strength of different paper tubes spanning a six-inch gap by experimenting with different thicknesses, lengths, and circumferences. Discuss different approaches and help students record key information in their Essential Question Notes.	Tool(s): Cooperative Structures; Essential Question Notes Style(s): Interpersonal; Understanding
Help students Perform or apply their learning?	Final challenge: Each group must create a paper tube that will hold the most weight possible. Test each group's tube and declare a winner.	Tool(s): Cooperative Structures Style(s): Interpersonal (Also Understanding and Self-Expressive as students apply concepts and create a product)
Help students Personalize their learning?	Students respond in their math journals to this question: Why are precision and accuracy so important when conducting experiments?	Tool(s): Reflective Writing Style(s): Interpersonal; Understanding (focus on explanation)

References

Beck, I. L., McKeown, M. G. & Kucan, L. (2002). *Bringing words to life: Robust vocabulary instruction.* New York: Guilford.

Blachowicz, C. & Fisher, P. (2002). *Teaching vocabulary in all classrooms.* Upper Saddle River, NJ: Prentice Hall.

Butler, F. M. (1999). Reading partners: Students can help each other learn to read! *Education and Treatment of Children, 22*(4), 415–426.

Chen, Z. (1999). Schema induction in children's analogical problem solving. *Journal of Educational Psychology, 91*(4), 703–715.

Cole, J. C. & McLeod, J. S. (1999). Children's writing ability: The impact of the pictorial stimulus. *Psychology in the Schools, 36*(4), 359–370.

Fuchs, D., Fuchs, L. S., Mathes, P. G. & Simmons, D. C. (1997). Peer-assisted learning strategies: Making classrooms more responsive to academic diversity. *American Education Research Journal, 34*(1), 174–206.

Geocaris, C. & Ross, M. (1999). A test worth taking. *Educational Leadership, 57,* 29–33.

Glasser, W. (1998). *Choice theory: A new psychology of personal freedom.* New York: HarperCollins.

Gregory, G. (2005). *Differentiating instruction with style.* Thousand Oaks, CA: Corwin Press.

Harmon, J. M., Wood, K. & Hedrick, W. B. (2006). *Instructional strategies for teaching content vocabulary: Grades 4–12.* Westerville,OH: National Middle School Association.

Hashey, J. M. & Connors, D. J. (2003). Learn from our journey: Reciprocal teaching and action research. *The Reading Teacher, 57*(3), 224–232.

Hunter, M. (1984). Knowing, teaching, and supervising. In P. Hosford (Ed.), *Using what we know about teaching* (pp. 169–192). Alexandria, VA: Association for Supervision and Curriculum Development.

Jenkins, J. R., Stein, M. L. & Wysocki, K. (1984). Learning vocabulary through reading. *American Educational Research Journal, 21*(4), 767–787.

Jung, C. (1923). *Psychological types* (tran. H. G. Baynes). New York: Harcourt, Brace.

Kentucky Department of Education. 2006 Combined Curriculum Document (CCD). Retrieved on August 13, 2007 from www.education.ky.gov/KDE/Instructional+Resources/Curriculum+Documents+and+Resources/Teaching+Tools/Combined+Curri culum+Documents/default.htm

King-Sears, M. E. & Bradley, D. F. (1995). Classwide peer tutoring: Heterogeneous instruction in general education classrooms. *Preventing School Failure, 40*(1), 29–35.

Mamchur, C. (1996). *A teacher's guide to cognitive type theory and learning style.* Alexandria, VA: Association for Supervision and Curriculum Development.

Marzano, R. J. (2003). *What works in schools: Translating research into action.* Alexandria, VA: Association for Supervision and Curriculum Development.

Marzano, R. J. (2004) *Building background knowledge for academic achievement: Research for what works in schools.* Alexandria, VA: Association for Supervision and Curriculum Development.

Marzano, R. J., Pickering, D., & Pollock, J. (2001). *Classroom instruction that works: Research-based strategies for increasing student achievement.* Alexandria, VA: Association for Supervision and Curriculum Development.

Marzano, R. J., Norford, J. S., Paynter, D. E., Pickering, D. J. & Gaddy, B. B. (2001). *A handbook for classroom instruction that works.* Alexandria, VA: Association for Supervision and Curriculum Development.

McCarthy, B. (1982). *The 4mat system.* Arlington Heights, IL: Excel.

Myers, I. B. (1962/1998). *The Myers-Briggs type indicator.* Palo Alto, CA: Consulting Psychologists.

National Council of Teachers of Mathematics (2000). *Principles and standards for school mathematics.* Reston, VA: National Council of Teachers of Mathematics.

Paivio, A. (1990). *Mental representations: A dual coding approach.* New York: Oxford University Press.

Pajak, E. (2003). *Honoring diverse teaching styles: A guide for supervisors.* Alexandria, VA: Association for Supervision and Curriculum Development.

Quia Homepage. Retrieved on March 16, 2007 from www.quia.com.

Reeves, D. (2002). *Reason to write.* New York: Kaplan.

Scieszka, J., & Smith, L. (1995). *Math curse.* New York: Viking.

Silver, H. F., Strong, R. W., & Commander, J. (1998). *Tools for promoting active, in-depth learning.* Ho-Ho-Kus, NJ: Thoughtful Education Press.

Silver, H. F., Strong, R. W., & Perini, M. J. (2001). *Tools for promoting active, in-depth learning* (2nd ed.). Ho-Ho-Kus, NJ: Thoughtful Education Press.

Silver, H. F., Strong, R. W., & Perini, M. J. (2007). *The strategic teacher: Selecting the right research-based strategy for every lesson.* Alexandria, VA: Association for Supervision and Curriculum Development.

Silver, H. F., Thomas, E., & Perini, M. J. (2003). *Math learning style inventory.* Ho-Ho-Kus, NJ: Thoughtful Education Press.

Sprenger, M. (2005). *How to teach so students remember.* Alexandria, VA: Association for Supervision and Curriculum Development.

Sternberg, R. J. (2006). Recognizing neglected strengths. *Educational Leadership, 64(1).*

Strong, R. W., Silver, H.F., & Perini, M. J. (2001). *Teaching what matters most: Standards and strategies for raising student achievement.* Alexandria, VA: Association for Supervision and Curriculum Development.

Taba, H. (1971). *Hilda Taba teaching strategies program.* Miami, FL: Institute for Staff Development.

Thomas, E. (2003a). *Styles and strategies for teaching middle school mathematics.* Ho-Ho-Kus, NJ: Thoughtful Education Press.

Thomas, E. (2003b). *Styles and strategies for teaching high school mathematics.* Ho-Ho-Kus, NJ: Thoughtful Education Press.

United States Department of Education, National Center for Education Statistics. *National assessment of educational progress, the nation's report card.* Retrieved on October 4, 2007 from http://nces.ed.gov/nationsreportcard/

United States Department of Education, National Center for Education Statistics. *International outcomes of learning in mathematics literacy and problem solving: PISA 2003 results from the U.S. perspective.* Retrieved on October 4, 2007 from http://nces.ed.gov/pubs 2005/2005003_1.pdf

United States Department of Labor, Bureau of Labor Statistics. *Consumer price indexes.* Retrieved on March 16, 2007 from http://www.bls.gov/cpi/

Wiggins, G. & McTighe, J. (2005). *Understanding by design* (2nd ed.). Alexandria, VA: Association for Supervision and Curriculum Development.

Wormeli, R. (2005). *Summarization in any subject: 50 techniques to improve student learning.* Alexandria, VA: Association for Supervision and Curriculum Development.

Index

The Corwin Press logo—a raven striding across an open book—represents the union of courage and learning. Corwin Press is committed to improving education for all learners by publishing books and other professional development resources for those serving the field of PreK–12 education. By providing practical, hands-on materials, Corwin Press continues to carry out the promise of its motto: **"Helping Educators Do Their Work Better."**